Safe Practice
in Physical Education and School Sport

People

Appropriate
challenge

▲

**PHYSICAL
EDUCATION**

▼

Acceptable risk

Context   Organisation

ISBN 1 902523 68 7

BRITISH ASSOCIATION OF
ADVISERS & LECTURERS
IN PHYSICAL EDUCATION

University College Worcester
Henwick Grove
Worcester
WR2 6AJ
Tel: 01905-855584
Fax: 01905-855594
E-mail: admin.baalpe@worc.ac.uk
Website: www.baalpe.org

Compiled by the BAALPE Safety Committee

Editor
Nicola Craine

Designers
Julia King and Sandra Flintham

Indexer
Glyn Sutcliffe MPhil, MCLIP (glyns@britishlibrary.net)

BAALPE would like to thank the following organisations and individuals
for their valuable input into this handbook:
CCPR, Chris Lowe (QGP Quick Guides), Department for Education and Skills, Department of Education in
Northern Ireland, General Teaching Council for England, Jenny Gray (Westminster Institute of Education),
Mountain Leader Training England, Ofsted, Physical Education Association of the United Kingdom,
Scottish Executive Education Department, Scottish Local Authority Network of Physical Education,
Sports Council for Wales, Youth Sport Trust

Published on behalf of BAALPE by

Coachwise Solutions

Coachwise Solutions
Coachwise Ltd
Chelsea Close
Off Amberley Road
Armley
Leeds LS12 4HP
Tel: 0113-231 1310 Fax: 0113-231 9606
E-mail: enquiries@coachwisesolutions.co.uk
Website: www.coachwisesolutions.co.uk

Contents

Chapter eleven: Accidents, incidents and first aid management

Part two: Specific guidance

Chapter twelve: Athletic activities

Chapter thirteen: Combat activities

Chapter fourteen: Dance activities

About this handbook

Welcome to the sixth edition of *Safe Practice in Physical Education and School Sport*. This edition has been fully updated to reflect recent developments in statute, case law and current practice in the field of physical education and school sport. It has also been extensively restructured and redesigned to ensure that it remains user-friendly.

The only publication of its kind, this handbook is essential reading for all those involved in the delivery of physical education and school sport in all types of educational establishments. The aim of the handbook is to provide a sound framework against which readers may analyse and adjust their own practice, and to help readers make informed judgements about safety and risk management in relation to their own circumstances. It is important that all pupils are involved in the assessment and management of risk at a level appropriate to their age, ability, experience and behaviour. The importance of safety education and risk education for pupils is evident throughout the handbook.

This handbook has been written by a group of qualified experts in the field of safety and risk management in physical education and school sport. It has also been reviewed by a wide range of relevant organisations to ensure that the guidance provided is relevant across the whole of the United Kingdom and across the full range of activities and sports included in the handbook. Numerous national organisations endorse or commend the contents to school staff, parents and other adults working in a school context. It is also used extensively by the legal profession.

The principles set out in this handbook are also relevant to other contexts (eg further and higher education, prison services and commercial providers) and other countries. All those involved in the delivery of physical education in such contexts should be able to apply the guidance provided to their own circumstances.

Structure

This handbook is divided into two main parts:

- **Part one** provides general guidance on the effective management of risk in physical education and school sport.
- **Part two** provides specific guidance on individual activities and sports.

The guidance provided in *Part one* applies to each of the individual activities and sports included in *Part two*. It is therefore essential to refer to the whole of *Part one* in addition to the relevant chapter(s) in *Part two*. The guidance in both parts is supplemented by a range of useful appendices (eg sample forms, letters and procedures), which are provided on pages 295 to 315.

Good practice in physical education and school sport reflects safe practice which, in turn, involves the effective management of risk. In this context, physical education may be defined as providing a balance between appropriate challenge and an acceptable level of risk. Figure 1 on page 2 displays the three key factors which impact on this balance and the key considerations relating to them:

- The **people** involved in a physical education activity
- The **context** in which the activity takes place
- The **organisation** of the activity.

Figure 1: Safe practice in physical education

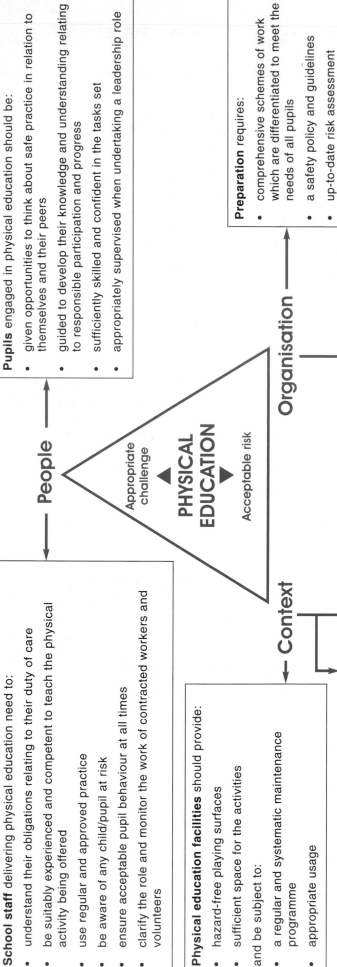

School staff delivering physical education need to:

- understand their obligations relating to their duty of care
- be suitably experienced and competent to teach the physical activity being offered
- use regular and approved practice
- be aware of any child/pupil at risk
- ensure acceptable pupil behaviour at all times
- clarify the role and monitor the work of contracted workers and volunteers

Physical education facilities should provide:

- hazard-free playing surfaces
- sufficient space for the activities

and be subject to:

- a regular and systematic maintenance programme
- appropriate usage

Procedures should involve:

- safety rules and regulations which are clearly understood by both pupils and staff
- consistently maintained attendance and assessment records
- all accidents and *near misses* being comprehensively logged and reported to the appropriate body where required
- communication with parents about school policies and practice

Pupils engaged in physical education should be:

- given opportunities to think about safe practice in relation to themselves and their peers
- guided to develop their knowledge and understanding relating to responsible participation and progress
- sufficiently skilled and confident in the tasks set
- appropriately supervised when undertaking a leadership role

Preparation requires:

- comprehensive schemes of work which are differentiated to meet the needs of all pupils
- a safety policy and guidelines
- up-to-date risk assessment

Teaching style and class organisation should ensure that:

- pupil capability is matched to task
- the methodology is appropriate to safety demands inherent within the activity
- pupils are always appropriately prepared and confident through progressive practices

Physical education equipment should be:

- inspected annually
- regularly maintained
- regularly monitored for wear and tear
- checked before use
- used appropriately and stored safely
- disposed of when condemned

People

Organisation

Context

Appropriate challenge

PHYSICAL EDUCATION

Acceptable risk

Reproduced with the kind permission of the Department for Education and Skills, Department of Education Northern Ireland, Scottish Executive and Sports Council for Wales

Figure 1 determines the structure of many of the chapters in this handbook. Where appropriate:

- relevant considerations are set out under each of the three key headings: *People*, *Context*, *Organisation*

- key risk management issues are listed under the same three headings towards the end of each chapter

- questions and answers relating to the content of the chapter are provided under the same three headings at the end of each chapter. The answers supplement the guidance provided in the main part of the chapter and are therefore essential reading.

The diagram in Figure 1 can be downloaded from the BAALPE website (www.baalpe.org). Printed copies are also available from the following organisations:

- England – Department for Education and Skills (tel 0845-6022260)

- Northern Ireland – Department of Education Northern Ireland (tel 028-9127 9279)

- Scotland – Scottish Executive Education Department (tel 0131-556 8400)

- Wales – Sports Council for Wales (tel 029-2030 0500).

Legislation

Health and safety legislation applies to all the home countries in the United Kingdom. However, other specific legislation may vary. Although the position in each of the home countries is broadly similar, those involved in the delivery of physical education and school sport in Northern Ireland, Scotland and Wales are recommended to visit the following websites for details of specific legislative requirements and policy documents:

- www.northernireland-legislation.hmso.gov.uk/legislation/northernireland

- www.scotland-legislation.hmso.gov.uk/legislation/scotland

- www.wales-legislation.hmso.gov.uk/legislation/wales

Further help

The aim of this handbook is to provide comprehensive guidance for all those involved in the delivery of physical education and school sport. Inevitably, it is impossible to account for all eventualities and readers may have specific queries or concerns, which are not answered by the relevant chapter(s) of this handbook. In these circumstances, readers are encouraged to seek further clarification from appropriate sources (eg local education authority support staff, higher education providers, other school staff) and/or BAALPE. A comprehensive list of useful contacts and website addresses is provided in Appendix 9 for this purpose.

Glossary of terms

Additional educational needs	Specific requirements relating to issues such as advanced ability, cultural background, ethnicity and language, which may have safety implications and should be considered by those delivering physical education and school sport
Adults	Occasionally used as a collective term for school staff, volunteers and paid coaches
Coaches	All those, who are not members of school staff, who are contracted (ie paid) to deliver an agreed physical education or school sport programme
Employers	Includes local education authorities, local authority Departments of Education and Education Service, Education and Library Boards, school governing bodies, trustees, managers of other premises (including school grounds and outdoor centres) and self-employed people
Head teachers	All those responsible for managing educational establishments (includes principals)
Helpers	Used specifically in the context of special educational needs
Key Stage 1	Pupils aged 5–7 years
Key Stage 2	Pupils aged 7–11 years
Key Stage 3	Pupils aged 11–14 years
Key Stage 4	Pupils aged 14–16 years
Out-of-school-hours learning (OSHL) activities	All sessions which take place outside of lesson time (formerly known as *extra-curricular activities*)
Parents	Includes carers, guardians and other next-of-kin categories
Physical education	Short for the term *physical education and school sport* – abbreviated to *physical education* for convenience
Pupils	All young people attending any form of educational establishment
School staff	Any employee of a school (in line with the principles of modernising school workforces)
Subject leaders	All those responsible for managing physical education and school sport in any phase or any educational establishment
Teachers	Used specifically in circumstances when qualified teachers have a particular responsibility (includes lecturers in further and higher education)
Volunteers	Adults (and young leaders under the age of 18 who are closely managed by school staff) who are not paid for their work within physical education or school sport programmes (includes trainee teachers)

Abbreviations

AALA	Adventure Activities Licensing Authority
AIDS	acquired immumo-deficiency syndrome
ASA	Amateur Swimming Association
BAALPE	British Association of Advisers and Lecturers in Physical Education
BHS	British Horse Society
BSAC	British Sub-Aqua Club
BS EN	British Standards European Norm
CPD	continuing professional development
CRB	Criminal Records Bureau[1]
DfEE	Department for Education and Employment (now DfES)
DfES	Department for Education and Skills (formerly DfEE)[2]
HIV	human immuno-deficiency virus
HSE	Health and Safety Executive
HSO	Health and Safety Officer
HSWA	The Health and Safety at Work Act 1974
IEP	individual education plan
ILAM	Institute of Leisure and Amenity Management
IRB	International Rugby Board
ISRM	Institute of Sport and Recreation Management
ITT	initial teacher training
LEA	local education authority[3]
NCSS	National Council for School Sport
NGB	national governing body
NPFA	National Playing Fields Association
NQT	newly qualified teacher
OAA	outdoor and adventurous activities
OSHL	out-of-school-hours learning
POCA	The Protection of Children Act 1999
QCA	Qualifications and Curriculum Authority
RFU	Rugby Football Union
RIDDOR	The Reporting of Injuries, Diseases and Dangerous Occurrences Regulations 1995
RLCEP	Rugby League Coach Education Programme
RLSS UK	Royal Life Saving Society UK
RoSPA	Royal Society for the Prevention of Accidents

(continued)

1 Home country equivalents include Disclosure Scotland.

2 Home country equivalents include Department of Education in Northern Ireland, Scottish Executive Education Department and Department for Training and Education in Wales.

3 Home country equivalents include local authority (LA) in Scotland and Education and Library Boards in Northern Ireland.

Abbreviations (continued)

RYA   Royal Yachting Association

SEN   special educational needs

SENCO   Special Educational Needs Coordinator

STA   Swimming Teachers' Association

Part one
General guidance

People

Appropriate
challenge

▲

**PHYSICAL
EDUCATION**

▼

Acceptable risk

Context   Organisation

Chapter one

Physical education and the law

1.1 Introduction

1.1.1 Common law[1] and statute law[2] impose duties on individuals and bodies. A breach of the law may give rise to a claim for damages (compensation) or, sometimes, to criminal penalties. Where statute law requires certain action to be taken, it is the duty of school staff to meet those requirements.

1.1.2 Incidents and injuries do occur, but some are foreseeable. School staff have a legal duty to work within a system that anticipates and reduces foreseeable risks. Head teachers must ensure that such a system is operable, even by recently appointed school staff.

1.1.3 All schools are required to have a formal health and safety policy, to review it periodically and to ensure that it is implemented effectively. A safe practice policy specifically for physical education could also be developed based on the *people*, *context* and *organisation* involved[3].

1.1.4 The National Curriculum for physical education requires that the risk assessment process be taught to pupils. They should receive clear guidance and experience (appropriate to their needs, age and intelligence), and a clear explanation of the need to follow required practice. This will help them to develop their own knowledge and understanding of safe practice. Pupils should not be caught out by their own ignorance. School staff should *teach safely* and *teach safety*.

1.1.5 The aim of this chapter is to raise the awareness of all those who work or help in schools of their legal duties and responsibilities in relation to safe practice. Subjects covered include:

   a duty of care

   b negligence

   c vicarious liability

   d voluntary assumption of risk

   e contributory negligence

   f employer's liability insurance

   g unions/professional associations.

1 Law based on judicial decision and custom.
2 Law prescribed by parliament.
3 See Figure 1 on page 2 for further information.

1.1.6   In addition, brief explanations of the following are provided:

Acts of Parliament

a The Health and Safety at Work Act 1974 (HSWA)

b The Occupiers' Liability Acts 1957 and 1984

c The Children Act 1989

d The Protection of Children Act 1999 (POCA)

e The Activity Centres (Young Persons' Safety) Act 1995

f The Special Educational Needs and Disability Discrimination Act 2001

Regulations

g The Adventure Activities Licensing Regulations 2004

h The Management of Health and Safety at Work Regulations 1999

i The Reporting of Injuries, Diseases and Dangerous Occurrences Regulations 1995 (RIDDOR)

j The Fire Precautions (Workplace) Regulations 1997

k The Provision and Use of Work Equipment Regulations 1998

l The Education (Specified Work and Registration) (England) Regulations 2003.

Please note that the intention is not to interpret the above Acts and Regulations, but merely to provide a general overview.

1.2   Duty of care

1.2.1   The law does not expect perfection. However, it does impose on those involved in physical education a duty of care to:

a identify foreseeable risks that may result in injury

b take reasonably practicable steps to reduce the risk to an acceptable level.

1.2.2   It has long been established that school staff must take reasonable care to avoid acts or omissions which they can reasonably foresee would be likely to cause injury to other people. In a judgement that effectively marked a turning point in the law relating to negligence, Lord Atkin (Donoghue v Stevenson, 1932) defined *other people* as:

'Persons who are so closely and directly affected by my act that I ought reasonably to have them in contemplation as being so affected when I am directing my mind to the acts or omissions which are called into question.'

This clearly applies to school staff when performing their duties whether during curriculum time or out-of-school-hours learning (OSHL), on or off the school premises.

1.2.3   As long ago as 1893, Mr Justice Cave stated:

'The person must take such care of the pupil as the careful parent would take care of the same.'

This was subsequently modified to mean that a teacher must take such care as would a reasonably prudent parent in the same situation as the teacher (Lyes v Middlesex County Council, 1962). This standard of care continues today.

1.2.4   There is no absolute standard of care required – this varies according to the expertise of the school staff, stage of development of the pupils and the demands of the activity. However, school staff are required to exercise a greater level of care than would be expected of the average *person in the street*. They are expected to possess a greater than average knowledge of the risks involved in the activities they teach and to take precautions appropriate to that knowledge and understanding. They are also expected to continually develop and apply new knowledge. Newly qualified teachers are normally expected to demonstrate the same level of competence as teachers with significant experience. Inexperience is not a defence against a charge of not meeting the expected professional standard of care.

1.2.5   School staff must consider the likelihood of an accident and the gravity of the consequences. The more severe the injury that may result, the more thorough the precautions required. However, school staff are not expected to take all precautions against every foreseeable risk – what matters is the degree of risk. This involves foreseeing substantial risk and taking steps to avoid it or reduce it to an acceptable level.

1.2.6   By their nature, some activities involve a higher risk than others. Indeed, without an element of risk, some activities would become meaningless. However, there must be a balance between the risks taken and the consequences of not reoognising, and taking account of, that rlsk. For example, in many games, tackling and bodily contact are inevitable and necessary. In such circumstances, there may be occasional injuries to pupils. Case law suggests that, when teaching techniques and skills, school staff should take into consideration the likelihood of a pupil being harmed during a tackle by an older, larger or more experienced opponent. Similarly, the use of an unsuitable surface may well be deemed to be less than satisfactory practice. Cases decided in court have influenced the development of safe practice and are likely to continue to do so.

1.2.7   School staff continue to exercise a duty of care when teaching pupils over the age of 18 in a school context.

1.2.8   School staff owe a higher duty of care to pupils with special educational needs (SEN) or additional educational needs.

1.2.9   When involved in educational visits (including residential visits and ventures abroad), school staff owe a constant duty of care to the pupils involved (ie 24 hours a day, seven days a week). Duty of care cannot be diluted or removed by any association of the words *holiday*, *abroad*, *weekend* or similar terms. This does not mean that school staff should be on duty for 24 hours each day. A rota of duties should be established to enable school staff to have rest periods.

Volunteers and paid coaches

1.2.10   Head teachers are responsible for ensuring that the competence (or otherwise) of volunteers and paid coaches is assessed, and the limits of their duties established. They may delegate this task to competent school staff.

1.2.11   Teachers should monitor and manage the role played by volunteers and paid coaches, even those who are directly managed by other school staff.

1.2.12   When a volunteer or paid coach is in charge of a group, that person owes the same duty of care to the pupils as if they were a teacher.

1.3 Negligence

1.3.1 In order for a claim for damages on the grounds of negligence to succeed, the complainant has to demonstrate that, on the balance of probabilities, negligence on the part of school staff directly resulted in his/her injury or loss. However, if the claim concerns a blatant act or omission (eg pupils permitted on a trampoline or to practise javelin throwing without supervision), the onus may be placed on the defendant to prove the absence of negligence.

1.3.2 Examples of cases in which allegations of negligence have been made include the following:

   a A pupil injured by a tackle performed by a teacher playing a full part in a pupils' game, using his greater skill, experience, strength and physique.

   b A pupil injured within a staff/pupil competitive match involving physical contact or an accelerating missile.

   c A pupil injured by the collapse of a rugby scrum where the referee was ignorant of the rules.

   d Equipment used for purposes other than that for which it was designed – either through improvisation or the introduction of a competitive element, such as in the game of *Pirates*[1] or an obstacle course using gymnastic equipment.

   e Excessive weight-bearing, such as in mass pyramids, or excessive unstructured physical contact, such as in the game of *British Bulldogs*, where the likelihood of injury is high.

   f Fun or *free* swimming sessions during which large recreational equipment that impeded lifeguard observation was introduced without the essential increase in vigilance.

1.3.3 Claims of negligence are normally made against employers[2]. Local education authorities (LEAs) and governing bodies are usually vicariously liable[3] for the negligent acts of their employees. It is most unusual for school staff to be sued personally. However, when damages have been awarded against an LEA or governing body on account of the grossly negligent act(s) of school staff, the member(s) of staff involved have occasionally been asked to contribute towards the damages.

1.4 Defence against charges of negligence

1.4.1 School staff are significantly protected against charges of negligence if good, regular and approved practice was followed, and the level of competence usually associated with the teaching profession was used.

1.4.2 Claims of negligence are easier to refute if school staff can demonstrate that the following good practice guidelines were followed:

People

   a Head teachers (and governors where appropriate) should be aware of, and approve, all physical education activities taking place in their school.

---

1 A chasing game over gymnastic apparatus.

2 This includes LEAs, school governing bodies, trustees, managers of other premises (including school grounds and outdoor centres) and self-employed people.

3 See pages 13–14 for further information about vicarious liability.

b School staff should be suitably competent to teach the activities in question, be appropriately qualified when required, and should provide appropriate supervision and assistance.

▶▶ See *Chapter three: Qualifications, competence and supervision* for further information.

c School staff and governors should have a knowledge and understanding of current safety developments. Professional development opportunities should be provided to enable school staff to influence and improve safe practice. This is particularly important for those who are newly qualified or inexperienced.

d All volunteers and paid coaches should be fully briefed, given clear roles and managed by identified members of school staff.

e Pupils should be informed about the importance of safety and good behaviour in a manner appropriate to their age, intelligence, and experience.

Context

f All reasonable steps should be taken to ensure the safety of the working environment and equipment.

g Appropriate risk assessments should be carried out.

h Parents should be well informed about forthcoming educational visits and outdoor and adventurous activities, and parental consent should be obtained before such activities take place. Senior managers are usually responsible for compiling a suitable form for this purpose.

▶▶ See *Chapter twenty: Educational visits* for further information.

i School staff should maintain accurate records (eg attendance registers, lesson preparation, assessment records) which demonstrate pupils' experience and abilities.

Organisation

j Pupils should be thoroughly prepared and equipped with appropriate clothing and footwear for the activities to be undertaken.

k Activities should be carried out in accordance with good, regular and approved practice adopted by other similar schools across the country. Over the years, school staff have developed effective practices and procedures which have prevented foreseeable accidents, without reducing challenge.

Vicarious liability

1.4.3 Employers (ie LEAs or governing bodies) are usually vicariously liable (ie held responsible) for the negligent acts of omission or commission made by school staff during the course of their normal employment (scope of contract). However, school staff should be aware that their employers are not vicariously liable for negligence that occurs outside the scope of their employment. For example, if school staff took a group of pupils away for a weekend without the knowledge and agreement of the head teacher, and someone was injured, this may well be judged to be outside the contract of employment of the school staff involved and their employer may therefore not be liable. School staff should always follow their school's policies.

1.4.4 School staff are strongly recommended to find out who is vicariously liable for their actions and whether liability is likely (or unlikely) to be assigned to them personally. They are also advised to take out their own insurance cover to provide financial support should the need arise.

Voluntary assumption of risk

1.4.5 In general, a willingness to participate in an activity may be deemed to be an acceptance of the risk of injury. However, this is unlikely to apply in a school situation in which pupils are involved. Participation in the school curriculum is not voluntary for pupils.

1.4.6 In addition, participation in some OSHL activities may not be considered to be voluntary, particularly if there are hidden pressures on pupils to participate and if it would be difficult to demonstrate that they were fully aware of the risks involved.

Contributory negligence

1.4.7 If the person injured can be shown to have contributed to the cause or aggravation of the injury by some irresponsible act or omission, they may be held partially responsible for the injury. In such circumstances, this may be taken into account when responsibility is determined. However, the younger the claimant, the less likely it is they will be deemed to have contributed to their injury.

1.5 Employer's liability insurance

1.5.1 Although LEAs are exempt from the Employer's Liability (Compulsory Insurance) Act 1969, the Department for Education and Employment (DfEE) Circular 2/94 *Local Management of Schools*[1] established that LEAs should either act as insurers or make other insurance arrangements to cover potential liabilities of their employers. The Employer's Liability (Compulsory Insurance) Regulations 1998 set the minimum cover at £5,000,000 for claims arising from any one occurrence.

1.5.2 Schools which are not maintained by an LEA are not exempt from the Employer's Liability (Compulsory Insurance) Act 1969 and must therefore comply with its requirements.

▶▶ See *Chapter ten: Insurance* for further information about insurance requirements for schools.

1.6 Unions/professional associations

1.6.1 All school staff should consider joining a union or professional association that offers legal advice and financial support to its members.

1.6.2 School staff involved in legal action should contact their union or professional association at an early stage.

1 See page 20 for full reference details.

1.7   The Health and Safety at Work Act 1974 (HSWA)

1.7.1   Under the terms of the Health and Safety at Work Act 1974 (HSWA), employers are required to do all that is reasonably practicable to ensure the health and safety of employees (eg school staff) and non-employees (eg pupils, parents and other visitors to the school premises) who are affected by their actions. This requirement extends to people who are not employers, but who have control of premises, whatever the extent. Such people are required to do all that is reasonably practicable to provide a safe environment and safe systems of work, including safe access to, and exit from, their premises.

1.7.2   The employer varies according to the type of school:

a   In community schools, the LEA is classed as the employer.

b   In voluntary-aided or foundation schools, the governing body is classed as the employer.

c   In independent schools (including city technology colleges and city academies), the proprietor or governing body is usually classed as the employer.

1.7.3   Under the terms of Section 2(3) of the HSWA, employers are required to prepare (and revise when necessary) a written statement containing a general policy relating to the health and safety at work of employees, and guidelines on its implementation. Employers must inform their employees about the statement and any revision of it.

1.7.4   The policy applies to all organised activities both on and off the school site.

1.7.5   The Health and Safety Executive (HSE) and local authority health and safety inspectors have powers to ensure that schools comply with the requirements of the HSWA. Failure to comply may result in prosecution.

1.8   The Occupiers' Liability Acts 1957 and 1984

1.8.1   The Occupiers' Liability Acts 1957 and 1984 impose a duty of care on those who manage premises to ensure that visitors (eg pupils and parents) are reasonably safe on the premises for the purposes for which they are invited or allowed to be there. School management teams are therefore responsible for ensuring that school premises are safe to use.

1.8.2   A higher duty of care is imposed on an occupier if children are involved. Objects that may, in legal terms, be classed as *allurements* should be safeguarded. It is essential to do so with equipment associated with physical education (eg javelins, trampolines). A warning notice does not necessarily absolve an occupier from liability, unless it enables visitors to be reasonably safe. It is only one of many factors which will be considered when deciding whether or not an occupier has exercised the duty of care required.

1.9 The Children Act 1989

1.9.1 Under the terms of the Children Act 1989, everyone who has substantial access to children is required to provide evidence of their suitability to work with children, which should be vetted by the authority concerned. In the context of education, this applies when recruiting school staff, volunteers and paid coaches.

1.9.2 Many LEAs and independent agencies now provide codes of conduct on purposeful physical contact with children. Those working with pupils in situations where physical contact is sometimes deemed to be necessary (eg when teaching certain gymnastic skills) should ensure that they are aware of, and follow, such guidance. Physical contact should only occur when it is necessary to ensure the safety of a pupil and when the pupil is aware that it will take place. Contact should be such that it cannot be misconstrued.

▶▶ See *Chapter six: Safeguarding children and young people* for further information about child protection issues relating to physical education.

1.10 The Protection of Children Act 1999 (POCA)

1.10.1 The Protection of Children Act 1999 (POCA) has four principal objectives:

a To make statutory the Department of Health Consultancy Service Index list – the *Protection of Children Act (POCA) List* – which contains names of people considered unsuitable to work with children.

b To amend Section 218 of the Education Reform Act 1988 to enable the Department for Education and Skills (DfES) to identify people placed on *List 99* because they are considered unsuitable to work with children.

c To amend Part V of the Police Act 1997 to enable the Criminal Records Bureau to disclose information about people who are included on the *POCA List* or *List 99*, along with their criminal records, thereby creating a *one-stop shop* system of checking people seeking to work with children.

d To require regulated childcare organisations to check the names of anyone they propose to employ in posts involving regular/substantial access to children against both the *POCA List* and *List 99*.

1.10.2 Sports organisations are not covered by the mandatory aspects of POCA 1999, as they are not childcare organisations. However, they are encouraged to refer names to be considered for inclusion on the *POCA List*.

▶▶ See *Chapter six: Safeguarding children and young people* for further information about child protection issues relating to physical education.

1.11 The Special Educational Needs and Disability Discrimination Act 2001

1.11.1 The Special Educational Needs and Disability Discrimination Act 2001 requires all schools to establish accessibility plans to take account of SEN and disabilities.

1.12 The Activity Centres (Young Persons' Safety) Act 1995 and Adventure Activities Licensing Regulations 2004

1.12.1 Under the terms of the Activity Centres (Young Persons' Safety) Act 1995 and Adventure Activities Licensing Regulations 2004, commercial providers of climbing, water sports, trekking and caving activities, in remote or isolated areas, for young people under the age of eighteen, are required to apply for a licence to offer such activities. All applicants must undergo an inspection and will only be awarded a licence if their safety management systems are deemed to be adequate.

1.12.2 In October 1997, it became a legal requirement that only licensed activity providers could offer outdoor and adventurous activities on a commercial basis. Some activity centres are exempt from licensing requirements (eg school-operated centres, non-profit-making centres).

1.12.3 School staff planning to take pupils to an activity centre should ascertain whether the planned programme falls within the remit of the Adventure Activities Licensing Authority (AALA) and, if so, whether the centre is licensed. Holding a licence demonstrates that the centre's safety management has been inspected and that it meets AALA requirements. However, a licence does not cover aspects of provision such as accommodation.

1.12.4 If the work of the centre falls outside the remit of AALA, school staff should be satisfied that the quality of the staffing, equipment and accommodation at the centre is adequate, and should advise the school governors accordingly.

1.13 The Management of Health and Safety at Work Regulations 1999[1]

1.13.1 Under the terms of the Management of Health and Safety at Work Regulations 1999, employers are required to carry out risk assessments by:

a formally identifying the hazards present in any undertaking

b estimating the extent of the risks involved, taking into account any precautions that are already in place

c introducing measures for planning, organising, controlling, monitoring and reviewing their management of health and safety.

1.13.2 Risk assessments are central to any health and safety system. Assessments must be made of the risks to which employees, pupils and others who visit the school premises are exposed, so that appropriate action can be taken to protect their health and safety.

1.13.3 All risk assessments must be suitable and sufficient, and should cover the following:

People

a The school staff and/or volunteers and paid coaches involved (ie competence, experience and relevant training)

b The pupils involved (ie their abilities, previous experience, behaviour and individual needs)

---

1 The Management of Health and Safety at Work and Fire Precautions (Workplace) (Amendment) Regulations 2003 – Regulation 22 has been amended to allow civil liability claims under the 1999 Regulations.

c The nature of the activity

d The premises

e The equipment

f The procedures to ensure a safe working environment

Organisation

g Preparation through reference to schemes of work and the assessment of significant hazards in terms of the likelihood of occurrence and the severity of outcomes

h Teaching style and class organisation to promote a safe working situation.

The consideration given to removing the hazards or minimising them to an acceptable level should also be documented.

1.13.4   Pupils should share in the assessment and management of the risks associated with physical education activities. This is an essential part of the learning process. Due to different abilities, the risk management process should be applied to individual pupils, to pupil groups and to the class as a whole.

1.13.5   Risk assessments should be recorded and there should be a review of any amendments made following previous risk assessments, together with an indication that they have been implemented.

▶▶ See *Chapter two: Risk management* for further information.

1.13.6   The governing bodies or management teams, and the school staff of the relevant premises, should work together to establish and implement effective health and safety policies. Employees should be well informed about these policies and receive adequate health and safety training.

1.14   The Reporting of Injuries, Diseases and Dangerous Occurrences Regulations 1995 (RIDDOR)

1.14.1   The Reporting of Injuries, Diseases and Dangerous Occurrences Regulations 1995 (RIDDOR) apply to accidents or occurrences which take place during both curricular or OSHL activities, both on and off the school premises (eg outdoor activity centres, sports centres).

1.14.2   The employer should be informed of any such accident or occurrence, as it is likely to manage the reporting procedure to the HSE, if required.

1.14.3   School staff should familiarise themselves with the requirements of the Regulations so that they are aware which accidents have to be reported. Failure to comply may result in prosecution.

▶▶ See *Chapter eleven: Accidents, incidents and first aid management* for further information about RIDDOR 1995.

1.15 The Fire Precautions (Workplace) Regulations 1997[1]

1.15.1 Under the terms of the Fire Precautions (Workplace) Regulations 1997, schools are required to carry out, and record, fire precaution checks and risk assessments. This includes checking emergency exits, the presence of fully serviced fire extinguishers, fire evacuation drills, communication systems (eg alarms and telephones) and the storage of potentially flammable materials (eg mats).

1.15.2 Such checks are a whole school responsibility, but subject areas may include relevant specific aspects in their subject risk assessments. School staff are recommended to do so in all risk assessments relating to physical education.

▶▶ See *Chapter two: Risk management* for further information.

1.15.3 In the event of a fire, the availability of completed attendance registers and a plan of the school buildings would be helpful to the fire and rescue services.

1.16 The Provision and Use of Work Equipment Regulations 1998

1.16.1 Under the terms of the Provision and Use of Work Equipment Regulations 1998, employers are required to ensure that work equipment is maintained in good working order. To achieve this, they should arrange for equipment to be inspected at regular intervals, particularly where a risk assessment has identified a significant risk arising from the installation or use of the equipment.

1.16.2 The extent of the inspection will depend on the type of equipment, its history, how it is used, how often it is used and the potential risks arising from its use or failure.

1.16.3 School staff are advised to ensure that specialist physical education equipment (eg gymnastic equipment) is inspected on an annual (or more frequent) basis. LEAs often make arrangements for an annual inspection of gymnastic apparatus in the schools for which they are responsible. The schools are subsequently responsible for implementing any recommendations made in the inspection reports.

1.17 The Education (Specified Work and Registration) (England) Regulations 2003

1.17.1 The Education (Specified Work and Registration) (England) Regulations 2003 impact on how adults, who are not qualified teachers, work within the school setting. They set out the conditions under which school staff other than qualified teachers may undertake the following *specified teaching activities* in schools:

a Planning and preparing lessons and courses for pupils

b Delivering lessons to pupils, including delivery via distance learning or computer-aided techniques

c Assessing the development, progress and attainment of pupils

d Reporting on the development, progress and attainment of pupils.

1 The Management of Health and Safety at Work and Fire Precautions (Workplace) (Amendment) Regulations 2003 – Regulation 22 has been amended to allow civil liability claims under the 1999 Regulations.

1.17.2   The Regulations ensure that all such specified teaching activities are supervised by a teacher. The degree of supervision is up to the professional judgement of head teachers. For example, it is not assumed that a teacher will always be physically present when a member of staff without qualified teacher status is carrying out specified teaching activities.

1.18   Transport

1.18.1   School staff must adhere to current legal requirements (however recent) relating to the use of cars, taxis, mini-buses and coaches for transporting pupils. Cost may not be used as an excuse for failure to comply with the requirements.

Further reading

- BAALPE, DfES (2003) **The use of volunteers and paid coaches (contractors) in physical education and school sport**[1]

- Clarke, R, Lowe, C and Szemerenyi, S (2004) **Quick guides CD: management of staff, management of pupils, and management of health and safety.** Northampton, QGP Ltd[2]

- Croner CCH Group Ltd (2004) **Schools' health and safety management.** Kingston upon Thames, Croner CCH Group Ltd. Ref no: SHS[3]

- Croner CCH Group Ltd (2004) **The head's legal guide.** Kingston upon Thames, Croner CCH Group Ltd. Ref no: HLG[3]

- Croner CCH Group Ltd (2004) **The teacher's legal guide.** Kingston upon Thames, Croner CCH Group Ltd. Ref no: TLG[3]

- DfEE (1994) **Circular 2/94: local management of schools.** London, DfEE

- DfEE (1998) **Health and safety of pupils on educational visits.** London, DfEE. Ref no: HSPV2[4]

- DfES (2004) **A guide to the law for school governors**. London, DfES Publications[5]

- Grayson, E (2001) **School sports and the law**. Kingston upon Thames, Croner CCH Group Ltd. ISBN 1 85524 610 4

- Health and Safety Commission (1998) **Health and safety guidance for school governors and members of school boards.** 2nd edition. Sudbury, HSE Books. ISBN 0 7176 1298 8

- Health and Safety Commission (2000) **Management of health and safety at work.** 2nd edition. Sudbury, HSE Books. ISBN 0 7176 2488 9

- HSE (1998) **Five steps to risk assessment.** Revised edition. Sudbury, HSE Books. ISBN 0 7176 1565 0

- HSE (1999) **A guide to the Reporting of Injuries, Diseases and Dangerous Occurrences Regulations 1995.** Revised edition. Sudbury, HSE Books. ISBN 0 7176 2431 5

- Lowe, C (2002) **Teachers' rights, duties and responsibilities.** Kingston upon Thames, Croner CCH Group Ltd. ISBN 1 85524 666 X

- Sport England and Health and Safety Commission (2003) **Managing health and safety in swimming pools**. Sudbury, HSE Books. ISBN 0 7176 2686 5

1   Visit the BAALPE website (www.baalpe.org) or DfES website (www.dfes.gov.uk) for further details.

2   Visit www.quickguides4schools.com for further details.

3   This manual and related updates are available via a subscription service (tel 020-8247 1630).

4   See also the related supplements listed on page 280.

5   Appropriate variations of this guide are distributed to different categories of schools – community (ref no: GTTLC2004), voluntary aided (ref no: GTTLVA2004) and foundation (ref no: GTTLF2004). They contain sections on managing health and safety, and the school site.

Chapter two

Risk management

2.1 What is risk management?

2.1.1   Risk management is a more current term for safe practice. It involves managing the risk (or possibility) of injury by:

a   assessing what could cause harm

b   judging whether the risk of injury is significant

c   controlling or reducing the risk of injury to an acceptable and reasonable level via some form of corrective action.

2.1.2   In the context of physical education, risk management involves providing a balance between appropriate challenge and an acceptable level of risk. Three factors affect this balance:

a   The people involved

b   The context

c   The organisation of the activity.

The risk management model in Figure 2 below illustrates the link between these three factors.

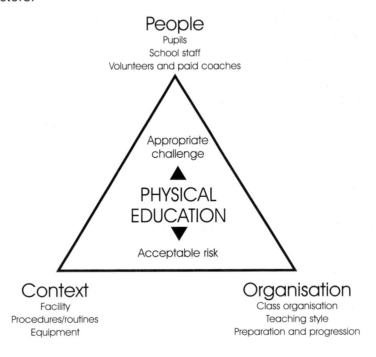

Figure 2: Risk management model

▶▶   See the *About this handbook*[1] section for further information about this risk management model.

---

1   See pages 1–3.

2.2 Why is risk assessment important?

2.2.1 Everyone has a right to be educated in a safe and healthy environment. However, physical education cannot be totally free from the possibility of injury because it is a practical activity that involves moving at speed and changing direction, often in a confined space.

2.2.2 School staff have a legal duty to take positive steps to ensure the health and safety of the pupils in their care.

2.2.3 There are three main types of risk assessment:

a **Generic risk assessment** – general principles which apply to an activity wherever it may take place.

b **Site- or activity-specific risk assessment** – usually carried out for each work area or activity with specific consideration of the people involved, the context and the organisation of the activity.

c **On-going risk assessment** – carried out while an activity or event is taking place, taking into account issues such as sudden illness, changes in climatic conditions or ineffective officiating.

2.2.4 The Health and Safety Executive (HSE) has the power to check that risk assessments are carried out.

2.2.5 Under the terms of the Management of Health and Safety at Work Regulations 1999, employers have a duty to ensure that periodic formal, activity- or site-specific risk assessments are carried out in the establishments for which they are responsible. In the context of schools, employer's (eg local education authorities (LEAs)) usually delegate this duty to head teachers and governors, as they have day-to-day responsibility for applying their employer's health and safety policies. A careful examination must be carried out of what could harm pupils, school staff or visitors to the school during all organised activities.

▶▶ See *Chapter one: Physical education and the law* for further information about the Management of Health and Safety at Work Regulations 1999.

2.2.6 Under the terms of the Fire Precautions (Workplace) Regulations 1997, schools are also obliged to include a specific, written fire risk assessment within their overall risk management schemes. In the context of physical education, this requirement could be met by ensuring that the following issues are considered within generic risk assessments:

a Escape routes in case of fire

b Enclosed areas from which there is no escape (eg storerooms)

c The storage of highly flammable items of equipment (eg mats)

d The location and type of fire extinguishers

e The implications of emergency evacuation in cold or inclement weather.

▶▶ See *Chapter one: Physical education and the law* for further information about the Fire Precautions (Workplace) Regulations 1997.

2.2.7 School staff assess risk (ie the likelihood of something causing injury) every working day by applying logic and commonsense. Forward planning before sessions, judgements made during sessions and post-session evaluations all involve on-going risk assessment to ensure a safe working environment. Frequent judgements such as these provide a sound basis for more formal, written, site-specific risk assessments.

2.2.8 Pupils should share in the assessment and management of the risks associated with physical education activities. This is an essential part of the learning process. Due to different abilities, the risk management process should be applied to individual pupils, to pupil groups and to the class as a whole.

2.2.9 Risk assessments are best carried out:

a as a team exercise, because this helps raise awareness of possible risks, establishes collective expertise and ensures that everyone involved understands the organisational requirements of the activity

b in or on the facility in/on which the activity will take place

c using the *People, Context, Organisation* model[1]

d based on existing documentation, procedures and practice, checking whether additional precautions are required, over and above those currently in place

e by thinking logically through a session format from start to finish (eg from when pupils begin to assemble through to changing into appropriate clothing, moving to the work area, taking part in the activity, returning to the changing area, changing and dispersing).

1 See page 21 for further information.

2.3   The risk assessment process

Generic risk assessment

2.3.1   Table 1 below lists generic risk assessment principles which should be considered during activity- or site-specific risk assessments. These should be modified as necessary to the specific circumstances of each school to ensure that risk assessments meet the particular needs of the school.

Table 1: Typical generic risk assessment principles

PEOPLE	School staff	• Qualifications/experience/confidence • Professional development needs • Knowledge of individuals and group • Observation and analysis skills • Teaching position in relation to pupils • Parents informed and involved as necessary
	Volunteers and paid coaches	• Qualifications/experience/confidence • Professional development needs • Aware of limits of role/responsibilities • Effective communication with school staff • Level and type of insurance cover • Disclosure certification
	Pupils	• Consistent and acceptable behaviour • Levels of responsibility known • Individual and group abilities • Medical conditions known • Awareness of routines and procedures
CONTEXT	Facility	• Hazard-free • Clean, non-slip floor/water clarity • Sufficient space for group size/activity • Shared use issues • Operating procedures known and applied • Fire regulations applied • Safety signs/notices in place • Access to facility
	Equipment and clothing	• Used for purpose for which designed • Suitable for activity • Handling/carrying/siting issues • Accessibility/storage • Safety/rescue equipment available • Annual/periodic inspection check • Checked before use • Careful consideration as to whether improvisation is wise • Routines for collection/retrieval/changing • Appropriate clothing • Personal effects • Adequate safety equipment/personal protection
	Procedures and routines	• Standard accident procedures (both on and off site) • First aid equipment/procedures/responsibilities • Carrying/moving/placing equipment • Safety policy applied
	Transport	• Roadworthiness • Safe embarkation • Seat belts used • Driver requirements/responsibilities • Passenger lists • Insurance and any other requirements for use of school staff's and volunteers' cars

(continued)

ORGANISATION	Preparation	• Written scheme of work setting out safety issues for consideration • Ability matches demands of activity
	Class organisation	• Group sizes • School staff/pupil ratio • Supervision at all times • Additional supervision if required • Numbers known/register check • Regular scanning/head counts • Group organisation/management procedures • Orderly movement to work area • Warm-up/preparation/safe exercise • Accurate demonstrations
	Teaching style	• Appropriate teaching style used • Adequate class control • Rules consistently applied • Regular and approved practice used • Policy on physical contact/substantial access • Support techniques known and applied • Intervention appropriate • Differentiated tasks
	Progression	• Progressive practices known and applied • Appropriate activities selected
	Emergency action	• Emergency/accident procedures and contingency plans known and applied

Activity- and site-specific risk assessment

2.3.2 School staff should decide whether to complete a risk assessment for each activity, each physical education facility, staff expertise, all the equipment or, more simply, for each facility, taking into account the range of physical activities which could occur in each one.

2.3.3 Any foreseeable hazards (ie what could cause harm) should be identified by referring to the risk management model on page 21 and the generic issues in Table 1, taking into account the:

a people involved

b facility

c equipment

d procedures

e nature of the activity

f way in which the activity will be taught.

2.3.4 Those at risk should then be identified. Will everyone be affected or just particular groups? Will the hazard(s) be a threat to school staff, pupils or visitors to the school? Are particular groups more likely to be affected than others (eg disabled pupils or pupils with behavioural problems)?

2.3.5 All risks should be evaluated. This involves making a professional judgement as to whether the hazard(s) identified is/are likely to cause significant injury[1].

2.3.6 Findings should be recorded as the risk assessment is carried out. There is no set format for formal written risk assessments – the only statutory requirements are to:

a demonstrate that the assessment has been carried out

b identify any significant risks and who is affected by them

c identify whether any further action is necessary, over and above the precautions and procedures already in place, to reduce the risks to an acceptable level

d record the assessment if there are more than five employees.

▶▶ A sample risk assessment form is provided in Appendix 1.

2.3.7 School staff should check with their employer (eg LEA) whether there are any local requirements in relation to risk assessments (eg recording assessments and/or rating the level of risk in a particular format). Local requirements must be met.

2.3.8 If further action is thought to be necessary, control measures should be implemented to reduce the risk to an acceptable level.

2.3.9 When procedures are amended, all those affected (eg school staff, pupils, visitors) should be informed. This could be done verbally or in writing (eg posters, amending schemes of work, extending guidance in the school handbook).

2.3.10 Written risk assessments should be reviewed on a regular basis. This involves repeating risk assessments annually or when circumstances change (eg new pupils, new school staff, change of programme of activities, member of school staff becomes pregnant).

▶▶ For further information on the risk assessment process, visit the HSE website (www.hse.gov.uk).

On-going risk assessment

2.3.11 During any activity or event, those responsible for the group of pupils should constantly re-assess the precautions included in the site- or activity-specific risk assessment. They should respond to any changes to the anticipated situation that may have an adverse effect on the safety of the group in order to maintain an acceptable level of safe management.

---

1 According to the Management of Health and Safety Regulations 1999, a significant injury is one which involves three or more days off school, or a trip to hospital for any reason and for any length of time.

2.4   Risk control

2.4.1   Most significant risks can be reduced to an acceptable level. The following guidelines will help school staff to minimise and control risk.

People

2.4.2   It is essential that all those involved in physical education work safely. This can be achieved by:

a   ensuring that school staff, volunteers and coaches are well qualified, trained and experienced

b   devising appropriate working procedures

c   maintaining discipline and control

d   providing appropriate supervision

e   ensuring that appropriate protective equipment and clothing are worn

f   developing observation skills.

Context

2.4.3   It is essential that physical education is delivered within a safe environment. This can be achieved by:

a   inspecting, repairing and servicing facilities and equipment on a regular basis

b   placing warning notices where risks persist

c   using good quality equipment

d   using equipment of an appropriate size and weight for the pupils concerned

e   teaching pupils how to use the equipment and/or the facility safely

f   establishing appropriate procedures.

Organisation

2.4.4   It is essential that physical education sessions are delivered in a safe and organised manner. This can be achieved by:

a   working to comprehensive schemes of work which address different abilities

b   matching pupil strength, experience, ability and confidence where physical contact is involved

c   explaining any inherent risks

d   providing support or standing by when necessary

e   amending the way an activity is carried out when necessary

f   teaching progressive practices thoroughly

g   using regular and approved practice.

Chapter three

Qualifications, competence and supervision

3.1 Qualifications and competence

3.1.1 Competence to teach physical education may be defined as having the skills, knowledge, understanding and expertise necessary to plan, deliver and evaluate the physical education programme.

3.1.2 School staff are not legally required to hold a specific award in order to teach a physical education activity. However, it is wise for them to be able to demonstrate that they are suitably trained, experienced and qualified to undertake the activities in which they engage with pupils.

3.1.3 Head teachers should recognise that it is unwise for school staff to work in areas in which they lack the appropriate experience and expertise.

3.1.4 Local education authorities (LEAs) and school governing bodies may establish their own policies and insist on certain minimum qualifications before school staff are allowed to teach some aspects of physical education, particularly those that involve significant risk. School staff should be aware of these local requirements and ensure that they meet the criteria before teaching the activities concerned.

3.1.5 Examples of potentially hazardous activities include swimming, trampolining, gymnastics, rugby football and many outdoor and adventurous activities. Those teaching these activities should hold recognised and current qualifications (eg national governing body (NGB) qualifications) to demonstrate their suitability to teach or coach the activities safely.

3.1.6 Evidence of accreditation can help head teachers when considering requests from school staff to introduce potentially hazardous activities into the physical education programme.

Primary schools

3.1.7 Primary school teachers may be required to teach gymnastics, dance, games, athletics, swimming and water safety, and some aspects of outdoor and adventurous activities. They should have satisfactorily completed an initial teacher training (ITT) course, which covered all the activities they will be required to teach.

3.1.8 However, those with little or no ITT in physical education run risks unless further training opportunities are provided. Such teachers should undertake appropriate professional development before being allowed to teach a full range of activities. Head teachers must be satisfied that all those who are required to teach physical education are able to do so in a safe environment, with a sound understanding of the needs and stages of development of all the pupils in their charge.

3.1.9   School staff should obtain the permission of their head teacher before introducing any new physical education activity into their school, whether during curriculum time or out-of-school-hours learning (OSHL). This is particularly important if the activity is potentially hazardous.

3.1.10   Some LEAs do not permit the use of certain items of equipment in primary schools. Examples include rebound jumping equipment (eg trampettes and trampolines), which require very specialised knowledge and teaching to be used safely. Head teachers should be aware of, implement and monitor all such policies.

Secondary schools

3.1.11   Teachers who are responsible for the planning and delivery of physical education programmes in secondary schools should have satisfactorily completed appropriate ITT and/or professional development courses which covered all the activities they will be required to teach.

3.1.12   As the National Curriculum develops, some schools may include new, emergent activities for which codes of safe practice are still under development. In these circumstances, head teachers should proceed with caution and should be prepared to contact their LEA advisory service, a relevant consultant, expert staff in other schools, their insurer or the relevant NGB to obtain the best advice available.

Professional development courses

3.1.13   Changes and developments in practice mean that those involved in physical education need to undertake professional development in order to keep abreast of what is acceptable and safe.

3.1.14   Professional development courses can provide additional training opportunities for physical education teachers. They may be necessary to compensate for omissions in ITT courses.

3.1.15   Some NGBs require qualifications to be revalidated periodically. This is not simply to endorse previous requirements but to inform of changes and developments which may have occurred in the interim period. Guidance should be obtained from the relevant NGB or LEA, or an expert consultant.

3.2   Supervision

3.2.1   There is no statutory requirement for pupils to be supervised at all times. However, analysis of case law provides a clear indication that the incidence of injury is much higher during unsupervised activities than supervised ones.

3.2.2   Direct supervision of pupils enables the adult in charge to intervene at any time. Decisions to supervise less strictly should not be taken lightly.

3.2.3   Where a degree of independence is required, progress towards remote supervision should be developed over time. The member of school staff involved maintains responsibility for the pupils, regardless of whether he/she is present.

3.2.4   The standards of expertise, discipline, relationships and risk management expected of all adults working with pupils need to be consistent with providing a safe working environment. This applies at all times and to all on- and off-site school-related activities.

Adults without teaching qualifications

3.2.5   The modernisation of school workforces and ever broadening opportunities in programmes offered to pupils, both on- and off-site, has led to supervision and teaching responsibilities being given to adults who may not hold a teaching qualification. In these circumstances, the teacher always maintains overall responsibility for what is taught and for the conduct, health and well-being of the pupils involved.

3.2.6   Adults working in schools usually fit into one of the following categories:

     a   **Employee** – a member of school staff paid under their contract of employment, whether a qualified teacher or not (eg learning assistant or coach employed on the school staff).

     b   **Contractor** – a person external to the school staff with whom the school/employer has a contract for the provision of services and who is paid under the terms of the contract (eg paid coach for specific services).

     c   **Volunteer** – a person external to the school staff who is not paid by the school/employer and therefore does not have a contract (eg trainee teacher in higher education, sports development officer, NGB coach, parent).

3.2.7   Contractors and volunteers may be used to:

     a   support the delivery of the National Curriculum during curriculum time

     b   develop out-of-school-hours clubs and teams on the school site

     c   deliver off-site activities, usually in the presence of a member of school staff.

3.2.8   It is good practice for school support staff[1], volunteers and paid coaches to benefit from an induction programme, opportunities for professional development and regular, systematic monitoring, which addresses whole school, physical education and sport-specific issues.

School support staff

3.2.9   School support staff[1] can make a significant contribution to pupils' learning by providing support to teachers and, thereby, pupils. However, they must always work under the direction of a teacher, whether in a whole class or group situation. The teacher should direct learning at all times.

Volunteers and paid coaches

3.2.10   Volunteers and paid coaches can be defined as any adults external to the school staff who work with pupils with the permission of the head teacher. Examples include coaches, instructors, sports development officers, sports leaders, ITT trainers, parents and other helpers.

3.2.11   Volunteers and paid coaches can enhance pupil experiences and make a valuable contribution to the range and standards of physical education, both during curriculum time and OSHL activities. They may work in schools in a variety of ways and circumstances.

3.2.12   As they are not employed as members of school staff, volunteers and paid coaches operate under different conditions to employees. Clear operating procedures therefore need to be established.

---

1   Any non-teacher directly employed by the school.

3.2.13   Parents should be informed when volunteers and paid coaches are used to enhance physical education programmes.

3.2.14   It is good practice for schools to keep a register of any volunteers and paid coaches used, including contact details and work undertaken, for future reference.

Determining levels of supervision

3.2.15   In the first instance, it is good practice for teachers to directly supervise school support staff, volunteers and paid coaches at all times in order to evaluate their competence. Direct supervision involves school support staff, volunteers and paid coaches working alongside a teacher in a supporting role, whereby the teacher can intervene at any time, if necessary.

3.2.16   At a later stage, distant supervision may be appropriate for school support staff and paid coaches (and in some cases for volunteers) according to their competence and the level of responsibility assigned to them. This would allow them to work at some distance from a teacher, possibly out of sight or in a different facility. However, frequent monitoring by the teacher would be essential.

3.2.17   The level of supervision required for school support staff, volunteers and paid coaches should be determined by a thorough risk assessment based on their competence in the following areas:

   a   Relationship with pupils[1]:

      •   Value, care for and respect all pupils

      •   Act as an appropriate role model (eg use of language, dress)

      •   Promote fair play and equality

      •   Promote the ethos of the school

      •   Work well with members of school staff.

   b   Knowledge of pupils[1]:

      •   Levels of confidence

      •   Levels of ability

      •   Special educational needs

      •   Medical needs

      •   Behaviour

      •   Age/development stage.

   c   Pupil management[1]:

      •   Use common and approved practice

      •   Match pupils' confidence, strength and ability in pair and group tasks

      •   Maximise participation

      •   Maintain effective pupil control and motivation

      •   Apply the school's standard procedures and routines (eg child protection, emergency procedures, jewellery, handling and carrying equipment).

1   All teachers should be able to judge competence in this area.

d Expertise in activities[1]:

- Understand how the activities undertaken fulfil or complement the relevant National Curriculum Programme of Study and/or wider curriculum

- Demonstrate an appropriate level of expertise to enable learning to take place during the activities undertaken

- Demonstrate understanding of the overall needs of the age group involved

- Use suitable space for the group, differentiated equipment, differentiated practice and effective progression

- Know and apply the relevant rules.

e Observation and analysis skills:

- Provide a safe learning and working environment

- Identify faults and establish strategies for improvement.

3.2.18 Direct supervision by school staff is always required when minors[2] (eg junior sports leaders) assist with the delivery of activities. Regardless of their experience and qualifications, minors cannot be legally responsible for a group of children and should therefore always work alongside a member of school staff, who is able to monitor them and intervene immediately, if necessary.

3.2.19 Head teachers should, on behalf of their employer, ensure that volunteers and paid coaches are appropriately managed at all times.

3.3 Partnership arrangements

3.3.1 The implications for schools of using off-site facilities or other partnership arrangements are significant. Schools must assess and monitor the quality of the management and teaching provided in such circumstances.

3.3.2 Schools should seek LEA advice on setting up safe partnerships with external agencies. Subject leaders of physical education should be asked to arrange and monitor partnership arrangements on behalf of the head teacher and school governing body. Whatever system is adopted, the following points should be addressed:

a Head teachers should be mindful of the fact that they have overall responsibility for the management of all aspects of the National Curriculum and for the safety of their pupils.

b A safety policy for the functioning of the physical education department should be included in the whole school safety policy and be approved by the governing body.

c The levels of expertise conferred by any NGB award or National Vocational Qualification held by volunteers and paid coaches should be known by, and be acceptable to, the school.

1   Teachers may need to seek guidance from others (eg specialist LEA representatives, consultants, senior managers or teachers) to help them judge competence in this area.

2   People under the age of 18.

d The school management system should require and enable all external assistance to be checked, tutored and monitored. This is a legal requirement under health and safety legislation. When external assistance is used, parents should be informed of the level of involvement of the volunteers and paid coaches involved.

Further reading

- BAALPE, DfES (2003) **The use of volunteers and paid coaches (contractors) in physical education and school sport**[1]

- BAALPE, PEA UK, Sport England, sports coach UK (2003) **Induction pack for teachers and adults other than teachers**. Leeds, Coachwise Solutions. ISBN 1 902523 44 X

Risk management

People

- Head teachers and governors are responsible for ensuring that school staff are competent to deliver physical educational activities.

- School staff should be knowledgeable, competent and skilled in the delivery of physical education activities. Employers may require school staff to hold particular qualifications for some activities.

- Professional development opportunities should be provided for all school staff.

- School staff should be vigilant in exercising their duty of care.

- School support staff, volunteers and paid coaches must be adequately supervised by qualified teachers.

Context

- Safety policies for physical education should be written and regularly reviewed.

▶▶ See *Chapter two: Risk management* for more detailed, general guidance on risk management issues.

1   Visit the BAALPE website (www.baalpe.org) or DfES website (www.dfes.gov.uk) for further details.

Questions and answers

People

Qu 1 **Is it acceptable for Year 11 pupils to use local, off-site sports centre facilities as part of an options programme for physical education? If so, will staffing at the centre be sufficient for supervisory purposes?**

Ans Providing your school's governing body and head teacher approve, parental consent is obtained and suitable arrangements can be made with the sports centre manager, using the sports centre may well provide a useful experience for the pupils involved, particularly if specialist physical education facilities at your school are limited.

You should carefully plan and agree the activity programme with the sports centre manager, so that the system will work well and there will be no misunderstandings on either side. You should make all the pupils who will be using the sports centre fully aware of their responsibilities during the planning stage.

Sports centre staff may work with the pupils during specific activities, although at least one member of school staff from your school should attend the sessions to exercise overall supervision and thereby meet duty of care requirements for the pupils involved.

Under no circumstances should the pupils go to the sports centre without a member of school staff from your school being present.

Qu 2 **Teacher colleagues from other departments and school support staff in my secondary school are timetabled to assist with some games in physical education. Is this acceptable practice?**

Ans In general, it is better if the physical education programme is delivered by those with specialist training in the subject, but this may not always be possible. Games is one area in which other school staff may be knowledgeable and experienced, and their support in the way you suggest acceptable, providing they have a sound appreciation of the rules and their essential implementation.

Physical education teachers should satisfy themselves that such colleagues are able to deliver the programme safely and effectively. This may require monitoring and assessment by specialist teachers in the early stages.

The use of non-specialist staff with expertise in only one game or activity may be a significant constraint in staffing the range of activities for pupils in a given year. This should be discussed with senior management where it may impinge on safety.

As an extension of this question, assistance from school staff during sports days requires very careful planning. They should be fully briefed well beforehand by a specialist teacher on the technical and safety requirements, particularly for potentially hazardous throwing and jumping events.

Qu 3 **As a primary school head teacher, I am concerned that some of my staff who are responsible for leading gymnastics sessions in the school hall have not received adequate training in this area. What advice can you give me?**

Ans   Current ITT courses in primary education sometimes do not provide sufficient time to meet the needs of trainee teachers and many newly qualified teachers may be deficient in some areas of the National Curriculum. In the case of gymnastics, there are safety implications, which I believe may be at the root of your concern. Other school support staff may have qualifications and experience.

Arrangements should be made with your employer for the teaching staff concerned to receive professional development in primary gymnastics as soon as possible. Until then, it will be necessary for them to modify their sessions to include only those activities which are relatively safe and low-risk, and which they feel competent and able to manage. A possible interim measure would be to arrange for them to work alongside a competent teacher during gymnastics sessions, providing a type of *on the job* training.

Organisation

Qu 4   **I am a secondary teacher involved in teaching rugby and, on occasions, I take teams away to play against other schools. At such times, I am often the only teacher present from my school. Is this a satisfactory arrangement?**

Ans   You would need to consider what you would do if one of the pupils from your team was injured and required medical treatment part-way through the game. Clearly, you would have a duty of care for all the pupils in your charge and your position of sole responsibility would place you in a dilemma. If you were to take the injured pupil for treatment, the other pupils would be left unattended.

It may be possible for school staff from the host school to assist during an emergency, but this would not be entirely satisfactory and could in no way be expected unless an agreement had been made beforehand.

One solution could be for the fixtures system to require two teams from your school, each with a member of school staff, to play away at any one time. Two members of school staff would then be present and the injury situation described above could be managed.

Alternatively, you could take a second responsible adult (eg parent) with you to away matches, who would be responsible for supervising the pupils if the need arose. It would also be useful to have an emergency contact number for your school.

Qu 5   **I am a male member of school staff and run an outdoor games club for pupils in Years 5 and 6 during one lunchtime and one evening after school. The club has proved very popular with both girls and boys, and about 60 pupils attend on a regular basis. This number presents organisational difficulties, but I am anxious not to turn anyone away. What advice do you have?**

Ans   It would be unwise to accept responsibility for a group greater in number than a usual class size. In the case of high-level competition where close refereeing may be required, the number of pupils should be such that control can be realistically maintained.

You might consider splitting the pupils into two groups, with half attending at lunchtime and the other half after normal school hours. The two groups could be switched round at suitable intervals (eg every half-term). Another possibility would be to split by gender but you would need to weigh up the benefits, or otherwise, of operating single-sex activities. It would be advisable to recruit a female colleague or volunteer to assist with out-of-school-hours sessions and to provide responsible support in case of an emergency.

Chapter four

Management and administration

4.1 Introduction

4.1.1 The management of safe practice is essential. It involves managing issues relating to the people, context and organisation involved. It is important that school staff, pupils, volunteers and paid coaches apply procedures and standards consistently.

4.1.2 Health and safety requirements are whole school issues. As a practical subject based on a premise of appropriate challenge within an acceptable level of risk, it is natural that physical education will make a significant contribution to whole school developments in health and safety.

4.1.3 Those involved in teaching physical education need to:

   a teach *safely*

   b teach *safety*

   c maintain good class control.

4.1.4 The guidance in this chapter will help school staff, volunteers and paid coaches to exercise their responsibility for safeguarding the well-being of pupils and others involved in physical education.

4.2 People

4.2.1 The employer is legally responsible for health and safety. Where the LEA is the employer, the day-to-day responsibility for health and safety is often delegated to the governors. However, the Department for Education and Skills (DfES) does not expect governors in community or voluntary-controlled schools to have health and safety expertise. LEAs have no health and safety responsibility for foundation or voluntary-aided schools.

4.2.2 Head teachers should:

   a ensure that regular inspections, risk assessments and adequate actions are carried out

   b submit reports to governors, the LEA or other agencies as appropriate

   c ensure that health and safety information is passed to the appropriate people

   d maintain overall day-to-day management responsibility for health and safety.

chapter four

4.2.3   Subject leaders of physical education should:

      a establish regular review procedures to ensure safe working environments and systems of work

      b carry out regular inspections and risk assessments

      c check that appropriate action is taken to safeguard pupils, visitors and other school staff

      d inform senior management of any relevant issues

      e make appropriate arrangements for staff training in safety

      f ensure that appropriate personnel are kept informed

      g manage effectively the work of any volunteers or paid coaches contributing to physical education and out-of-school-hours learning (OSHL) activities (ie provide essential information, share planning, check competences and monitor delivery standards).

        ▶▶ See *Chapter three: Qualifications, competence and supervision* for further information about managing volunteers and paid coaches.

4.2.4   All school staff, volunteers and paid coaches have a responsibility for safety. This involves:

      a following the policies and guidelines provided

      b checking that work areas are safe

      c participating in inspections and risk assessments

      d taking appropriate remedial action as soon as possible to eliminate or minimise risk

      e reporting any safety-related issues to their line manager/senior manager.

4.3   Context

Safety policies

4.3.1   Whole school and subject policies should be established in accordance with the Health and Safety at Work Act 1974 and LEA and governing body requirements. A policy statement for health and safety should explain the purpose, rationale and context for risk management in physical education.

      ▶▶ See *Chapter one: Physical education and the law* for further information about the Health and Safety at Work Act 1974.

4.3.2   The purpose of developing risk management in physical education is to:

      a offer physical education within a well managed, safe and educational context

      b establish common codes of practice

      c provide common administrative procedures

      d ensure that statutory and local requirements, and other national guidelines (eg codes of practice), are followed.

4.3.3   The rationale for teaching risk management in physical education is to:

    a   enable pupils to participate in physical education sessions which provide appropriate challenge, with acceptable risk, but no danger

    b   educate pupils about risk management in order for them to participate independently in physical activity later in life

    c   fulfil the requirements of the National Curriculum for physical education.

4.3.4   Risk management in physical education should be developed and taught in a context in which:

    a   activities take place in a safe environment and are adequately supervised

    b   regular and approved practices are used

    c   pupils are taken through progressive stages of learning and challenge

    d   a system of advice and the practice of warning are established

    e   equipment is only used for the purpose for which it was originally intended

    f   basic care is provided in the event of an accident.

4.3.5   A safety policy is based on forethought and sound preparation. It should be developed as a team exercise and may involve governors, pupils and other stakeholders as appropriate. The policy should be reviewed on a regular basis. This could be achieved by ensuring that safety issues are a standard agenda item for meetings which take place at least once each year – preferably, more regularly.

Physical education handbooks

4.3.6   Many subject leaders of physical education in primary, secondary and special schools produce a handbook containing relevant information to enable anyone teaching the subject to follow required procedures and programmes. The handbook should:

    a   include a copy of the safety policy and any procedural arrangements to be followed (eg registration at the start of lessons in secondary schools)

    b   include a scheme of work

    c   be readily available and familiar to all those to whom it is relevant, including support and supply staff and trainee teachers on school placement

    d   be reviewed regularly and updated as necessary.

Monitoring and evaluation

4.3.7   Safety issues should be addressed as soon as possible. Staff meetings, either on a whole school basis in primary schools or as a department in secondary schools, will provide regular opportunities to raise and discuss safety matters.

4.3.8   The sharing of information is a vital first step in raising awareness of safety issues, which in turn can lead to more informed and, therefore, better practice.

4.3.9   Periodic monitoring and review of hazards should be established. This is an important aspect of risk management. Monitoring may be carried out in a number of ways – by peer observation of sessions, checking planning against schemes of work, pupil records, accident report forms and discussion at staff meetings.

Informing parents

4.3.10 Parents should be kept fully informed of activities and related safe practice arrangements in physical education. This could be done via the school prospectus, letters, newsletters and brochures.

4.3.11 Parents should be informed about their child's involvement in OSHL activities. It is helpful if the school prospectus explains that pupils are likely to be involved in OSHL activities at some point in their school career. When this opportunity arises, the parents of the pupils involved should be kept informed. This may involve providing them with relevant information at the start of each term, such as the items listed below:

   a Fixture list for each sport

   b Practice schedule for OSHL activities.

4.3.12 In exceptional circumstances (eg a visit to an international match), written parental consent may need to be sought for the pupils involved.

   ▶▶ A sample parental consent form for educational visits is provided in Appendix 2.

4.3.13 All information relating to OSHL activities should also be made available to the main school office so that parents who are unsure of arrangements can contact the school for confirmation.

Community use of physical education facilities

4.3.14 Arrangements for the community use of physical education facilities should ensure that consistent procedures and standards are applied across the different groups using the facilities. Written safety policies for the facilities should be developed with, and made known to, community user groups, with due regard to liability and insurance matters. It is good practice to include specific safety requirements (eg staffing levels, qualifications, insurance requirements and procedures) in written letting agreements.

Risk management

People

- **Pupils should share in the assessment and management of the risks involved**.

- The employer is responsible for health and safety.

- Head teachers and governors are responsible for the day-to-day management of health and safety.

- Subject leaders should monitor the application of procedures and standards in physical education.

- School staff should:

  - follow set policies and procedures

  - report health and safety issues

  - take all possible action to minimise the risk of injury

  - *teach safely* and *teach safety*.

Context

- Policy statements for health and safety should explain the purpose, rationale and context for risk management in physical education.

- Subject leaders are recommended to produce physical education handbooks.

- Safety issues should be raised and discussed as soon as possible.

- Periodic monitoring and review of hazards should be established.

- Parents should be kept fully informed.

- Procedures and standards should be applied consistently across the school (including community use of facilities).

▶▶ See *Chapter two: Risk management* for more detailed, general guidance on risk management issues.

Questions and answers

People

Qu 1   **I was recently asked to supervise the work of a coach who, through the local football club, was assigned to help with my class's football lesson. Feelings flared a little when I told him that I wanted my class to spend most of their time working on basic skills rather than just playing 5-a-side. He told me that he would decide what they would do since he was a qualified FA coach. My class contains a mixture of seven- and eight-year-olds. Should I have given in to the football coach?**

Ans   This question raises the issue of safe management. Even if the coach's football skills are superior to your own, the legal fact is that you, the teacher, are the person responsible for the well-being of your pupils.

You would know better than the coach whether it was totally safe for such young pupils to be encouraged to play the team game, rather than to concentrate on simple skills practices and consolidation before setting up small-sided games (not necessarily five-a-side competitions). You would be expected to know and to decide whether every pupil was sufficiently mature to take part in sophisticated *grown-up* type games. You would be the one aware of the dangers of mismatched children and what might happen to them during the hurly-burly of full-sized games.

In this instance, you were therefore right to overrule the football coach.

Context

Qu 2   **What is the need for, or value of, parental consent for pupil participation in any given activity?**

Ans   If school staff involve pupils in an activity which is not part of the curriculum normally offered by the school, it is advisable to inform parents and to seek their consent prior to the activity taking place. Doing this will in no way reduce the duty of care required of the school staff, although it will prevent a parent from pleading ignorance of their child's involvement in the activity.

LEAs and head teachers are experienced in this area and may be expected to provide an appropriate parental consent form. The legal departments of teachers' unions and professional associations may also be able to provide advice on appropriate wording and formats for consent forms.

▶▶ A sample parental consent form is provided in Appendix 2.

Chapter five

The curriculum and out-of-school-hours learning

5.1 Introduction

5.1.1   In addition to the requirements of the National Curriculum in physical education, most schools provide a voluntary and varied programme of out-of-school-hours learning (OSHL) in which pupils may take part on a voluntary basis. This may take place beyond the school day and its premises. Both curricular and OSHL activities require the same duty of care from school staff.

5.1.2   Awareness of safety is an integral part of the education process and its development enables pupils to accept and exercise greater responsibility as they mature. The knowledge gained can be applied outside and beyond school, where the principles of safe practice underpin the tasks and challenges of daily living. Safety is a general requirement and an integral part of the *knowledge and understanding of fitness and health* aspect of learning within the National Curriculum in physical education. It is most effectively demonstrated and applied in the practical areas of learning and nowhere more so than in physical education.

5.2 People

5.2.1   School staff should know and apply the accepted techniques for learning an activity and the progressive stages leading up to that activity.

5.2.2   School staff should be aware of any recorded individual needs of pupils, including special educational needs (SEN), disabilities or medical conditions. Lack of awareness by school staff in this regard has sometimes been significant in cases of alleged negligence.

5.2.3   School staff should be aware of any medical treatment, particularly drugs, which a pupil may be receiving and take account of its known effects on the sensory perception, motor control and coordination of the pupil.

5.2.4   Pupils should be physically capable of undertaking the tasks with which they are presented. Factors such as size, weight, strength, mobility and endurance should be taken into account when assessing whether or not individual pupils may reasonably be expected to take part in an activity.

5.2.5   The stages of growth and development of young people, particularly during adolescence, and the individual differences which occur at such times, must be taken into account when pupils take part in physical activities. Periods of relatively rapid body change, when *growth spurts* take place, significantly influence performance and may, in some instances, cause temporary regression of physical skill, strength, endurance and coordination. Empathy, understanding, and explanation by school staff will help to ensure that physical activities are appropriately modified to meet these changing individual circumstances.

5.2.6   Pupils should share in the assessment and management of the risks associated with physical education activities. This is an essential part of the learning process. Due to different abilities, the risk management process should be applied to individual pupils, to pupil groups and to the class as a whole.

Pupils with special educational needs

5.2.7   It is most important for head teachers to request information from parents on any significant physical or mental medical conditions and associated needs of pupils. School staff, particularly physical education teachers, should be informed accordingly.

> ▶▶ See *Chapter seven: Pupils with special educational needs or medical needs* for further details.

5.3   Context

5.3.1   During journeys to and from inter-school events which take place at venues other than their own school, pupils should be accompanied by at least one member of school staff, supported by other responsible adults according to the size of the group. Arrangements should be made for them to travel as a group or in several groups where large numbers are involved.

5.3.2   Procedures should be written into a safety policy and adopted by all school staff involved in the delivery of physical education activities.

Parental consent

5.3.3   Parents should be informed of any educational visit which takes place during curriculum time or out of school hours.

> ▶▶ A sample letter for informing parents about educational visits is provided in Appendix 3.

5.3.4   Parental consent should be obtained for senior pupils when direct supervision cannot be provided during educational visits.

> ▶▶ A sample parental consent form for educational visits is provided in Appendix 2.

5.3.5   Indemnity forms seeking to absolve the school of responsibility for injury have no standing in law. Parents sign participation agreements (eg consent forms) without removing the school's duty of care.

Parental notes

5.3.6   A note from a parent requesting that a pupil be excused active participation in physical education on given grounds should always be treated seriously and accepted where a specific illness or injury is stated. Subsequent tactful enquiries may be appropriate in cases of reasonable doubt.

5.3.7   Prolonged periods of inactivity through ill health or injury on the part of a pupil should result in a letter from the school to the parent(s) expressing concern for the pupil's well-being and requesting an explanation. If there is no response, home school workers should be asked to investigate.

5.4 Organisation

5.4.1 All physical education activities should take place in the context of learning about safety.

Preparation

5.4.2 Schemes of work should be constructed to provide appropriate content for the ages and stages of educational development of the pupils involved. These should provide cohesion, continuity and progression to ensure that pupils' experiences are at all times appropriate, with risks assessed and managed so that safe practice is addressed and implemented. A safe system will identify pupils with any SEN or medical needs, or additional educational needs and ensure that pupils are not exposed to unreasonable challenge. Record-keeping is therefore vital.

5.4.3 Individual pupils will vary in their stages of development and capacities to meet and respond to challenge. It is essential that pupils are not challenged beyond their individual capabilities. The use of tasks, equipment and time must allow for differentiated inputs and outcomes. If a specific skill is taught, school staff must be satisfied that it is appropriate for the pupils concerned, whether as a whole class, a group or individually. No pupil should be placed at risk by attempting a skill or activity for which he/she is not ready or capable.

5.4.4 Particular care should be taken when determining the appropriate nature and level of an activity for pupils who are inexperienced or immature, have a disability or experience behavioural disorder.

5.4.5 Physical education activities should be planned carefully, paying particular attention to the inherent risks involved and how these will be managed.

5.4.6 An activity should never proceed if an inherent hazard cannot reasonably be managed and safety may therefore be compromised.

Teaching

5.4.7 Pupils should always be supervised when taking part in physical education, both during curriculum time and OSHL activities.

5.4.8 School staff/pupil ratios should be modified according to the maturity, competence, intelligence, experience and behavioural/emotional characteristics of the pupils and the nature of the activities in which they are involved.

5.4.9 Class numbers should be checked at the start of, and during, a lesson or OSHL activity. In the case of swimming and cross-country running, an additional check should also be made at the end of the activity.

5.4.10 School staff should adopt a position where they can safely and effectively supervise all pupils while they are working.

5.4.11 Pupils should be monitored for signs of fatigue. This is generally associated with prolonged activity and is demonstrated by a reduced level of concentration, slower reaction time and deterioration in quality of performance.

5.4.12 Where fatigue is apparent, activity should stop and the pupil should rest. This is particularly important during activities such as gymnastics, trampolining, distance running and swimming.

Progression

5.4.13   Activities should be broken down into progressive stages and each stage should be learned and consolidated by the pupils. The rate of progress will vary according to their respective abilities. All pupils should follow the appropriate sequence and consolidation before moving on.

5.4.14   Continuity in learning is an important element of safe practice. Where pupils experience a significant break in their learning, particularly when illness is a factor, school staff should carefully consider the reintroduction of these pupils to the programme of work being followed. In such circumstances, it may be necessary to revisit and consolidate activities previously undertaken before pupils progress further. Special consideration should be given to pupils who move between schools and join classes as new pupils.

Further reading

- BAALPE, DfES, NCSS (2004) **Guidance on the organisation of inter-school fixtures and area sports events**[1]

Risk management

People

- **Pupils should share in the assessment and management of the risks involved.**
- School staff should have appropriate levels of expertise in the activities to be undertaken.
- School staff should have knowledge of the pupils':
  - ability
  - behaviour
  - medical conditions
  - confidence.

Context

- School staff should be familiar with the facility being used.
- All equipment used should be appropriate to the needs of the pupils.

Organisation

- Group sizes should be appropriate.
- School staff should decide whether additional supervision is necessary.
- Class numbers should be checked before, during and after activities.

▶▶ See *Chapter two: Risk management* for more detailed, general guidance on risk management issues.

---

1   Visit the BAALPE website (www.baalpe.org) for further details.

Questions and answers

Organisation

Qu 1   **When inter-school games matches are played out of school time, is it acceptable for pupils to travel independently to and from the venue?**

Ans   Pupils should not be asked to undertake difficult journeys without supervision unless their age, experience and maturity is sufficient to cope with the problems involved and parental consent has been obtained.

It is first necessary to assess that the risks are reasonable and then to provide the pupils involved with details of the travel arrangements. Whenever possible, pupils should travel together or in groups.

Chapter six

Safeguarding children and young people

6.1 Introduction

6.1.1 The welfare of all children and young people is paramount.

6.1.2 All children and young people have the right to protection from abuse, regardless of their age, culture, disability, gender, language, racial origin, religious beliefs and sexual identity. They should be made aware of this right and also informed about where to seek help in relation to child abuse, including bullying.

6.1.3 Physical education should take place in a safe, positive and encouraging environment. All school staff, volunteers and paid coaches should:

a promote a culture that ensures that children and young people are listened to and respected as individuals

b know how to respond appropriately to concerns about children and young people

c know how to respond appropriately to allegations of child abuse committed by other adults

d know how to respond appropriately to allegations of child abuse committed by other children and young people.

6.1.4 Each school will have its own child protection policy and procedures, but subject leaders need to satisfy themselves that they are sufficient for the purposes of physical education, in line with the guidance provided in this chapter.

6.2 Recruitment procedures

6.2.1 All schools should have clear procedures for the recruitment of school staff and other adults (eg volunteers and paid coaches) who will work with children and young people. These should include:

a application

b interview

c references

d self-declaration[1]

e Criminal Records Bureau[2] (CRB) checks

f induction

g mentoring

h review.

---

1 See Section 6.3 on pages 50–51 for guidance on disclosure certification.

2 Or home country agency such as Disclosure Scotland.

6.2.2 All schools need to satisfy themselves that all school staff, volunteers and paid coaches are suitable to work with children and young people, and should ensure that all the necessary checks are carried out before any person takes up such a position.

6.2.3 The following Department for Education and Skills (DfES) documents[1] contain useful guidance in this respect:

a *Child Protection: Preventing Unsuitable People from Working with Children and Young Persons in the Education Service* provides details of the pre-appointment checks that should be carried out on all people who will have contact with children and young people, and explains the role of the CRB.

b *Criminal Records Bureau: Managing the Demand for Disclosures* provides further advice for head teachers on checking the suitability of volunteers.

6.3 Disclosure certification

6.3.1 Disclosure certification is a way of checking adults' suitability to work with children and young people and is intended to provide an effective recruitment monitoring process for employers and voluntary organisations.

6.3.2 Anyone appointed to work with children and young people without supervision, whether in a paid or voluntary capacity, should be asked by the employer to provide a disclosure certificate. This is a document containing information held by the police and relevant Government departments (eg DfES, Department of Health), and is available from the CRB.

6.3.3 The employer (local education authority (LEA)/governors/trustees) will determine whether a certificate is needed and, if so, at what level. Schools are advised to check with their employer if they are unsure as to whether any adult, who is not a member of school staff, needs to provide disclosure certification.

6.3.4 The information contained in disclosure certificates is confidential and is not passed on to schools by the employer. Schools will simply be informed whether or not the information received makes the applicant suitable to be appointed to a particular post.

6.3.5 A criminal record does not automatically make someone unsuitable to work with children and young people. Suitability for employment should be judged in relation to:

a all pre-employment checks

b the nature of any offences

c the nature of the appointment

d the age of the offence

e the frequency of the offence

f the circumstances of the offence

g changes in the applicant's circumstances.

1   See page 55 for full reference details.

6.3.6 Volunteers and paid coaches are responsible for applying for their own disclosure certificates. This can be done in two ways:

a Phone the CRB and provide the details requested. The CRB then inputs the details into the application form, prints it off and sends it to the applicant for signing and submission to a registered body (usually the employer).

or

b Complete an application form provided by the employer.

6.3.7 The completed form should be submitted to whoever originally requested it (eg school), along with any necessary originals of identity documents. The employer will countersign the form.

NB Head teachers of LEA schools cannot countersign on behalf of an LEA.

6.3.8 If an individual has a number of jobs with different employers for which disclosure certification is required, he/she may ask a new employer to accept sight of his/her first disclosure certificate rather than applying for another one. Whether or not the employer will accept this will depend on:

a the level of certification

b how long ago it was awarded

c the nature of the position for which it was issued.

6.3.9 Certification will usually be logged by employers before destroying the disclosure certificate. All certificates must be destroyed after six months and employers must justify the need to retain certificates beyond this time.

6.4 Child Protection Coordinators

6.4.1 In accordance with DFE Circular 10/95 *Child Protection: The Role of the Education Service*[1], all schools should have a senior teacher with designated responsibility for child protection.

6.4.2 During off-site educational visits and out-of-school-hours learning (OSHL) activities, all adults should be aware of their responsibilities in relation to child protection issues and should report any concerns to the teacher in charge.

6.5 Child protection policies

6.5.1 All schools should have a child protection policy. This should:

a be clear and unambiguous, and understood by school staff, volunteers and paid coaches

b include appropriate guidance and training to help teachers, volunteers and paid coaches meet the requirements of the school's child protection procedures

c be publicised and promoted within the school

d be mandatory

e be reviewed every three years.

1 See page 55 for full reference details.

6.6 Child protection procedures

6.6.1 In accordance with DFE Circular 10/95 *Child Protection: The Role of the Education Service*[1], all schools should have clear and unambiguous child protection procedures that comply with LEA and Area Child Protection Committee guidance. All teachers, volunteers and paid coaches working with children and young people in, or on behalf of, a school should be aware of these procedures and operate in accordance with them.

6.6.2 Child protection procedures should cover the following areas:

a Reporting suspicions and allegations of child abuse

b Reporting concerns about unacceptable behaviour by other members of school staff, paid coaches or volunteers

c Dealing with unacceptable behaviour by an adult, child or young person

d Supporting an adult, child or young person who is suspected of inappropriate behaviour towards a child or young person

e Recording incidents

f Confidentiality and information-sharing

g Dealing with complaints.

6.6.3 Any concerns relating to child abuse should be referred in accordance with local Area Child Protection Committee procedures.

6.6.4 All suspicions and allegations of abuse should be taken seriously and responded to swiftly and appropriately.

6.7 Safeguarding adults

6.7.1 In order to protect themselves against allegations of abuse, school staff, volunteers and paid coaches should act in an appropriate way, which is unlikely to cause concern to other adults or harm children and young people. This should be in line with relevant published codes of conduct, good practice and ethics, and/or other guidance on expected and acceptable behaviour towards children and young people.

6.7.2 All disciplinary measures and sanctions should be non-violent and should not involve humiliating children and young people.

6.7.3 School staff, volunteers and paid coaches should attend relevant training courses to raise their awareness of child protection issues[2].

---

1 See page 55 for full reference details.

2 See Section 6.8 on page 53 for further details.

6.8 Education and training

6.8.1 In order to safeguard children and young people, and minimise the risk of abuse, all school staff, volunteers and paid coaches should have access to appropriate guidance and training in the following areas:

a Expected and acceptable behaviour towards children and young people (eg codes of conduct for adult/child behaviour and child/child behaviour, good practice guidelines)

b Appropriate ratios of adults to children and gender-specific supervision

c Filming and photographing at sports events[1]

d Using digital imagery on websites[1]

e Supporting and handling pupils (to improve performance or for demonstration purposes)

f First aid (including the appropriate handling of injured pupils)

g Physical contact by adults in contact sports

h One-to-one coaching

i Journeys in cars, taxis and minibuses

j Conduct on school trips

k Other relevant issues.

6.8.2 In order to raise awareness of child abuse and overcome the barriers which children, young people and adults may experience to reporting their concerns, all school staff, volunteers and paid coaches should have access to appropriate training and guidance in the following areas:

a Recognising and responding to signs and indicators of child abuse

b Responding to a child or young person who reports an allegation of abuse.

6.9 Digital imagery

6.9.1 The development of digital technology (eg digital cameras and video recorders) has opened up an exciting and highly effective way of enhancing learning in schools. Physical education is a subject in which a great deal of visual learning takes place. Digital photographs and video clips can provide pupils with clear images of performances and specific techniques, as well as immediate visual feedback on their own movements. New software enables this process to be managed easily during physical education sessions.

6.9.2 However, certain procedural and protocol issues need to be addressed to ensure that digital images are managed effectively and securely. This is particularly important since they can now be transmitted and manipulated easily. Great care should be taken to safeguard children and young people when storing and using digital images in an educational context.

---

1 See Section 6.9 for further details.

Parental consent

6.9.3   Parental consent should be obtained prior to filming or photographing pupils. It is good practice to include relevant details on school admission forms to inform parents that digital imagery is used in education to support learning, and to reassure them that it will only be used in specific circumstances.

▶▶   A sample parental consent form for the use of digital imagery in schools is provided in Appendix 4.

In-house use of images

6.9.4   In-house use of digital imagery occurs within a school or group of schools as part of a defined educational project or partnership (eg between a secondary school and its feeder primary schools). The way the images are used should be controlled by the school or project at all times.

6.9.5   Access to the images should be controlled by authentication mechanisms (eg password protection and/or identification of specific computers).

6.9.6   Manipulation of the images must be restricted to appropriate formatting and display purposes (ie to enhance the content for educational use).

6.9.7   School staff should be aware of the dangers of distributing the images via e-mail or CD-ROM. This leads to a loss of control of the images by the user group.

6.9.8   The following filming guidelines should be followed:

a   Pay particular attention to the background. Clutter-free backgrounds focus the attention of the learner on the specific performance issues.

b   Care should be taken over the angles chosen for filming higher risk sporting situations (ie swimming, gymnastics, trampolining, some athletics events). Profile shots (side-on) are generally more informative and less prone to risk of misuse.

c   Filming pupils on the poolside should be avoided.

d   Some specialist sports clothing (eg swimming costumes, gymnastic leotards) can create added risk.

e   Names of pupils should not appear in images used on websites. If this is not possible, the images should not be used.

Publishing images

6.9.9   The publishing of images occurs when they are distributed beyond a defined group via videotape, DVD, CD-ROM or a website/internet.

6.9.10   Publishing images, particularly of minors in a physical education environment, has obvious associated risks. Following appropriate filming guidelines[1] will help teachers to reduce these risks and enhance their feedback to pupils.

---

1   See paragraph 6.9.8 for further details.

6.9.11 The following additional guidelines will help school staff to reduce the risks associated with the publishing of video clips:

    a Use general view shots to establish the theme.

    b Shots held for a maximum of three seconds reduce risks (this makes the clip very difficult to manipulate).

    c Any pupil shown in a video clip should not be identified by name.

    d Interviews should only show the head and shoulders of the pupils involved. They should not be identified by name (this includes voice-overs and text-overs).

    e Group shots should be in wide vision.

6.9.12 Further information can be obtained from the DfES document *Superhighway Safety Pack – Safety for Schools*[1] and other relevant publications/organisations.

Storage guidelines

6.9.13 First generation content (ie master tapes) should be stored in a secure environment since these are more readily manipulated if they fall into the wrong hands. Second generation video copies and compressed digital video (eg Windows Media Files) are less of a risk since manipulation is more difficult.

6.9.14 Libraries of tapes should be managed with care. Unnecessary storage of material should be avoided. Tapes should be stored in a locked cabinet and saved for a maximum of five years.

6.9.15 The reuse of tapes, which have not been erased first, can increase the risk of unwanted images being used inappropriately.

Further reading

- BAALPE, PEA UK, Sport England, sports coach UK (2003) **Induction pack for teachers and adults other than teachers.** Leeds, Coachwise Solutions. ISBN 1 902523 44 X

- DFE (1995) **Circular 10/95: child protection – the role of the Education Service.** London, DFE

- DfES (2002) **Child protection: preventing unsuitable people from working with children and young persons in the Education Service.** London, DfES Publications. Ref no: DfES/0278/2002

- DfES (2002) **Criminal Records Bureau: managing the demand for disclosures**. London, DfES Publications. Ref no: DfES/0780/2002

- DfES (2003) **Superhighway safety internet – safety for schools.** London, DfES Publications. Ref no: SAFEREV2JUNE2003

- Home Office (2004) **Keep your child safe on the internet.** London, Home Office Communication Directorate. Ref no: ICP2

- NCH (2004) **Child abuse, child pornography and the internet**. London, NCH. ISBN 0 9009 8479 1

- sports coach UK (2001) **Code of conduct for sports coaches.** Leeds, Coachwise Solutions

- sports coach UK (2001) **Safe and sound (leaflet).** Leeds, Coachwise Solutions

- sports coach UK (2002) **Protecting children: a guide for sportspeople.** 3rd edition. Leeds, Coachwise Solutions. ISBN 0 947850 50 3

1 See below for full reference details.

Risk management

People

- All schools should have a designated Child Protection Coordinator.
- The work of volunteers and paid coaches should be managed and monitored.
- Employers' disclosure certification requirements should be followed.

Context

- Physical education should take place in a safe, positive and encouraging environment.
- Child protection procedures should comply with LEA and Area Child Protection Committee guidance.
- Whole school child protection policies and procedures should be applied to physical education.
- Volunteers and paid coaches should be informed about child protection procedures and monitored in relation to them.

Organisation

- Awareness of child abuse issues should be raised and appropriate training opportunities provided to all teachers, volunteers and paid coaches.
- All allegations of abuse should be taken seriously.
- Parental consent should be obtained before photographing/filming pupils.
- The use of photographs and video clips should be planned before actually shooting any material.
- Schools should control the use of any photographic and video material they produce.
- All visual material involving pupils should be stored securely.

▶▶ See *Chapter two: Risk management* for more detailed, general guidance on risk management issues.

Questions and answers

People

Qu 1   **We use coaches quite often at my school. They have been CRB checked by the LEA, so do I always need to be in charge or in vision when they are working with our pupils? If so, does this change once they have provided high quality coaching over a reasonable period of time and I feel I can trust them?**

Ans   Technically, your head teacher is responsible for making this decision. The coaches should have been monitored and made aware of all school procedures relating to behaviour, discipline, first aid, evacuation and end-of-session arrangements. If they are deemed to be working in a responsible and safe manner, they may work at distance from the supervising school staff. However, a member(s) of school staff must be responsible for the management of the coaches and should be on site whenever they are working with pupils. All coaches working off site should be accompanied by a member of school staff other than in exceptional circumstances.

Qu 2   **I have been told that anyone who is not a member of school staff, and who assists with the delivery of physical education activities, must have an enhanced CRB disclosure certificate. Is this correct?**

Ans   Employers are responsible for this policy decision. Teachers should check what their local requirements are. These will be based on DfES guidance, but may vary from one school/LEA to another.

Context

Qu 3   **What action should I take if I see a pupil with an unusual injury?**

Ans   Follow your employer's guidelines. Observe and note the nature and extent of the injury, and the time and date. Report the details to your school's Child Protection Coordinator and/or head teacher. If you are on an off-site educational visit, report the details to the teacher in charge.

Qu 4   **I am organising an educational visit. How important is it to address the gender issue when arranging first aid provision?**

Ans   It is good practice to arrange both male and female cover where possible. However, in the event of an emergency, the most immediately available member of school staff should respond.

Qu 5   **A pupil reports an incident which raises concerns about their safety or well-being. What action should I take?**

Ans   Follow your employer's guidelines. Remove the pupil from the situation if necessary. Make a note of the time, date and pupil's comments, and report the details to your head teacher/Child Protection Coordinator.

Qu 6   **A bus driver verbally abuses/accuses some of my pupils. What should I do?**

Ans   Remove the pupils from the situation and try to resolve it. Report the incident to your head teacher/Child Protection Coordinator to ensure that the manager of the bus company involved is informed.

Organisation

Qu 7 **What would be the most appropriate way to check rooms/dormitories during a residential visit? Does this depend on the age of the pupils involved?**

Ans Only male school staff should enter boys' rooms/dormitories and female school staff girls' rooms/dormitories. In an emergency situation, male and female members of staff should support each other. If a cross-gender situation is the only solution, school staff are recommended to operate in pairs after having confirmed that all occupants of the rooms/dormitories are in a decent state of dress.

▶▶ See also Qu 1 in *Chapter nineteen: Swimming, diving and lifesaving activities* (page 274).

Chapter seven

Pupils with special educational needs or medical needs

7.1   Introduction

7.1.1   For many years, physical education has made a unique contribution to the physical, social, emotional and intellectual development of pupils with special educational needs (SEN) in mainstream primary, secondary and special schools.

7.1.2   The inclusion of pupils with SEN in physical education has risen up the agenda in recent years to such an extent that many pupils are now being educated in mainstream schools, while still acknowledging the value of special schools and the role that they play.

7.1.3   The SEN Code of Practice (2002) outlines the nature of support and provision available to pupils and places significant responsibility for action on schools through the four stages of: School Action, School Action Plus, Formal Assessment and Statement of SEN. It is essential that any school staff involved in teaching pupils with SEN consults his/her school's Special Educational Needs Coordinator (SENCO) in order to ensure that all relevant educational, pastoral and managerial policies are followed.

7.1.4   The SEN and Disability Act (2001) offers pupils with SEN and their parents a fundamental right to access a mainstream education, and/or to ensure that appropriate provision is available to meet individual pupil needs. In addition, the National Curriculum (2000) Statutory Inclusion Statement establishes clear duties and expectations of school staff to set suitable learning challenges, respond to individual pupils' diverse needs and overcome potential barriers to learning and assessment.

7.1.5   This chapter aims to build on the excellent safe practice developed in the special education field in order to provide guidance relevant to both mainstream and special schools.

7.2   Philosophy

7.2.1   The social model of disability recognises that, in order for pupils with SEN to access physical education, school staff should be prepared to modify and/or adapt their existing practices in order to meet individual pupil needs. Consequently, in the context of planning for the inclusion of pupils with SEN in physical education, activities should be delivered with equal worth, challenge and appropriateness to individual pupil needs. As with all physical education activities, it is essential that they are delivered within a safe and secure environment.

7.2.2　　　Pupils with mild forms of some of the disabilities covered in this chapter (eg asthma, epilepsy, diabetes) have been attending mainstream schools for many years. However, school staff are advised to regularly reassess teaching practices to ensure the continued provision of safe learning environments, while considering the more complex range of pupil needs now entering mainstream schools.

7.2.3　　　All pupils with SEN should take part in regular physical education; it is vital to their growth and development. Often, such pupils need more, rather than less, physical education.

7.2.4　　　When teaching physical education, it is important to adopt positive attitudes and to have open minds and high expectations of pupils with SEN. The planning of activities for pupils with SEN should be an integral part of their teaching and learning philosophy.

7.2.5　　　For pupils with SEN, the way to a free and independent life is not only through being well cared for, but also through learning to care for themselves.

7.2.6　　　The effectiveness of any programmes of study will be influenced by the involvement of the pupils concerned. They should be encouraged to participate in the decision-making process and should, where possible, be educated to understand, and take some personal responsibility for, their own safety.

7.3　　Prior consultation

7.3.1　　　Prior to any pupil with SEN taking part in a physical education programme, consultation and discussion must take place between his/her teacher, parents and other relevant professionals (eg doctor, physiotherapist, school nurse). The pupil should be involved in these discussions whenever practical.

7.3.2　　　The discussions should result in the development of a medical profile/health care plan for the pupil concerned, covering issues such as:

　　　　　a　personal health care equipment (eg inhalers, syringes, incontinence pads)

　　　　　b　body splints and aids

　　　　　c　*valves* and *shunts*

　　　　　d　administration of drugs

　　　　　e　incontinence

　　　　　f　mobility aids

　　　　　g　ranges of physical movement

　　　　　h　daily living aid

　　　　　i　care assistance

　　　　　j　any activities identified as contraindicative by the medical profession.

7.3.3 Adults[1] in charge of a pupil with SEN must:

a know the nature of the pupil's learning difficulty, disability, emotional or behavioural disorder

b be aware of any constraints on physical activities as a result of the disability or regime of medication

c be able to provide the emergency treatment necessary if physical activities exacerbate the disability

d be prepared for problems such as:

- limited coordination

- lack of spatial concept or perception

- slow reaction time

- variable levels of concentration

- short concentration span

- cardiovascular inhibition

- muscle spasm

- sensory loss

- limited fine/gross motor skills

e have examined the need for:

- mobility aids

- dependence on learning support/care

- special handling

- toileting and waste disposal

- special showering requirements

- special resources

- special/adapted equipment.

f have determined that they:

- have sufficient background knowledge about the pupil

- are confident in their approach to teaching pupils with SEN

- have the knowledge and techniques necessary for safe teaching.

7.3.4 If insufficient information is available to ensure safe practice, school staff must seek guidance and advice from the pupil's parents and other relevant professionals (eg doctor, physiotherapist, school nurse). Further assistance could be obtained via the *Contact a Family Directory*[2].

---

1   Includes school staff, volunteers and paid coaches.

2   See page 80 for full reference details.

7.4 Disabling conditions and their implications for physical education

Arthritis (Still's Disease)

7.4.1 Arthritis, or Still's Disease, is a progressive condition, which mainly affects the joints but sometimes influences other body systems. Rheumatoid arthritis causes inflammation of the joints, which become swollen and tender. The surrounding tissues become thickened and mobility is impaired. The pain and stiffness experienced may vary from day to day, but it is likely to be most severe early in the morning. Some children affected by arthritis have to wear splints on their wrists and ankles.

7.4.2 Adults should be aware of the following:

a It is essential that advice is sought from pupils' parents and physiotherapists before any physical activity is undertaken.

b Jumping activities should be very limited and jumping from a height avoided.

c Gripping can cause problems (eg in the gymnasium, in some games activities).

d Due to pain and stiffness in the joints, pupils may require more time for general movement.

e General clumsiness may be evident.

f Swimming is very beneficial as this is a non-weight-bearing activity.

Asthma

7.4.3 Asthma is a common ailment, which appears to be increasingly prevalent in young people. The condition narrows or restricts the passages of the lungs. The most noticeable symptoms of asthma are shortness of breath, wheezing and coughing. The severity of an attack may vary considerably from mild (which may need no special treatment) to severe (which will require prompt medical assistance).

7.4.4 Adults should be aware of the following:

a Pupils with asthma should be encouraged to take part in physical education. Reluctance to participate should be discussed with the parents, teachers and the pupil.

b A thorough warm-up is essential. Attacks can often be prevented by using a bronchiodilator inhaler. Asthmatic pupils, for whom these have been prescribed, should be encouraged to carry one with them. Alternative treatment requires a tablet to be taken about twenty minutes before the start of a physical education session. The use of appropriate drugs will usually allow asthmatic pupils to participate normally.

c Exhaling should be emphasised in the event of an attack.

d Pupils with asthma may participate in all physical activities, but care should be taken to avoid prolonged strenuous exercise.

e Swimming is particularly beneficial. Endurance work should be avoided.

Behavioural difficulties

7.4.5   Many children displaying severe behavioural difficulties attend day and residential special schools. They greatly benefit from physical education designed to meet their specific needs. Mainstream schools are not likely to be able to support such pupils. However, some behaviourally disturbed children can cope with the corporate school ethos and, given sensitive teaching support and an appropriate physical education programme, they can both contribute to, and benefit from, their participation.

7.4.6   Generally, these pupils will display an aggressive attitude towards physical education, either verbally or physically, or by simply opting out. Many pupils with severe behavioural problems have a poor self-image and consequently poor self-esteem. The main task will be to improve the former in order to enhance the latter.

7.4.7   Adults should be aware of the following:

    a   Some pupils with behavioural difficulties will cope well with team games, but many will have difficulty coping with peer relationships. Individual and small group activities should therefore be explored in depth prior to larger team games.

    b   Swimming, basic trampolining, simple challenge gymnastics, small group games and stamina-focused circuit training can be undertaken with care.

    c   Teaching groups should be small to ensure that suitable and satisfactory supervision is provided.

    d   If a pupil with unpredictable aggressive behaviour takes part in a physical education session, extra support will be required. In extreme cases, it may be necessary to consider excluding the pupil from the session in order to ensure the safety of other pupils.

Brittle bones (Osteogenesis Imperfecta)

7.4.8   Brittle bones is a condition which is usually inherited and is the result of an abnormality of the protein structure of the bones, which causes them to break more easily than normal. Joints are often more mobile than is generally the case. Occasionally, hearing may be impaired.

7.4.9   For some children, fractures may occur without warning and for no apparent reason but, nevertheless, it is important not to overprotect them. In more severe cases, children are small and the bones are twisted as a result of frequent fractures. These children can rarely join in group activities physically, but enjoy taking responsibilities as judges or umpires.

7.4.10   Children with this condition usually require regular physiotherapy. More severely affected children use special wheelchairs for safety and support[1]. Those with lesser impairment may use sticks and crutches. Most children with brittle bones have severely restricted mobility.

---

1   See Section 7.5 on pages 76–78 for further guidance on pupils in wheelchairs.

7.4.11   Adults should be aware of the following:

a   Because of the nature of this condition, many forms of physical education – especially contact activities – are not suitable. However, some exercise is essential for general fitness.

b   Swimming is ideal, as are other non-weight-bearing activities.

c   Care must be taken in the general handling of pupils with brittle bones when getting in and out of swimming pools.

d   Consultation with parents, doctors and physiotherapists must take place before any physical activity is undertaken. Evidence of this consultation should be obtained prior to pupils participating in physical education.

e   Crowded corridors, changing rooms and playgrounds should be avoided to minimise the risk of bumping and knocking. Pupils with brittle bones need to be given space. Careful planning and selection of appropriate material is essential.

Cardiac conditions and congenital heart disease

7.4.12   Congenital heart disease signifies that a heart defect has been present from birth. In some cases, the condition may be very mild and needs no treatment. The most common condition is called a *hole in the heart*. Children awaiting surgery, and those whose condition cannot be completely cured, require special consideration, but some may be able to join in certain aspects of physical education.

7.4.13   Generalisations should not be made about heart conditions. School staff must seek expert advice from a pupil's parents and doctor about the advisability of participation in physical activity, appropriate levels of activity and the pupil's capabilities.

7.4.14   Adults should be aware of the following:

a   Some pupils with heart disease can lead normal lives and should be allowed to participate in physical education.

b   When heart disease causes circulatory problems, these may be evident through breathlessness and blueness of the lips and nail beds. Pupils will tire very quickly when active.

c   When swimming, special consideration should be given to the water temperature and the procedures which must be followed in the event of a pupil becoming exhausted in the water.

Cerebral palsy

7.4.15   There are three main forms of cerebral palsy – *spasticity*, *athetosis* and *ataxia*.

7.4.16   Cerebral palsy is caused by damage to, or lack of development of, the part of the brain which controls movement. The effects of cerebral palsy vary widely, from slight disability (eg unsteady gait) to severe multiple disabilities.

7.4.17   Adults should be aware of the following:

a Spatial and/or perception difficulties are common.

b Some pupils may have poor motor organisation. Careful attention to correct sequencing is necessary.

c Holding and supporting is often difficult, and care is required during climbing activities.

d Swimming in warm water can assist relaxation. Pupils with spasticity should normally be introduced into the water in the *face upwards* (supine) position. They often have difficulty exhaling, so the importance of controlled breathing and reverting to the supine position should be stressed. After swimming, care must be taken to return the pupil gradually to normal body and air temperature. Severe chilling can induce spasms.

e Some pupils may have more problems with balance and may be more prone to falling over than other pupils.

f Dressing and undressing may be difficult. Allow pupils sufficient time.

g Pupils with an appreciable disability may tire more easily as they need to use more energy to achieve the same goals.

Clumsiness (dyspraxia): developmental coordination difficulties

7.4.18   Clumsiness (minimal motor dysfunction) is relative. This section deals with pupils who appear to be clumsy in attempting most physical tasks, lack coordination of their physical movements and frequently display behavioural disorders.

7.4.19   There is no one example of the typically clumsy pupil and the condition is not necessarily related to intelligence. It is important that clumsiness is identified early and that all those working with a clumsy pupil understand his/her needs and work together towards a remedy.

7.4.20   Adults should be aware of the following:

a A carefully constructed physical education programme can aid the development of clumsy pupils.

b Activities in which pupils respond to tasks at their own level of ability will be helpful. Effort and success should be acknowledged and praised.

c Gross and fine motor skills will usually need to be broken down into the smaller stages of progression.

d Spatial and perceptual difficulties are common.

e Poor motor organisation may be evident. Care is required during climbing activities.

f The *buddy* system (ie working with a friend or peer) may be appropriate.

Coeliac condition

7.4.21 Coeliac condition is caused by sensitivity to the protein gluten. The condition can cause damage to the small intestine and/or a skin condition of small irritating blisters. It may develop at any stage. It is treated by strict dietary means.

7.4.22 Adults should be aware of the following:

a Absolute compliance with diet is necessary.

b Particular care should be taken to ensure that dietary requirements are met during educational visits (eg day trips, excursions).

Cystic fibrosis

7.4.23 Cystic fibrosis is a genetically determined disorder which causes thickening of the mucus secreted by the body, leading to reduced breathing efficiency of the lungs. Regular respiratory education and physiotherapy, together with modern drugs and diet supplements, have greatly improved the survival rate and lifestyles of children with the condition.

7.4.24 Pupils with cystic fibrosis will cough a lot and this helps to clear the lungs. Adults should look out for excessive coughing, breathlessness, blueness around the lips and over-tiredness. In such circumstances, the pupils must rest.

7.4.25 Adults should be aware of the following:

a It is essential to cooperate with parents and medical advisers (particularly pupils' physiotherapists).

b Exercise is helpful and, for some pupils, it is essential. Activities requiring shorter bursts of energy may be more beneficial than endurance activities (eg cross-country running). Otherwise, pupils with cystic fibrosis should be able to participate in all aspects of physical education.

c At secondary school level, pupils with cystic fibrosis should know how much they can reasonably do and know when to rest or to withdraw to clear the lungs.

d At primary school level, awareness of the associated problems is more critical.

e Adults should be aware of any special prescribed inhalants to be used by pupils.

f Swimming is very beneficial. Racing, which may demand too much from pupils, should not be encouraged.

g In hot weather, excessive perspiring will cause loss of salt from the body; this can be detrimental to the condition.

Diabetes

7.4.26 Diabetes is a condition in which the body is not able to absorb sugar and starch properly due to a lack of the hormone insulin. Treatment is usually by means of injections of insulin and/or a controlled diet.

7.4.27 Adults should be aware of the following:

a Pupils with diabetes can normally participate in most physical education activities. However, because exercise can use up sugar in the blood quickly, they may need to have a suitable snack (eg sugar, biscuits, chocolate) before, and sometimes after, exercise.

b Strenuous activities should be supervised by an informed adult.

c Adults should be aware of the symptoms of hypoglycaemia (ie drowsiness, untypical behaviour, excessive sweating or vomiting) and react accordingly.

d The likelihood of the need for extra sugar should be established through consultation with pupils' doctors and parents. It is useful for adults to ensure that a supply of sugar is available in case the symptoms listed above occur. Pupils should also be encouraged to carry sugar in case it is needed.

Down's syndrome

7.4.28 Down's syndrome is a congenital condition in which a baby is born with a chromosome irregularity. A child may have unusual features and may also have learning difficulties. Additional disabilities, such as hearing loss, poor eyesight and heart defects, may also be present.

7.4.29 Atlanto-axial instability may also affect a small minority of these children. In this condition, the two upper cervical vertebrae of the spine are more mobile than normal. In such cases, severe pressure can produce dislocation, or may even cause the spinal cord to sever. These children may need special care[1]. Some Down's syndrome children attend mainstream schools.

7.4.30 Adults should be aware of the following:

a Most Down's syndrome pupils are able to participate in all physical education activities.

b Down's syndrome pupils present a wide range of physical abilities. Some will be well coordinated and able; others will be flat-footed, overweight and clumsy.

c For pupils with atlanto-axial instability, the following activities must be avoided:

• Gymnasium: rolling activities, high level gymnastics, trampolining

• Swimming pool: diving, butterfly stroke, breast stroke

• Games and athletics: martial arts, boxing, high jump

• High-level contact activities: scrummaging or tackling in rugby.

d Any additional disabilities present must be taken into account in accordance with the relevant guidance provided in this chapter.

e Some pupils will have a very short concentration span; reinforcement and perseverance are vital. Most pupils will respond to constant encouragement and praise.

1 See paragraph 7.4.30c for further details.

Eczema

7.4.31   Eczema is an itchy, sore and sometimes very unpleasant skin condition. It is not infectious.

7.4.32   Adults should be aware of the following:

a At times, joints become stiff and sore, and pupils may find physical education activities difficult.

b Pupils should be protected from extremes of temperature.

c Some pupils will be sensitive to chlorinated water. Discussion with parents should take place prior to pupils taking part in a swimming programme.

Epider molysis bullosa

7.4.33   Epider molysis bullosa occurs when the collagen fibres between the layers of skin malfunction and blisters form between these layers.

7.4.34   Adults should be aware of the following:

a Gentle exercise is needed to keep the skin, muscles and joints in good condition.

b Body contact should be avoided.

c Team games, in which contact can occur, are generally unsuitable.

d Swimming is beneficial, but medical approval should first be sought.

Epilepsy

7.4.35   Epilepsy is a symptom of a disorder of the nervous system which manifests itself in the form of an epileptic seizure (fit or attack). There are three types of seizure – *grand mal*, *petit mal* and *temporal lobe epilepsy*. School staff should check medical or school records to ascertain which type an individual pupil has.

Grand mal

7.4.36   This is a major seizure during which pupils may make a strange cry, fall suddenly, stiffen and then relax, before lapsing into convulsive movements. After several minutes they should recover consciousness, although they will feel dazed and confused. This condition is often controlled by drugs and rarely happens at school.

Petit mal

7.4.37   This is manifested by brief interruptions of consciousness and may be difficult to detect. Although brief, the absences can be frequent.

Temporal lobe epilepsy

7.4.38   This results in partial seizures taking the form of a period of partial consciousness in which abnormal behaviour such as lip smacking, head turning and plucking at clothes may occur. These signs can be mistaken for silliness or psychological disturbance.

7.4.39   Adults should be aware of the following:

    a Advice from parents and doctors should be sought. However, pupils with epilepsy are normally able to participate in all physical education activities.

    b During swimming activities, pupils should normally be partnered with strong swimmers using the *buddy* system.

    c A person should be present on the poolside, whose primary duty is to watch pupils with epilepsy.

    d If a seizure occurs in the water, it is essential that the *buddy* or the person on the poolside is capable of holding the pupil's head above water.

    e Working at high levels in the gymnasium or participating in higher risk activities (eg rock climbing, sailing) should be undertaken with extreme caution (especially if pupils are taking drugs and if seizures are not uncommon). As well as checking with parents and doctors, school staff are advised to ensure that pupils always work with responsible partners.

    f Adults must fully understand the following procedures for coping with a seizure:

- Allow the seizure to take its course.

- Cushion the pupil's head and do not restrain.

- Do not give the pupil a drink.

- Carefully loosen the clothing around the pupil's neck.

- Only call an ambulance if the pupil does not regain consciousness after 15 minutes. (The standard procedure for calling an ambulance should be written, displayed and known by all adults.)

- After the seizure, place the pupil in the recovery position and allow time to rest.

    g Careful consideration should be given to pupils with epilepsy wearing distinctive coloured caps when swimming, so that they can be identified more easily.

Freidrich's ataxia

7.4.40   Freidrich's ataxia is an inherited disease of the central nervous system which causes a progressive deterioration of coordination and muscle control.

7.4.41   Adults should be aware of the following:

    a Regular exercise is required.

    b Physical education programmes should be designed in association with a physiotherapist.

    c Pupils need to be kept mobile for as long as possible.

Haemophilia

7.4.42   Haemophilia is an inherited condition whereby there is a lifelong deficiency in the clotting factor in the blood. Children with haemophilia may bleed for much longer than normal after injury and may suffer frequent pain due to stiffness in the joints.

7.4.43   Adults should be aware of the following:

a Most pupils with haemophilia can participate to some extent in physical education activities and restrictions should be kept to a minimum.

b The likelihood of damage to the tissues is reduced by general fitness; swimming usually provides one of the best forms of exercise.

c Contact sports (eg rugby, football, basketball) should be avoided.

d School staff should liaise with parents about the extent to which pupils should participate in physical education activities.

e It is essential for school staff to consult with parents about appropriate procedures for treating injuries (eg check whether normal first aid is appropriate for small cuts). Pupils with haemophilia must receive prompt, correct assistance.

f When treating injuries, adults should pay due regard to advice issued by the Department for Education and Skills (DfES), the local health authority and the local education authority (LEA) on possible contact with the AIDS virus.

Hearing impairment

7.4.44   There are two basic types of hearing impairment:

a **Conductive deafness** affects the outer and middle ear, and can result from obstruction or malformation.

b **Sensori-neural deafness** affects the inner ear. It results from malfunction in either the inner ear or the auditory nerve, and prevents the proper transmission of sounds to the brain. Hearing loss may be permanent and severe, but in some cases may be alleviated by the use of hearing aids. Mixed conductive and sensori-neural deafness may occur in some children.

7.4.45   Adults should be aware of the following:

a Pupils with partial hearing are generally allowed to participate in all physical education activities and this should be encouraged. However, it may be necessary to restrict certain activities (eg swimming) if a pupil has a middle ear infection, a perforated eardrum or a post-operative condition.

b Pupils should be able to see the adult's face easily when lip-reading will be used. As far as possible, the adult should endeavour to:

• be near to the pupils

• be at the same horizontal level as the pupils

• be still when speaking and look towards the pupils

• face the light so that his/her face is not in shadow

• avoid shouting and use normal rhythm and intonation.

c Hearing aids:

• must be removed before swimming

• tend to amplify background noise and do not make speech clearer.

d Communication between deaf pupils and adults can be a source of frustration. It is useful to devise signals whereby the pupils can alert adults to the fact that an instruction or task has not been understood.

e Normal audio warning signals may not be heard. Visual signals may be necessary, especially in swimming pools. Another pupil may be designated to ensure that a hearing-impaired pupil is aware of the warning (ie the *buddy* system).

f Peripatetic teachers of the deaf are a valuable source of help and information.

Hydrocephalus

▶▶ See paragraphs 7.4.66 to 7.4.69 on pages 74 to 76 for information about spina bifida and hydrocephalus.

Kidney disorders

7.4.46 There are two main types of kidney disorders – *severe kidney infection* (which usually responds to treatment) and *kidney failure* (which results in the need for an organ transplant or for regular dialysis). Anaemia and associated fatigue are common. Children can become irritable and/or confused.

7.4.47 Adults should be aware of the following:

a Consultation with pupils' doctors and parents will be necessary to ascertain an appropriate physical education programme for both categories.

b Strict dietary control is required for renal failure. Particular care should be taken to ensure that all requirements are met during out-of-school-hour-learning activities.

c Pupils on dialysis could be involved in day trips, providing the programme is not too physically demanding.

Loss of limb

7.4.48 Children may be born without, or lose through an accident, a limb or partial limb. Artificial limbs encourage the development of muscle strength and patterns of movement.

7.4.49 Adults should be aware of the following:

a Parents and physiotherapists should be consulted about the removal of artificial limbs.

b The development and maintenance of physical fitness, including muscle strength, is essential.

c Physiotherapists should be consulted about any specific exercise programmes which may be required.

d Pupils with lower limb loss will need extra work on body balance.

e Control of wheelchairs[1], through lack of balance, can be a problem.

Moderate learning difficulties

7.4.50 Many pupils with moderate learning difficulties are now being educated in mainstream schools. This condition is not an illness or a disease; it is an intellectual impairment usually caused by genetic factors, or sometimes the result of an illness or accident. However, many pupils will have perceptual and coordination difficulties, and their skill level, both physically and cognitively, should be assessed prior to physical activity.

1 See Section 7.5 on pages 76–78 for further guidance on pupils in wheelchairs.

7.4.51   Adults should be aware of the following:

a Pupils with moderate learning difficulties should be able to participate in all
   activities, although some forms of activity may need to be modified.

b Many pupils will experience difficulties in activities involving cooperation.

Muscular dystrophy

7.4.52   There are several forms of muscular dystrophy, all of which are progressive.
          Either gender may generally be affected. The essential characteristic is a
          progressive breakdown of muscle fibre, resulting in the gradual weakening of all
          muscle groups. It first affects the extensor muscles of the hips, knees and
          shoulder girdle.

7.4.53   At about eight to ten years of age, children will start to use a manual wheelchair[1]
          and, as the arms weaken, an electric chair will be needed. Splints on the ankles
          and a body brace to keep the spine as straight as possible will probably be worn.
          At this stage, children will become prone to chest infections.

7.4.54   Children with muscular dystrophy should be encouraged to use all the movement
          they have for as long as possible. Medical advances are extending their life
          expectancy.

7.4.55   Adults should be aware of the following:

a As pupils age, a gradual reduction in mobility levels should be anticipated.
   However, these pupils should be included in all aspects of physical education
   for as long as possible.

b Pupils will tire easily.

c Adaptations to work and equipment will need to be introduced gradually and
   carefully to avoid frustration.

d Because of the weakness of the muscles in the shoulder girdle, pupils can
   rarely use sticks or rollators.

e Swimming in warm water is one activity which can be maintained for a
   relatively long time. However, pupils should be observed closely in case their
   bodies tip over and their heads become immersed in the water, as they may
   not be able to return to an upright position without assistance.

f Consultation with parents and physiotherapists is essential. Physiotherapists
   will be able to advise on appropriate exercise programmes to maintain fitness
   for as long as possible, as well as lifting and handling techniques.

g Pupils will need assistance from adults for many activities (eg dressing and
   undressing, getting in and out of a swimming pool). Due to the weakness of
   the shoulder girdle, particular care is needed when lifting pupils. Adults
   should:

   • not attempt to lift a pupil by holding his/her arms – the pupil could slip
     through their grasp

   • not hold a pupil's hands in order to pull him/her up

   • ask a physiotherapist to demonstrate correct lifting procedures.

1   See Section 7.5 on pages 76–78 for further guidance on pupils in wheelchairs.

Poliomyelitis

7.4.56 Poliomyelitis injures the nerve circuit between the spinal cord and the peripheral nerve endings of muscles. This results in non-functioning or partially inactive flaccid muscles. Large or small areas of the body can be affected, ranging from the muscles of just one limb to those of all four limbs and the trunk.

7.4.57 There will be a loss of muscle tone and unequal muscle strengths, leading to an imbalance of the body. The deformities of some limbs may require children to wear splints, callipers or body braces. Poor circulation in affected limbs is usual. However, intellectual functioning is not impaired.

7.4.58 Adults should be aware of the following:

a Depending on the severity of their condition, pupils will be able to participate in most physical education activities. However, some modifications and adaptations may be necessary.

b Swimming in warm water is particularly beneficial. Pupils should not be allowed to become cold. If their legs are affected, the supine position should be adopted first as flaccid limbs float more easily.

c A pupil with balancing problems may be prone to falling over easily. The use of aids such as callipers, sticks or body braces may overcome this problem to a degree. The pupil's physiotherapist should be able to confirm whether the brace aids may be taken off for physical education.

d Pupils will tire easily.

e Advice should be sought from pupils' parents, doctors and physiotherapists.

Raynaud's disease

7.4.59 Raynaud's disease is a condition in which the blood supply to the fingers and toes, and sometimes the ears and nose, is temporarily slowed down because the blood vessels go into spasm and restrict the flow of blood. Symptoms are usually worse in winter, but a slight change of temperature during other times of the year can initiate an attack.

7.4.60 During an attack, the hands take on a white, wax-like appearance and feel dead and useless. They may turn blue/purple and then red when the blood starts to flow back. This can be accompanied by considerable pain and numbness.

7.4.61 Adults should be aware of the following:

a Pupils' own knowledge of their capacity to withstand cold should be heeded. However, physical activity is good for pupils with Raynaud's disease.

b Pupils should keep warm by wearing suitable clothing. Parents should be consulted about the need for thermal underwear, tracksuits, gloves and a hat.

c An attack of Raynaud's disease could result in a loss of grip. This has obvious implications for climbing activities.

d Consultation with parents Is essential prior to pupils taking part in swimming programmes.

Short stature

7.4.62   Short stature can be divided into two main categories:

a **Proportionate short stature** – this is a condition whereby the whole of the body growth is restricted. It can usually be treated if it is diagnosed early.

b **Disproportionate short stature** – this is an abnormality of some aspect of bone and cartilage development, and cannot be treated.

7.4.63   Adults should be aware of the following:

a Pupils with short stature are usually in good health.

b Pupils tend to be robust, but are more prone to tiredness than their peers.

c Pupils should be encouraged to participate in the full physical education programme, apart from contact sports.

d Swimming is beneficial and should be encouraged.

e Medical advice should be sought when pupils are eager to participate in a more intensive programme of physical activity.

Sickle cell disease

7.4.64   Sickle cell disease is an inherited condition affecting the haemoglobin factors in the blood. The sickle cells create blockages in small blood vessels. This is known as *sickling* or a *sickle cell crisis*.

7.4.65   Adults should be aware of the following:

a Medical advice should be sought about the extent and limitations of the physical education programme.

b *Sickling* can be brought on by strenuous exercise.

c Pupils can usually take part in normal physical education activities, but prolonged and strenuous exercise should not be attempted.

d Pupils know their own limitations and should be allowed to rest if they get tired.

Spina bifida and hydrocephalus

7.4.66   Spina bifida and hydrocephalus often occur together, but may occur independently.

7.4.67   Spina bifida is a congenital condition whereby the bones of the spine (vertebrae) are incomplete and the spinal cord is exposed. The physical consequences depend on the amount of damage to the spinal cord. The resulting paralysis can range from minimal to complete. Eye defects and epilepsy are sometimes associated with spina bifida.

7.4.68   Hydrocephalus is caused by a build-up of fluid, which may exert pressure on the brain. When this does not drain of its own accord, a device known as a *shunt* is implanted to serve this purpose. This will usually work very well, but some children will occasionally experience problems with shunts which become blocked.

7.4.69   Adults should be aware of the following:

a Pupils with more severe forms of spina bifida are usually paralysed in the lower parts of the body. They move around with the aid of a wheelchair[1], sticks or crutches. Risk assessment will be necessary.

b Pupils may wear special boots or callipers. If long-leg callipers are worn, advice on taking them on and off should be sought from a physiotherapist. If the callipers are the type worn below the knee only, most pupils can manage by themselves. Boots and the ferrules of sticks and rollators should be regularly examined for signs of wear.

c Damage to the spinal cord may cause lack of sensation to pain, temperature and touch, and also poor circulation to the lower limbs. In these circumstances, the following precautions should be taken:

- During sliding activities, the legs and feet should be covered to avoid friction burns.

- Pressure on one part of the body over a sustained period of time (eg pressure on the bottom when sitting) could cause bruising and pressure sores.

- Impact on the floor, apparatus or sides of a swimming pool could cause fractures.

- Pupils should be reminded to take care of the position of their legs during all activities to avoid accidental damage.

d Exercise is vital to all pupils using wheelchairs and other mobility aids. They should be encouraged to participate as far as they are able, in order to keep fit and healthy. Physical activity aids circulation and improves muscle tone, as well as helping the functioning of the many organs of the body. Pupils' physiotherapists should be consulted about forms of physical education which will provide maximum therapeutic benefit.

e Activities which strengthen the upper body are generally considered valuable.

f Swimming is generally considered to be beneficial. The water temperature should be warm. Pupils who are paralysed in the lower limbs will often *ride high* in the water; they are therefore recommended to start in a semi-sitting supine position. Great care should be taken when entering and leaving the water to avoid limbs scraping and banging against the side of the pool.

g Incontinence of the bowel and/or bladder may be a problem for pupils with the more severe form of spina bifida.

h Advice on special hygiene arrangements should be sought before proceeding with any physical activity.

i Time, privacy and possibly assistance will be required. Some pupils will be able to manage their own toilet arrangements quite independently, but it may be necessary to provide a private changing area.

j Pupils with hydrocephalus may have slightly enlarged heads which will be quite heavy, so extra care should be taken with movement and they should not be rushed.

k Special considerations, modifications and adaptations to the physical education programme may be necessary. However, many pupils with spina bifida, hydrocephalus, or a combination of both conditions, are able to participate satisfactorily in most physical education activities.

---

1 See Section 7.5 on pages 76–78 for further guidance on pupils in wheelchairs.

l Medical assistance should be provided immediately if a pupil develops a high temperature or severe headache, becomes drowsy or vomits.

m It is helpful for a full-length mirror to be available in the changing area, so that pupils can visually check that their clothing is not disarranged.

Visual impairment

7.4.70 There are two categories of functional loss of vision – *problems with focus and problems with the field of vision (peripheral vision)*. Peripheral vision is important for mobility and for the perception of moving objects. It is used for scanning the environment and detecting moving objects.

7.4.71 Adults should be aware of the following:

a Apart from the more obvious implications, eye defects are variously responsible for difficulties in coordination, orientation, position in space, object identification and tracking.

b Glasses should be worn during physical education sessions if pupils find them helpful. They should have shatterproof lenses and should be adequately secured.

c Good light is important.

d Safe practice in all activities should be fully understood by pupils. Adults must be aware that visually impaired pupils will not necessarily see dangerous situations or stray missiles.

e The positioning of apparatus and equipment should be as constant as possible. Any changes to normal practice should be made clear to visually impaired pupils. Unnecessary equipment must be tidied away and not left lying about in a haphazard fashion.

f Visually impaired pupils need to be as independent as possible, but it is often useful to designate friends to assist them (ie the *buddy* system), without taking away their confidence.

g The following points should be considered in relation to swimming activities:

• When it is not possible for pupils to wear their glasses, they should be well informed about the geography of the pool (ie depth, width, length, points of entry and exit, rails and troughs).

• Orientation is easier in the prone than in the supine position.

• School staff should obtain medical approval before allowing pupils to enter chlorinated water.

h If appropriate, school staff should seek advice on suitable strategies for assisting visually impaired pupils in physical education.

7.5 Pupils in wheelchairs

7.5.1 It is important that pupils who depend on wheelchairs for mobility are able to control them and make the necessary adjustments to body positions. Wheelchair skills need to be taught and assessed. For example, the Royal Society for the Prevention of Accidents (RoSPA) Wheelchair Proficiency Award provides a useful means of assessment.

7.5.2 Most pupils who use wheelchairs are very safety conscious, but those with spatial problems will require constant reminders about safe practice. Adults should understand the problems associated with the use of wheelchairs.

General issues

7.5.3   Regular maintenance is essential. School staff should determine who is primarily responsible for this (eg home, agency, school) and act accordingly.

7.5.4   Tyres, wheels and brakes should be subject to regular checks and repairs.

7.5.5   Footrests should be at the correct level so that the feet are well supported and neither feet, nor legs, are at risk from other chairs.

7.5.6   A strap of webbing or leather at least five centimetres wide should be attached to each of the telescopic uprights of the footrest. This strap should be positioned in such a way as to ensure that the feet cannot slide off, touch the ground or get caught in the wheels.

7.5.7   Cushions (where used) should be well fitted and should not affect the balance of the pupil nor impede the movement of the chair.

7.5.8   Adults should be aware of the individual needs of the pupil when getting into and out of the wheelchair, and should be able to help as necessary.

7.5.9   The pupil should not stand on the footrests.

7.5.10   Care should be taken to ensure that the wheelchair does not become a hazard for other pupils.

7.5.11   Lifting and carrying a disabled pupil requires specialist training to avoid injury to both the pupil and the handler. The advice of a physiotherapist should be sought in the acquisition of these techniques.

Sport-related issues

7.5.12   Sports and racing wheelchairs should be:

      a   adapted to each individual

      b   specific to the demands of the activity

      c   checked for stability

      d   inspected to ensure that they are mechanically safe and sound.

7.5.13   Efficient training is the most effective way to ensure safe practice in wheelchairs. This should be based on the RoSPA Wheelchair Proficiency Scheme.

Athletics

7.5.14   Adults should be aware of the following when pupils in wheelchairs take part in athletic activities:

      a   Calf straps should be used when racing.

      b   During throwing events, chairs should be anchored below pupils' centre of gravity by a holding device. If this is not feasible, the chair should be held by an experienced adult while the throw is executed.

Games

7.5.15 Adults should be aware of the following when pupils in wheelchairs take part in games activities:

a Deliberate *blocking* using wheelchairs should be discouraged.

b Pupils' legs should be secured.

Swimming

7.5.16 Adults should be aware of the following when pupils in wheelchairs take part in swimming activities:

a Pupils must not be strapped into wheelchairs while at the side of the pool.

b Chairs should be stripped of cushions prior to entering the pool area.

c Pupils in wheelchairs should not be left unattended while in the pool area.

7.6 Hydrotherapy pools

7.6.1 Hydrotherapy pools in special schools provide the opportunity for pupils to exercise in warm water. This is of particular benefit to pupils with complex physical difficulties.

7.6.2 Hydrotherapy pool activity programmes usually involve team teaching by the swimming teacher, class teacher, learning support/care assistant and physiotherapist.

7.6.3 The adult/pupil ratio should not be determined in accordance with any written guidelines that may exist. A safe ratio can only be determined by carefully examining individual pupils' medical profiles and health care plans in conjunction with relevant medical staff.

7.6.4 Safe practice in hydrotherapy pools should be as rigorous as in swimming pools. In addition, a *pool watcher* should be present on the poolside, whose sole duty is to observe all pool activities and to draw attention to any problems developing in the water.

▶▶ See *Chapter eight: Environment and equipment* and *Chapter nineteen: Swimming, diving and lifesaving activities* for further information about safe practice in swimming pools.

7.6.5 As the pool will be used by pupils with complex physical difficulties, particular attention should be given to the development of risk management schemes for:

a lifting and carrying pupils

b transporting pupils between the changing rooms and the pool

c dressing/undressing areas and support staff

d emergency equipment and procedures.

7.6.6 Regular maintenance of the plant, filtration system and sterilisation system, and a comprehensive programme of water testing, are essential to ensure the safe use of hydrotherapy pools.

7.7 Multisensory environments

7.7.1 Pupils with severe and complex difficulties can benefit from physical activity in multisensory environments (eg soft play rooms, sensory light rooms, interactive hydrotherapy pools).

7.7.2 Multisensory environments enhance sensory learning by providing interactive experiences, which can enhance communication and physical movement.

7.7.3 When working in these environments, it is essential to follow risk management guidelines issued by the supplier and LEA/Government guidelines on electrical installation and equipment.

7.8 Supporting pupils with medical needs

Health and safety policy

7.8.1 Under the terms of the Health and Safety at Work Act 1974, employers (usually school governing bodies or LEAs) are responsible for ensuring that schools have a health and safety policy. This should include procedures for supporting pupils with medical needs such as those listed below:

a Consultation process involving parents, school health service, doctors

b Adequate training for all adults involved

c System for the management of medication (ie storage, access, administering)

d Written record of pupils and their medical needs

e Health care plans for pupils with medical needs

f Emergency procedures.

▶▶ See *Chapter one: Physical education and the law* for further information about the Health and Safety at Work Act 1974

7.8.2 Head teachers should ensure that all parents are aware of the school's health and safety policy and procedures.

7.8.3 Further guidance on health and safety policies and procedures is provided in the DfEE publication *Supporting Pupils with Medical Needs in School*[1].

Administering medication

7.8.4 School staff are not legally required to administer medication – this is a voluntary duty. Those who agree to do so should:

a have a clear understanding of their legal responsibilities

b be protected by an effective system of medication management

c be adequately trained to ensure that they have the understanding, expertise and confidence required

d be familiar with normal precautions for avoiding infections

e be issued with written confirmation of insurance cover to provide specific medical support.

1 See page 80 for full reference details.

Risk assessment

7.8.5   School staff should be aware that existing risk assessments will need to be
reviewed and updated when pupils with medical needs enter their school.

Further reading

*   Contact a Family (2004) **The contact a family directory 2004**. London, Contact
    a Family

*   DfEE (1996) **Supporting pupils with medical needs in school**. London, DfEE.
    Ref no: CIR14/96

*   Mortimer, H (2002) **The SEN code of practice in early years settings**. Lichfield,
    Qed. ISBN 1 898873 28 3

*   sports coach UK (2003) **Coaching disabled performers**. 2nd edition. Leeds,
    Coachwise Solutions. ISBN 1 902523 60 1

*   sports coach UK (2003) **How to coach disabled people in sport**. Leeds,
    Coachwise Solutions. ISBN 1 902523 54 7

Questions and answers

People

Qu 1 **I teach in an infant school and am often asked by a parent to give a prescribed medicine to a child at lunch time. We have discussed this problem in the staff room and would like advice.**

Ans It could be argued that, because of your duty of care for the pupils in your charge, a parent could ask you to administer a prescribed medicine that has to be taken during school hours. However, this would be a voluntary task and you could not be forced to do it.

As a caring community, most schools would try to accommodate parents' and pupils' wishes in this matter. Schools should determine a policy that is known to staff and parents alike, and rigorously applied. This could include the following points:

a Participation in the scheme is voluntary.

b Medicines must never be sent to school with a pupil.

c A responsible adult should hand the medicine to a member of the school staff.

d Written instructions regarding dosage and frequency must accompany the medicine. Information on the side of medicine containers will not be accepted as a substitute.

Your head teacher should check that your LEA's/governing body's insurance policy covers school staff who administer drugs on behalf of parents.

Context

Qu 2 **A number of our pupils need to use wheelchairs to get to the side of the swimming pool. Sometimes, the wheelchairs and/or support cushions get wet and are still wet when the pupils return to their classroom. Should we be carrying the pupils to the poolside rather than using their wheelchairs?**

Ans It would be very unwise to carry the pupils from the changing rooms to the poolside. Not only would this raise concerns about lifting and carrying techniques, but the risk of slipping on the wet floor would also be high.

You should invest in special plastic shower chairs, which can be used to transport disabled pupils between the changing rooms and the poolside, as well as under showers. These chairs are lightweight, have brakes on the wheels and can be manoeuvred by either the pupils or adults.

Qu 3   **Do I need to purchase specific equipment to ensure that pupils with SEN can be taught effectively?**

Ans   The National Curriculum 2000 for physical education states that teachers should plan activities that respond to individual pupils' needs and ensure that suitable learning challenges are met. One way of including pupils may be to ensure that a variety of equipment is available. This would benefit all pupils, not just those with disabilities.

For example, when teaching games activities, it would be beneficial to have a range of coloured balls of various sizes and densities, and a range of hitting implements with short, as well as full-sized, handles.

Adapted equipment (eg posts with adjustable targets, hand bats, balls containing sound modules) can be purchased from specialist retailers who cater for the educational needs of children.

Organisation

Qu 4   **Are there any activities in which it is dangerous for pupils with SEN to take part?**

Ans   There may be specific activities that pupils with SEN should not participate in. However, this would generally be the exception rather than the norm. As part of a school's health and safety policy and risk assessment, pupils with SEN's medical profiles should identify any physical education activities, which the medical profession has stated to be contraindicative. This may be due to ranges of movement, cardiovascular inhibition, sensory loss and special handling requirements.

It is important to recognise that, more often than not, pupils with SEN can be fully included in physical education if schools are prepared to adopt flexible approaches to their teaching and learning activities.

If you are concerned about any activity, you should consult a SENCO, the pupil's individual education plan (IEP), a school nurse or a medical adviser if necessary.

Qu 5   **For a considerable number of years, my school has embraced the inclusion of pupils with SEN. I have been informed that my risk assessments, which include all pupils, are not sufficient and that I require separate risk assessments that deal specifically with SEN.**

Ans   Your school's standard risk assessment should satisfy the health and safety needs of all pupils and adults, regardless of individual needs. Consequently, there is no need to have separate risk assessments. However, it is vital that the specific needs of pupils with SEN are fully considered when and where necessary in your general risk assessments and included in the pupil's statement.

As part of the risk assessment for pupils with SEN, it is advisable to consult your SENCO and review the content of the pupils' IEPs. When carrying out a risk assessment for pupils with SEN, the intention should be to ensure that a safe and secure learning environment is created for them, rather than to use the risk assessment as an excuse for excluding them.

Qu 6   **My LEA's *Swimming Policy Document* states ratios of adults to pupils when teaching swimming or when using therapy pools. Do I have to abide by these, as they are very prescriptive and expensive in terms of teaching time?**

Ans   Having primary responsibility for health and safety in its schools, your LEA has rightly stated its position with regard to swimming ratios. You should not exceed its ratio of pupils to adults.

However, due to specific pupil needs, your risk assessment may determine the need for additional adults than that stated in your LEA's policy document. This is good risk management.

Qu 7   **Is it dangerous to other pupils in a physical education lesson to allow a wheelchair user free access to the lesson?**

Ans   As part of the risk assessment process during the planning stage, adults should consider the potential risk arising from the inclusion of a wheelchair user in the lesson.

Adults will need to plan carefully to create a safe environment in which ambulant pupils and wheelchair users can work together. There are many occasions when pupils in wheelchairs can work alongside others during warm-ups and team and reciprocal activities, and this should be encouraged.

Sometimes, in competitive, fast-moving activities, pupils may need to play in zones. Occasionally, it may be more appropriate to organise either separate or disability sport activities.

Chapter eight

Environment and equipment

8.1 Introduction

8.1.1 Working environments for physical education include:

a gymnasiums, school halls or dining rooms

b dance studios

c sports halls

d fitness rooms

e swimming pools

f playgrounds and other hard paved areas (eg tennis courts)

g playing fields and all-weather surfaces.

8.1.2 Schools may access some of these working environments off site (eg outdoor centres, swimming pools and leisure centres).

8.2 People

8.2.1 School staff should be familiar with school policies on the safe use and maintenance of the physical education environment.

8.2.2 Pupils should:

a show respect for physical education facilities

b be taught how to handle physical education equipment safely and recognise the importance of doing so

c share in the assessment and management of the risks associated with the physical education environment and equipment. This is an essential part of the learning process. Due to different abilities, the risk management process should be applied to individual pupils, to pupil groups and to the class as a whole.

8.3 Context

Facilities

General guidance

Floors

8.3.1 Floors should be kept clean and swept regularly. Economies in floor cleaning arrangements can make planning a safe physical education programme difficult. Whenever possible, school staff should be involved in decisions about cleaning schedules. Following the guidance below will promote safe practice:

a The cleaning and/or polishing of floors should not leave a slippery finish.

b Patches of condensation and residual wet mopping after school meals should be dealt with before activity begins.

c Loose boards, splintering, cracking and lifting edges sometimes occur with heavy use, creating an irregular surface level which requires attention.

d Non-slip tiles must be used in shower areas.

Natural and artificial lighting

8.3.2 Apparatus and activities should be organised so that there is no risk of pupils or school staff losing visual focus when in the working area. Following the guidance below will promote safe practice:

a Any risk of being dazzled by sunlight coming through windows or reflected on water must be managed.

b Artificial lighting should be made from unbreakable materials or set in protective cages.

c Strip lighting which produces a flickering or stroboscopic effect must be avoided, as this could impair visual focus and induce disorientation.

Walls and doors

8.3.3 Walls in working areas should be smooth to avoid friction injury if body contact occurs. Following the guidance below will promote safe practice:

a Protection must be provided if walls in working areas have sharp edges.

b Broken wall tiles in shower areas can be razor sharp and should be replaced immediately.

c Essential features other than physical education apparatus should be positioned well above working height whenever possible, or recessed where this requirement cannot be met.

d Glass doors can be hazardous. Where they are necessary, the glass should be smoked or coloured for visibility, unbreakable, reinforced and resistant to impact fracture. If a pane is cracked, it should be replaced as soon as possible.

e If doors are glazed around hand-pushing height, there should be wooden push battens across the door on both sides.

f Main access doors should have some system of closure control. This is especially important on exposed or windy sites to minimise the risk of doors opening or slamming unexpectedly.

g Fire exits must remain clear at all times and it must be possible to open fire doors from the inside of the facility.

Heating

8.3.4   Heating systems should provide an adequate working temperature and should be adjustable to accommodate varying conditions. Following the guidance below will promote safe practice:

a Heating systems should be designed so that there is no danger of any pupil being adversely affected by burns, fumes or other hazards to health.

b Heating systems should be subject to a regular inspection and maintenance programme.

c Shower water mixer valves should be regulated by one control key, which should be positioned out of reach of pupils to reduce any risk of scalding.

d Mixer valves should be checked and cleaned at regular intervals to remove limescale.

Specific guidance

Fitness rooms

> Please read the general guidance provided in paragraphs 8.3.1 to 8.3.4[1] before reading this section. This will ensure that you have a comprehensive awareness of safe practice issues affecting physical education facilities.

8.3.5   Schools should have an induction process for all fitness room users, including school staff, pupils and visitors. Following the guidance below will promote safe practice:

a Working surfaces should be firm and stable.

b Equipment should be positioned so that adequate space is always maintained between working areas.

c Great care should be taken when using equipment such as free weights, weight stations and multi-gyms.

d Weight stations and multi-gyms should be subject to the same regular inspection and repair programmes by recognised specialists as other physical education equipment.

e Notices on safe weight training procedures should be clearly posted in working environments.

f The floor may need to be protected by mats in areas where free weights are used.

g Free weights should be stored on purpose-built stands and should not be allowed to remain loose on the floor.

h Collars on free weights should have devices which lock the discs firmly in position when in use.

i If wedge-shaped floor bases are used for leg squat exercises, they should be fixed or sufficiently weighted to prevent them from slipping.

▶▶ See *Chapter seventeen: Health-related exercise* for further guidance on fitness facilities.

1 See pages 86–87.

Swimming pools

> Please read the general guidance provided in paragraphs 8.3.1 to 8.3.4[1] before reading this section. This will ensure that you have a comprehensive awareness of safe practice issues affecting physical education facilities.

8.3.6   It is reasonable to expect owners of public swimming facilities to provide a safe working environment for users under the terms of the Occupiers' Liability Acts 1957 and 1984. However, school staff accompanying pupils, together with specialist swimming staff, should ensure that they know and implement the normal operating procedures and emergency action plan for the facility being used.

▶▶ See *Chapter one: Physical education and the law* for further information about the Occupiers' Liability Acts 1957 and 1984.

8.3.7   School staff have a duty to react to any unacceptable changes in the pool environment and to protect their pupils accordingly. Examples include:

a seasonal overcrowding by the public

b unruly or even dangerous behaviour by other swimmers

c lack of poolside attendants and poolside cover

d inadequate supervision of changing rooms

e lack of life belts and other essential emergency recovery equipment

f poor water clarity.

8.3.8   In addition, the following safe practice guidance applies to school pools:

a The principles of safe practice recommended by the Health and Safety Executive are the same for both public and school pools, and should be clearly understood.

b Schools must operate swimming pool cleaning systems which meet acceptable hygiene standards.

c Schools should operate a system whereby water temperature and chemical levels are monitored at the beginning of the day and at regular times throughout the day.

d At no time should chemicals be added to water directly when swimmers are present. School staff should ensure that the chemical balance of the water is appropriate. It is important to check this at the start of each day, particularly on Monday mornings when variations may have occurred over the weekend.

e If school staff suspect water contamination and health risks (eg irritation to the eyes), pupils should be instructed to leave the pool and the matter should be reported for further investigation.

f Clear signs should be posted relating to water depths. In addition, notices about safe procedures/behaviour should be clearly visible.

1   See pages 86–87.

g Swimming pool surrounds should be kept clear at all times. Pool equipment (eg floatation aids, emergency equipment, lane markers) should be stored appropriately, taking into account the need for safe access to and from the pool.

h An adult, who is able to effect a rescue from the water, must be present on the poolside. In the event of an emergency, all adults present must be aware of their roles and responsibilities within the emergency action plan.

i Adequate, well-maintained life-saving equipment must be readily available in known locations and staff (and pupils as appropriate) must be trained in its use.

j A pool logbook should be regularly completed by the pool manager and made available to school staff.

k Those responsible for the management of pools should ensure that outlet pipes at the bottom of pools have grilles in place that are securely fastened. Holes in the grilles should not be large enough for fingers to become trapped. When using off-site pools, school staff should obtain assurance that all grilles are securely in place.

▶▶ See *Chapter nineteen: Swimming, diving and lifesaving activities* for further guidance on swimming pools.

Playgrounds and other play areas

Please read the general guidance provided in paragraphs 8.3.1 to 8.3.4[1] before reading this section. This will ensure that you have a comprehensive awareness of safe practice issues affecting physical education facilities.

8.3.9   Following the guidance below will promote safe practice:

a Play areas should be sited to prevent the risk of running into walls or other obstacles.

b Play area surfaces should be maintained in good condition, with no loose materials present in the playing area.

c Reasonable measures should be taken to avoid allowing vehicles on playgrounds. Where this is not possible, close and careful monitoring by school staff is essential.

d Car parking areas should be separate from those used for pupil play.

e The presence of oil on playground surfaces must be prevented. It makes surfaces slippery, can cause them to deteriorate prematurely and is therefore a potential hazard.

▶▶ See *Chapter twenty-one: Play in the school environment* for further guidance on playgrounds and other play areas.

---

1   See pages 86–87.

Playing fields and all-weather surfaces

> Please read the general guidance provided in paragraphs 8.3.1 to 8.3.4[1] before reading this section. This will ensure that you have a comprehensive awareness of safe practice issues affecting physical education facilities.

8.3.10   Safety on playing fields can be adversely affected by the aftermath of trespass. Broken glass, cans and other rubbish generally deposited on these sites create serious risks to pupils. Deposits of dog or cat faeces infected by Toxocara (roundworm) can cause toxocariasis in humans, with symptoms which include blindness, asthma, epilepsy and general aches and pains. All practical measures should be taken to keep animals off playing surfaces and to encourage owners to remove any offending deposits immediately.

8.3.11   Pitches should be:

a   marked out safely so that playing surfaces are, and remain, level (corrosive substances should not be used)

b   regularly maintained to provide a safe playing area

c   positioned so that there are adequate run-off areas at the sides and ends.

▶▶   See *Chapter twenty-one: Play in the school environment* for further guidance on play areas.

Procedures

8.3.12   Schools should have stated policies designed to ensure safe working methods and environments. Following the guidance below will promote safe practice:

a   All physical education working areas should be locked when not in use to prevent unauthorised access.

b   Pupils should be taught how to handle equipment safely.

c   Schools should develop their own systems for the daily monitoring of equipment. Activity on apparatus should not begin until such procedures have been completed.

8.3.13   Pupils should be encouraged to dry off thoroughly after showering before proceeding to the main changing area.

Equipment

8.3.14   When buying new physical education equipment, care should be taken to ensure that it meets current British Standards European Norm (BS EN) requirements.

8.3.15   Equipment should be stored consistently and securely. In teaching and learning situations, it should be easily accessible to school staff and pupils.

1   See pages 86–87.

8.3.16   Schools should have their own systems for monitoring equipment whenever it is used. Activity should not begin until such procedures have been completed.

8.3.17   The improvised use of equipment for which it was not primarily designed should only take place with great forethought and care, and following a thorough risk assessment. Improvisation should not take place if safe practice may be compromised.

8.3.18   Equipment should be inspected regularly for signs of wear. All items in need of replacement or repair should be identified and listed. Any items that are beyond reasonable repair must be marked accordingly and disposed of so that they are no longer available for use. Equipment with frayed wires should not be used until the defective parts have been replaced.

Free-standing goalposts

> Please read the general guidance provided in paragraphs 8.3.14 to 8.3.18[1] before reading this section. This will ensure that you have a comprehensive awareness of safe practice issues affecting physical education equipment.

8.3.19   Free-standing goalposts are commonly used for soccer, five-a-side football and other (sometimes improvised) team games, particularly when storage, portability and flexibility of placement are important factors. Such posts are often made from metal, have folding side sections and are light enough to carry.

8.3.20   Past accidents involving pupils (including several fatalities) have highlighted the need for great care when using free-standing goalposts. The advantages of portability and lightness are countered by a very real danger that the posts may be unstable and fall over. Following the guidance below will promote safe practice:

a   Free-standing goalposts should:

  * be obtained from recognised sports equipment manufacturers

  * be assembled in accordance with manufacturers' instructions

  * be regularly inspected and maintained

  * not have any sharp edges

  * be properly stabilised when in use, so that they do not fall over when knocked.

b   Netting should be well fitted and should not extend beyond the area covered by the base of the posts.

c   Safe lifting and carrying techniques should be used when moving and positioning free-standing goalposts.

d   Pupils should be made aware of the dangers of misusing free-standing goalposts. Under no circumstances should they be allowed to climb or swing on them.

e   When not in use, free-standing goal posts should be anchored in position or moved to a locked storeroom.

1   See pages 90–91.

Gymnastics apparatus

> Please read the general guidance provided in paragraphs 8.3.14 to 8.3.18[1] before reading this section. This will ensure that you have a comprehensive awareness of safe practice issues affecting physical education equipment.

8.3.21   Gymnastics apparatus used in schools mainly consists of fixed and portable equipment such as climbing frames, ropes, benches, boxes, trestles, ladders, poles, nesting tables, movement tables, planks and wall bars.

8.3.22   In primary schools, some portable apparatus may be kept in a storeroom attached to the hall when not in use, with the remainder, plus fixed apparatus, located at points around the perimeter of the working area.

8.3.23   Following the guidance below will promote safe practice:

a   Apparatus should be stored in a reasonably accessible place.

b   Apparatus should be assembled and dismantled systematically. It should be checked immediately before use, adequately spaced out and adjusted to meet the needs of individuals. Pupils are able to participate in this process at all stages of their education. They should be encouraged to check that apparatus is safe and to report any wrong adjustments or loose fittings immediately.

c   After use, apparatus should be returned to its usual place so that pupils become familiar with storage locations. It should be stored in a stable position.

d   Apparatus should be suitable for pupils to handle and manage after having received appropriate training under the direction of a member school staff/coach.

e   Arrangements should be made for professional equipment engineers to inspect gymnastics apparatus at least once a year. Certificates of *safe usage* should be issued after the inspection has been completed. Any apparatus deemed unsafe should be clearly labelled and removed from the working area until it has been repaired or replaced.

f   Only apparatus that has been officially provided or approved should normally be used for gymnastics. Improvised apparatus should be checked and approved by an appropriate specialist adviser. The use of chairs for gymnastic purposes is unacceptable.

1   See pages 90–91.

8.3.24   Table 2 below contains a list of checks which school staff/coaches should carry out before specific items of gymnastics apparatus are used:

Table 2: Gymnastics apparatus checklist

Beating boards and springboards	Check that: • there are no cracks in the boards or supports • the take-off surface is non-slip and free from splinters
Benches and planks	Check that: • the wood is not warped and that there are no splinters • the rubber buffers are in place (these should make contact with the floor when the bench is inverted) • the fixing hooks are covered with leather or plastic, and the screws are firm • the bracing brackets on the legs are firm • the rubber pads on the base are in good condition and free from any build-up of dirt or polish • the hinged fixing hooks on benches are laid flat when the apparatus is used in the inverted position
Climbing ropes and other suspended apparatus	Check that: • drag lines are not worn and that there is a securing cleat on the wall to stabilise the ropes when fully extended • the runway operates smoothly • ropes are free of knots • caps at the base of the ropes are not worn or missing and stitching is not working loose • securing nuts are tight
Hinged type apparatus fixed to a wall	Check that: • bracing wires are taut and stable, and are not fraying at points of frictional contact • castors are running smoothly and the contact surface is free from grit • sockets in the floor are free from sweeping compounds and other dirt • locking nuts are secure • securing bolts are firmly fixed to their base and engage properly with the appropriate floor fitment • any securing bolts that fix the apparatus to the wall have not worked loose • wooden components are free from cracks or splinters
Portable freestanding apparatus (trestles)	Check that: • the horizontal stays are sufficiently wide apart to avoid the risk of a hand or foot getting trapped • all securing pins are fully engaged
Scrambling nets	Check that the: • ropes are not worn and all fixing devices are secure • nets are stabilised so there is no unexpected movement *(continued)*

Single and double beams	Check that: • the hauling cables are free-running and not frayed • the trackway has been oiled so that the upright post runs smoothly • the wooden beams have no cracks and shackle pins are firmly located on the hauling wires • there are sufficient pins and wedges • floor sockets are free from obstructions and the bolts locate fully and lock • the beams move smoothly when hauled
Vaulting apparatus	Check that: • the wood is free from splinters • the covers are free from tears • leather covers are rough and not highly polished through age or excessive use • there are no cracks or loose screws • fitted height adjustment mechanisms work smoothly • all rubber stops are firmly fixed and in good condition, and no screws are in contact with the floor • where sections interlock, the angular interlocking surfaces are not rounded through use, allowing dangerous movement in the apparatus when struck during a vault • the wheeling system works efficiently, with wheels clear of the floor when the equipment is in use

▶▶ See *Chapter sixteen: Gymnastic and trampolining activities* for guidance on gymnastic activities.

Mats

General guidance

Please read the general guidance provided in paragraphs 8.3.14 to 8.3.18[1] before reading this section. This will ensure that you have a comprehensive awareness of safe practice issues affecting physical education equipment.

8.3.25 The way in which mats have been used or abused has featured prominently in many court cases involving physical education. It is therefore essential that school staff/coaches understand the structure and use of mats within physical education programmes. Following the guidance below will promote safe practice:

a Mats should be seen as equipment designed to cope with planned and foreseen landings. When used with this deliberate intent, they should reduce impact shock. Pupils should be taught to use mats in a disciplined way and should understand the importance of doing so.

1 See pages 90–91.

b Over the years, considerable improvements have been made to the design and specification of mats that have enhanced safety. Mats should be carefully selected to meet the needs of the pupils and activity involved. Whenever possible, pupils should be informed why certain mats are used for specific activities (eg high jumping, advanced gymnastics), how mats offer protection and how their position can enhance safety.

c When buying new mats, care should be taken to ensure that they meet current BS EN requirements and fire regulations. Advice should be sought from appropriate fire service authorities to ensure satisfactory storage arrangements and fire alarm provision.

d Mats should be covered with material which is easy to clean. It may be necessary to clean the underside of mats from time to time.

e Mats should have a stable base and lie flat when in contact with the floor.

f Mats should be free from holes or tears.

g Mats should be light enough for pupils to handle easily. In general, it is better for at least two pupils to carry a mat, as this prevents folding and subsequent damage to the core and cover of the mat.

h Mats should be checked regularly to ensure that no dangerous objects (eg pins, stones) are concealed in the fabric and that the core is intact and not disintegrating to a point where there is a risk of pupils *bottoming out* (ie making contact with the floor) on impact.

i Thicker weight-absorbing mattresses should be regularly checked for signs of disintegration or thinning of the sponge foam interior, which may result from normal usage over time.

j As with other physical education apparatus, mats should be subject to an annual inspection and repair/replacement programme. Mats deemed unserviceable should be marked accordingly and removed from use.

Gymnastics

> Please read the general guidance provided in paragraph 8.3.25[1] before reading this section. This will ensure that you have a comprehensive awareness of safe practice issues affecting mats.

8.3.26 Following the guidance below will promote safe practice when using mats for gymnastic activities:

a Mats are primarily used in gymnastics sessions to:

- provide a cushioned area for floor work

- identify areas on which pupils will deliberately plan to land feet-first when jumping from apparatus.

b General-purpose mats, which are approximately 25 millimetres thick, are adequate for most landing needs in school gymnastics.

---

1 See pages 94–95.

c If the force of a pupil's landing is increased by factors such as their weight, the height of flight and the speed of the activity, thicker weight-absorbing mattresses, which are at least 10 centimetres thick, may be more appropriate. School staff should seek national governing body (NGB) advice on the appropriate density of mats required to avoid *bottoming out* (ie making contact with the floor) on impact.

d Mats should never be placed indiscriminately on the floor where their use is unclear and where pupils may inadvertently trip over them.

e School staff/coaches should be wary of placing mats in anticipation that a pupil may fall. It would be better to arrange the apparatus and modify the demands on the pupils in such a way that the risk of falling is minimised.

f Pupils must be taught to absorb their body weight effectively during a feet-first landing from a moderate height, by flexing at the knees and hips on impact. A typical 25 millimetre thick mat, which is often used in schools, will provide some slight cushioning to complement pupils' actions. However, the main function of the mat is to determine the landing site.

g The need to provide mats in a prescribed way is vital where landing impact cannot be accommodated by the body. There are times, however, when gymnasts become so skilful in their movements that they can manage and absorb their body momentum without the need for mats.

h Pupils should be made aware of the limitations of mats in protecting them if they fail to execute a safe landing when descending from apparatus.

i School staff/coaches may be aware from past experience and knowledge of their work that mats may be required by inexperienced pupils during the very early stages of traversing apparatus at a height (eg a ladder or bar suspended between trestles). Once pupils have developed sufficient shoulder strength to avoid the need to drop down, the mats may no longer be necessary.

j When thicker weight-absorbing mattresses, or several mats on top of and to the sides of each other, are used to provide greater weight absorbency during landings, great care should be taken not to leave gaps in which pupils may land and injure themselves.

k Foot or leg injuries can occur if pupils land on the very edge of thicker weight-absorbing mattresses, with their toes and heels at different levels on impact. Landing areas should therefore be large enough to minimise the likelihood of this happening.

l Thicker weight-absorbing mattresses should not be relied on to prevent injury during any kind of landing. Competent physical support may be needed to ensure that pupils land feet first and in control during the progressive stages of learning a prescribed skill, particularly when a high momentum is generated or rotation is involved.

m Both school staff/coaches and pupils should be involved in checking and positioning mats in accordance with requirements. Mats may move slightly during periods of active use and should therefore be checked and adjusted regularly. Pupils should report any defects they notice in mats to school staff/coaches.

▶▶ See *Chapter sixteen: Gymnastic and trampolining activities* for guidance on gymnastic activities.

High jump landing modules

> Please read the general guidance provided in paragraph 8.3.25[1] before reading this section. This will ensure that you have a comprehensive awareness of safe practice issues affecting mats.

8.3.27   Following the guidance below will promote safe practice when using mats for high jump activities:

a   When using high jump landing modules, particularly during outdoor practices where a running approach is used, care should be taken to ensure that they are large and deep enough to meet the landing needs of all the pupils involved.

b   School staff should seek NGB advice on the appropriate density of mats required to avoid *bottoming out* (ie making contact with the floor) on impact.

c   Multiple modules should be locked firmly together, preferably with a coverall pad.

d   Pupils should be trained to check that landing areas are safe.

e   The use of high jump landing modules for other physical education activities requires very careful consideration. Rather than absorbing pupils' weight, they can have unexpected effects (eg secondary recoil action).

▶▶   See *Chapter twelve: Athletic activities* for guidance on high jump activities.

Long jump

> Please read the general guidance provided in paragraph 8.3.25[1] before reading this section. This will ensure that you have a comprehensive awareness of safe practice issues affecting mats.

8.3.28   Following the guidance below will promote safe practice when using mats for long jump activities:

a   The use of gymnastics mats of any kind is not recommended for indoor long jump activities involving a run-up.

b   25 millimetre thick mats may be suitable for standing (horizontal) jumps.

▶▶   See *Chapter twelve: Athletic activities* for guidance on long jump activities.

Portable games posts

> Please read the general guidance provided in paragraphs 8.3.14 to 8.3.18[2] before reading this section. This will ensure that you have a comprehensive awareness of safe practice issues affecting physical education equipment.

1   See pages 94–95.
2   See pages 90–91.

8.3.29   Pupils should be taught how to move, adjust and position portable games posts (including wheeled equipment) safely and should always be carefully supervised when doing so.

Trampolines and trampettes

> Please read the general guidance provided in paragraphs 8.3.14 to 8.3.18[1] before reading this section. This will ensure that you have a comprehensive awareness of safe practice issues affecting physical education equipment.

8.3.30   Unfolding, folding and positioning trampolines is a highly disciplined activity, which pupils must be properly trained to carry out as a team. They should be taught how to erect and fold away school model trampolines. This should always take place under the direct supervision (and often with the physical assistance) of school staff/coaches. Larger trampolines (club and competition models) are heavier and may require additional adult assistance.

8.3.31   The procedures used must be systematic and clearly understood by all involved. Following the guidance below will promote safe practice:

a   Trampolines should be placed well away from any overhead obstruction (eg hanging beams, lights). There should be an overhead clearance of at least five metres from the floor to the lowest hanging object. Some trampolines may require even greater clearance.

b   Once removed, wheel units should be placed carefully in a storage position well clear of the working area.

c   The space under and around trampolines should be clear and free from obstructions.

d   When unfolding a trampoline, care should be taken to ensure that:

  • feet are kept well away from the wheels

  • the trampoline is angled and lowered carefully, and the lower leg section held firmly, so that it does not crash to the floor

  • the frame sections are opened with a firm, continuous movement, with steady force applied and maintained to prevent them from springing back

  • fingers, elbows and wrists are kept clear of all hinges.

e   Before allowing a trampoline to be used, school staff/coaches should check that:

  • all the leg braces have been properly fitted and the hinge units are securely housed

  • all adjustments are tight

  • the hooks of the springs/rubber cables are properly attached, with the hooks pointing down

  • the springs/cables are all in good condition

  • the safety pads are fitted and entirely cover the springs/cables

  • allen screws are tight (if present)

---

1   See pages 90–91.

- the bed is clean

- the wheeling devices are operating smoothly and the pivotal housing on the frame holds the hub of the wheeling mechanism at right angles without any movement of the hub and the housing

- any weight-absorbing mattresses used are of a sufficient size and weight-absorbency to meet the requirements of body impact.

f   When folding a trampoline, care should be taken to ensure that:

- the wheels are securely housed

- the frame sections are closed using a firm, continuous movement, with steady force applied and maintained to resist the tension of the springs or cables

- fingers, elbows and wrists are kept clear of all hinges

- feet are kept well away from the wheels

- the lower frame and leg sections are positioned inside the upper frame and leg sections as the trampoline is rotated from the horizontal to the vertical.

g   Once folded, trampolines should be locked to prevent unauthorised use. This can be done by locking together two links of one of the leg chains. Trampettes should also be *disabled* in some way when not in use to prevent unauthorised use.

h   When provided, overhead support rigs should be supplied and fitted by recognised specialist manufacturers and engineers. On no account should improvised rigs be used. Training in the correct use of rigs is essential.

▶▶   See *Chapter sixteen: Gymnastic and trampolining activities* for guidance on trampolining activities.

8.4   Organisation

8.4.1   School staff, volunteers and coaches should carefully examine all the working environments in which they place themselves and their pupils. Identifying and managing any potential hazards should remove, or significantly reduce, the incidence of accidents.

8.4.2   It is advisable to carry out a visual sweep of the playing area before all games sessions and to carefully remove, or make safe, all hazardous objects. Outdoor surfaces may vary according to weather. The effects of rain, snow and frost need to be assessed and acted upon according to their degree. Games should not be played if conditions present a foreseeable risk of injury.

8.4.3   There should be adequate space to accommodate the game(s) being played and the sizes of the pupils playing.

8.4.4   Play activities should be managed to ensure pupil safety in whatever space is available.

8.4.5   Activities involving balls should take place well away from glass windows.

8.4.6   Schools should have stated procedures for teaching pupils how to handle equipment safely and early sessions should focus on them.

8.4.7   Pupils should be involved in handling gymnastic equipment as part of their physical education programme at all key stages of learning and commensurate with their known abilities.

8.4.8   School staff, volunteers, coaches and pupils should be ready to react to changes that may occur while equipment is being used (eg mats moving, fixings slackening).

8.4.9   When pupils are challenged with new tasks, care should be taken to ensure safe working conditions which reflect the capabilities and developmental stages of all the pupils involved.

Risk management

People

- **Pupils should share in the assessment and management of the risks involved.**

- Pupils should show care and respect for physical education facilities.

- Pupils should be able to handle physical education equipment safely and recognise the importance of doing so.

- School staff should be familiar with school policies on the safe use and maintenance of the physical education environment.

Context

- All facilities should be subject to a regular maintenance programme (eg cleaning).

- Equipment should generally only be used for the purpose for which it was designed. Great care should be taken when using improvised equipment.

- Arrangements should be made for all physical education equipment to be inspected, maintained and repaired on an annual basis.

Organisation

- All school staff, volunteers and coaches (and pupils where appropriate) should be aware of the action to take if physical education equipment or facilities become unsafe.

▶▶ See *Chapter two: Risk management* for more detailed, general guidance on risk management issues.

Questions and answers

Context

Qu 1   **Is the tidiness, or otherwise, of storerooms a safe practice issue?**

Ans   Yes, it is. Equipment should be consistently stored in a logical place and should not be left lying around in a haphazard manner where someone may inadvertently step on or fall over it.

Adequate storage facilities should be provided, but this is not always the case in many schools. The provision of appropriate wall fittings, shelving and containers can help to overcome this.

Qu 2   **In the primary school in which I work, stage blocks are stored at one end of the hall. Would it be acceptable to use them during the apparatus section of gymnastics sessions with my class?**

Ans   The improvised use of apparatus/equipment for purposes other than that for which it has been designed and provided, requires great care and forethought. The key criteria to consider are the suitability of the apparatus/equipment for the activities to be undertaken and the nature of the hazards and attendant risks. If these matters can be satisfactorily resolved, the use of the stage blocks for gymnastics should be acceptable.

Qu 3   **Following an annual inspection of gymnastics apparatus, the specialist firm that carried out the inspection has condemned two benches and a mat, and has advised that they should be replaced. Do I need to follow this advice?**

Ans   It is important to ensure that all large apparatus and fixed equipment used for physical education purposes is formally inspected by a specialist firm on an annual basis. If any apparatus/equipment is condemned as a result of the inspection, this should be clearly stated in the specialist firm's written report. The designated items should be marked accordingly and immediate action should be taken to remove them from all use.

Organisation

Qu 4   **During a curriculum lesson in athletics, the contracted agent arrived to cut the grass on the activities area. The pupils were told to take care and to stop whatever they were doing whenever the machine came near. Unfortunately, a stone flew up from the cutting blades and struck a child, causing a wound that needed treatment. Was this an accident or would the contractor have been liable for the injury caused?**

Ans   This is a good example of the need for ongoing risk assessment. Problems associated with grass-cutting and other maintenance requirements can arise. The principle must be that grass-cutting constitutes a potential hazard and should not take place on areas and at times when physical education activities are in progress. Contracts between schools and grass-cutting agents should ideally include a clause which prevents grass-cutting being carried out during timetabled use of playing areas.

The person responsible for the class at your school had a duty of care for the pupils and should have taken one of two steps to safeguard them and prevent this unfortunate occurrence:

a He/she should have negotiated with the contracted agent to delay the grass-cutting until the athletics lesson had finished.

or

b He/she should have moved the pupils and activities to a position well away from the grass-cutting area (space and facilities permitting).

The contracted agent should have been aware that grass-cutting is hazardous when young people are in close proximity and should not have started work until a satisfactory arrangement had been negotiated with the teacher.

In the circumstances, it is possible that liability for the injury to the pupil would have been apportioned to both the school and the contracted agent for not taking reasonable care.

Chapter nine

Clothing, personal effects and protection

9.1 Introduction

9.1.1 Clothing is an important aspect of safe practice in all forms of physical activity. It serves to insulate the body during the warm-up phase and may be reduced to maintain an equitable working state during the main part of the session. It should be well suited to its function and generally neither too loose to flap around, nor too tight to restrict movement.

9.1.2 Personal effects (eg jewellery, religious adornments, watches, hair slides, belts, spectacles, hearing aids) constitute a hazard if worn while participating in physical activity and should be removed beforehand whenever possible. Accidents have been recorded where the wearing of such items during physical activity has caused injury. Exceptions to the rule of removing all personal effects should be occasional and closely managed. The final decision as to whether a pupil may participate without removing all personal effects rests with the teacher.

9.1.3 Personal protection requirements vary according to the nature of the physical activity and the predicted hazards. Protective devices (eg shin guards, cricket helmets) have developed significantly in recent years, largely as a result of progress in technology and design. Good practice in this area is continually changing and school staff should keep abreast of the latest recommendations.

9.1.4 Schools are advised to have a written policy on clothing, personal effects and personal protection for pupils in physical education, stressing the importance of safety and hygiene. All pupils and their parents should be informed of the policy. This will promote consistent practice across the school and minimise potential problems that may otherwise arise.

9.2 Clothing

General guidance

9.2.1 School staff, volunteers and paid coaches should wear appropriate clothing for their work in physical education sessions. Consideration should be given to general movement around the working area and the movement of apparatus or equipment.

9.2.2 Fashion inevitably impacts on what pupils may choose to wear for physical activity and this requires very careful assessment. Trends in footwear (eg laces not tied, tongues flopping out, platform soles) are clearly hazardous and should not be allowed.

9.2.3 Where fashion in clothing may compromise safety, it is important that the issues are addressed and that pupils understand the limits which must be applied to ensure their own well-being and that of others during physical activity.

9.2.4   Some cultures require particular garments to be worn to conform to their religious traditions and beliefs. This should be discussed with the parents and/or the leadership of the groups concerned. Satisfactory arrangements should be made for the pupils involved to wear suitable clothing to ensure their safe participation in physical education sessions.

9.2.5   Different clothing may be worn for sessions which take place indoors (eg gymnasium or sports hall) and outdoors (eg games field). If clothing is removed during physical activity, it should be placed somewhere safe where pupils will not trip, slide or fall over it.

9.2.6   Footwear should be flexible and close-fitting, with soles that provide good traction and *feel* for the surface on which physical activity takes place. Bare feet are most appropriate for gymnastics and dance, providing the floor surface is suitable. Pupils must never work in socks or stockinged feet (apart from during trampolining activities).

Specialist clothing

9.2.7   Some activities require specialist clothing/equipment to be worn (eg helmets and harnesses for climbing and caving), which has implications for acceptable safe practice. It is important for school staff to have a clear understanding of the requirements and to ensure that all pupils are properly fitted and attired prior to taking part in such activities.

9.2.8   If specialist clothing/equipment is provided by the school, careful planning will be necessary to ensure that sufficient stocks and sizes are available when they are needed and that the items distributed are checked for individual suitability as they are fitted.

9.2.9   Pupils should be properly fitted under supervision with the specialist clothing or individual equipment that they will need. They should be informed on the correct use of such items when they are first issued, together with any constraints which may apply.

9.2.10   Specialist clothing/equipment which pupils may provide for their own use should always be carefully checked by school staff in good time to make any necessary adjustments.

9.2.11   Bright clothing or reflective strips should be made available when visual factors apply (eg when a walk takes place during the evening or when cycling on roads).

9.2.12   All specialist clothing/equipment should be regularly checked for defects and repaired or replaced when necessary. Defective clothing or equipment must be removed from the allocation system until repairs have been carried out or the items replaced.

▶▶ See *Chapter eight: Environment and equipment* for further information about physical education equipment.

9.3 Personal effects

9.3.1 The wearing of non-essential personal effects by pupils can pose a difficult management problem in physical education, since such items need to be removed for safety reasons before active participation takes place. Schools are recommended to include a section in their prospectus, which explains the rationale for the removal of personal effects.

9.3.2 The following principles should be applied:

a All personal effects should be removed.

b If they cannot be removed, the adult in charge should take action to make the situation safe (eg adjust the activity for the individual pupil or group).

c If the situation cannot be made safe, the individual pupil should not actively participate.

9.3.3 Some pupils may need to wear personal effects such as spectacles or hearing aids. In these circumstances, the adult in charge should determine whether it is more or less hazardous for the pupils to actively participate wearing such items, both in terms of their own safety and that of the other pupils.

9.3.4 Body jewellery may be hidden. Pupils should be asked at the beginning of physical education sessions whether they are wearing it. If they disclose this information, the principles described in paragraph 9.3.2 should be applied. If this information is not disclosed, the session may proceed as planned. However, if the adult in charge becomes aware that body jewellery is being worn during the session, he/she should apply the principles described in paragraph 9.3.2 as soon as he/she becomes aware of the situation.

9.3.5 Taping over ear studs is sometimes used to make the situation safe. However, the adult in charge should be confident that this strategy will be effective.

9.3.6 When medical bracelets have to be worn, they should be covered with sweat bands secured by adhesive tapes.

9.3.7 Any willingness on the part of parents to indemnify teachers for allowing a pupil to wear personal effects should be declined. Indemnities have no legal status, as pupils may bring retrospective action against teachers in their own right within three years of reaching adult age[1].

9.3.8 Long hair should be tied back to prevent it obscuring pupils' vision or becoming entangled in apparatus during physical activity.

9.4 Personal protection

9.4.1 The use of personal protection will vary according to the nature of the predicted hazards and the levels of performance. Activities may need to be conditioned or modified to reduce risks to acceptable levels. For example, a tennis ball could be used instead of a cricket ball during a net practice or game where helmets would otherwise be used.

1 See paragraph 5.3.5 on page 44 for further information.

9.4.2 Protective devices (eg mouthguards, body armour for goalkeepers in hockey, helmets for batters and close fielders in cricket) enable wearers to take part in physical activity by reducing *high risk* to *reasonable risk*. Although not compulsory, it is good practice for pupils to wear mouthguards to protect their teeth and gums in invasion games such as rugby, hockey and lacrosse[1].

9.4.3 School staff should keep abreast of developments in this area and the associated recommendations from appropriate organisations. Any items used during physical education activities should either be provided by the school or, if this is not possible, made known to pupils and their parents, so that they can provide their own.

9.4.4 Tracksuit trousers and long-sleeved shirts are recommended when playing on artificial plastic or sand-filled surfaces due to the likely risk of friction burns from falls. Such injuries can be very painful and long-lasting, and preventative measures are therefore strongly advised.

▶▶ Refer to the relevant chapter in *Part two* of this handbook for details of particular protection requirements for specific physical education activities.

Weather conditions

Exposure to sun

9.4.5 The thinning of the ozone layer above the earth's atmosphere in recent years has increased the intensity at its surface of the two bands of ultra violet light from the sun. This can be problematic for some people. Both bands are believed to pose a risk of skin cancer as well as other changes in the skin.

9.4.6 Young people exposed to prolonged spells of sunshine (eg when playing a cricket match or taking part in outdoor athletics) may be at risk unless suitable preventative measures are taken. School staff are recommended to take the following common-sense precautions:

a Do not allow pupils to be over-exposed to direct sunlight. A little is good for them; too much is likely to be harmful.

b Teach pupils when and how to cover their bodies with loose-fitting, lightly-woven material that will screen them from the sun. However, such clothing should not be so loose as to endanger them during physical activity.

c Be particularly vigilant with fair-skinned pupils and very young pupils, whose skin reacts quickly to sunburn.

d Encourage pupils to wear wide-brimmed hats, which will effectively screen the head and neck, and good quality sunglasses.

e Be aware of the particular vulnerability of pupils with freckles or moles on their skin. Set up a sensible system of checking and helping pupils to check for themselves without causing unnecessary alarm.

f Seek parental approval before pupils use sunscreen, which their parents should provide.

Exposure to cold

9.4.7 Additional clothing should be allowed in cold conditions. This will enable pupils to be active without subjecting them to risk from the effects of cold.

---

1 See Qu 1 on page 108 for further information.

Risk management

Clothing

- Clothing should be appropriate for the intended activity and conditions.
- All clothing removed during physical activities should be put in a safe place.
- Specialist personal clothing and equipment should be properly fitted.

Personal effects

- Personal effects should be removed (or made safe where removal is not possible) prior to the start of physical activity.
- Physical activities should be modified when necessary to ensure safety.

Personal protection

- Appropriate body protection should be worn when necessary.
- Appropriate measures should be taken to protect pupils from the effects of sunlight and the cold.

▶▶ See *Chapter two: Risk management* for more detailed, general guidance on risk management issues.

Questions and answers

Context

Qu 1   **Are mouthguards required when playing some invasion games?**

Ans   Mouthguards are a useful means of protection for the teeth and gums for rugby, hockey and lacrosse players. Whenever possible, they should be properly modelled and fitted by a dental practitioner. *Off-the-shelf* mouthguards may not provide the same level of protection. Parents should be informed about issues relating to the wearing of mouthguards during games activities.

On no account should mouthguards ever be exchanged or shared by pupils; neither should the wearing of mouthguards cause pupils to engage in activities more robustly than they would otherwise do. In order to prevent or minimise the risk of injury, play should be well controlled in accordance with the rules, using skills that have been thoroughly learned and consolidated through practice.

Qu 2   **Is it acceptable for a headdress, worn by a female pupil for religious reasons, to be worn during physical education lessons?**

Ans   It is accepted practice in physical education that pupils should wear appropriate clothing for the activities in which they take part. All reasonable measures should be taken to achieve this. Clothing for physical education should be included in school health and safety policies, and made known to pupils and parents.

If there is a problem, it should be fully discussed with the parents of the pupil involved and will normally be resolved. However, if a parent and/or pupil is not able or willing to conform to the school's health and safety policy, a risk assessment will need to be applied.

In your case, the wearing of a headdress during physical activity clearly constitutes a hazard, particularly during gymnastics sessions and when apparatus is used. In all such circumstances where there is foreseeable risk, the girl wearing the headdress will need to remove it or sit out and observe.

Qu 3   **I am a teacher in an infant school responsible for a reception class. My young pupils take part in indoor activities wearing their vests and pants. Is it acceptable for them to be taken outside onto the playground for some (games type) lessons wearing this clothing?**

Ans   It is normal and accepted practice for infant children to take part in physical education activities wearing vests and pants, and with bare feet. They are too young to be able to change into physical education clothing – this will apply later at the junior school stage.

It should be possible to provide a suitable programme of gymnastics, games and dance using an indoor hall space. However, if your pupils are to be taken outside, then suitable footwear (eg plimsolls) will be necessary and possibly additional clothing if they need to keep warm. Footwear should be well fitted and not able to slip off the feet during activity.

Chapter ten

Insurance

10.1 Introduction

10.1.1 The organisation and management of physical education activities may attract legal liabilities. Risk assessment of what is involved is very important, so that adequate insurance cover can be arranged where necessary.

10.1.2 The provision of insurance and understanding insurance arrangements are very important issues. The responsibility for providing insurance and the scope of provision may vary from one school to another, according to its status and the possible delegation of funding to schools. School staff should clarify who is responsible for providing insurance cover, for what aspects and to what levels. It may be the responsibility of the local education authority (LEA), as the employer, through the central retention of funding, or the individual school through delegated funding or school status.

10.1.3 Insurance policies are legal documents that define the range and level of cover provided. They usually contain conditions and exclusions. School staff should be aware of the detail set out in the policies. Clarification should be sought if necessary.

10.1.4 Three types of insurance cover are relevant to physical education:

    a Property risks – the owner of the property will determine whether cover against material damage is taken out.

    b Liability risks – cover for employers', hirers', public (or third party) and professional liabilities.

    c Personal injury risk – cover for school staff or pupils.

10.1.5 All those involved in the delivery of physical education should understand whether they have or need:

    a personal injury insurance in case of injury incurred during an activity

    b public liability insurance in case of injury, loss or damage involving a third party (eg a pupil or other adult)

    c professional indemnity against poor advice or management within their work

    d additional insurance for special events

    e transport insurance when carrying pupils in a school vehicle or their own car.

10.1.6 Parents should be informed whether or not cover is provided, for what purposes, the level of compensation and any exclusions. For general programmes of physical education activities, this could be done via usual systems of communication (eg school prospectus). For specific activities (eg ski course), parents may be informed via a meeting during which written details of the cover provided should be made available. Having been suitably informed, parents may subsequently decide whether or not to take out any cover where none is provided, or additional insurance cover beyond that provided. It is very important that parents understand and accept the insurance arrangements.

10.2 Personal injury insurance

10.2.1 Personal injury insurance pays out regardless of who was at fault. Members of staff, volunteers and paid coaches on school business can be insured against accidental injury and deliberate assault. Separate personal injury insurance cover may also be taken out for pupils.

School staff

10.2.2 Employers may opt to provide:

   a cover for accidental injury to school staff

   b cover only against the risk of assault

   c neither of the above.

10.2.3 School staff may have a possible claim against their employer's liability insurance if they sustain any bodily injury arising out of, or during the course of, their employment. Such claims can only be substantiated when injury can be proved to be due to the negligence of the employer or another employee.

Volunteers

10.2.4 Insurance arrangements for volunteers (ie anyone not paid by the school to provide agreed services) may differ from one school to another. In most cases, volunteers would not be covered by personal injury provision by the school. Clarification should be sought from the employer.

Self-employed personnel

10.2.5 All self-employed personnel are responsible for making their own personal injury insurance arrangements.

Pupils

10.2.6 Schools have a legal duty to ensure the safety and well-being of the pupils in their care. However, there is no requirement for schools to make provision for loss through personal injury to pupils where no blame may be attached to the school. Parents are responsible for arranging personal injury insurance cover for pupils, although schools may wish to inform them of any relevant scheme that may be available. Similarly, cover for loss or damage to personal property is a parental responsibility.

10.3 Public liability insurance

10.3.1 Public liability insurance[1] is provided by an employer in case of a legal claim being made by someone other than an employee, for injury or damage caused by a defect in the premises or equipment, which it is the employer's responsibility to maintain.

10.3.2 This cover also applies to any injury or damage sustained by a party other than an employee, as a result of an activity organised by, or involving, employees or approved volunteers, whether on or off the school premises, during curriculum time, out-of-school-hours learning activities, weekends or holiday periods.

---

1 Sometimes referred to as *third party liability.*

10.3.3 Public liability insurance may include the provision of poor professional advice to another party within the remit of one's contract. This is sometimes referred to as *officials' indemnity*.

10.3.4 School staff are covered by their employer's public liability insurance. In many cases, volunteers are also covered, but it should be noted that insurance arrangements for volunteers may differ from one school or employer to another. It is important that subject leaders understand the precise insurance arrangements affecting anyone working within physical education and that they share this information with all those involved.

10.3.5 Arrangements vary for school staff involved in sport beyond their school remit (eg district, county or national sports associations). Some employers deem such involvement to be an extension of their contract and provide relevant cover. Others do not, interpreting it as being beyond the employment remit and, therefore, the responsibility of the individual or the regional/national governing body. All involved in sport beyond their school remit should clarify whether they are covered by their employer's public liability insurance. It is advisable to obtain written confirmation.

10.3.6 All independent users hiring premises should have their own public liability cover. Letting agreements drawn up by the agent of a school (eg governing body) should make this requirement clear. Parent-teacher associations and other school-related bodies (eg former student groups) are very likely to be considered to be independent hirers and clarification as to any public liability should be sought.

10.3.7 When premises are taken over by another agency, whether for a fee or not, the employer should take out indemnity against claims for injury.

10.4 Additional insurance for special events

10.4.1 Commercial companies usually provide an element of insurance cover within the cost of an agreed package. Those responsible for the management of a commercially organised event should check the scope of cover and levels of compensation provided. The following should be included:

a People:
- Public liability
- Personal injury
- Medical treatment
- Confirmation of whether any particular medical conditions are exempt from the cover
- Bereavement

b Context:
- Confirmation of whether specialist or adventurous activities are exempt from the cover
- Confirmation of whether programmed and non-programmed activities are covered
- Damage or loss of personal or hired equipment
- Emergency transport and accommodation expenses

c **Organisation**:

- Cancellation or delay

- Loss of baggage and personal effects

- Legal assistance for claims recovery

- Failure or bankruptcy of the commercial companies involved.

10.4.2   Additional cover may be necessary for participants with existing medical conditions.

10.4.3   If a school organises the different elements of a special event itself, rather than using a package from a commercial company, the scope of insurance cover should be commensurate with the demands of the event. School staff arranging such events should check with their employer, well in advance of the event, as to what insurance provision exists and what additional cover may need to be taken out. Special arrangements may be necessary to obtain insurance for activities abroad.

10.4.4   Insurance arrangements for outdoor and adventurous activities may need to be considered separately.

10.4.5   Parents should be informed of the scope and level of cover provided, so that they may take out additional insurance independently if they so wish.

10.5   Transport insurance

10.5.1   When using commercial transport companies (eg coaches, mini buses, taxis), the event organiser should check that the company used has appropriate insurance.

10.5.2   If a school minibus is used, the event organiser should check with whoever is responsible for the minibus to ensure that the insurance policy is appropriate for the journey being undertaken. There are additional insurance and licence requirements for travelling abroad. When travelling abroad, the insurance certificate (or a copy of it) should be taken on the journey.

10.5.3   Employers' policies on adults using private cars to transport pupils vary considerably. Some do not allow it. School staff intending to use their own or others' private cars should enquire about the licensing, insurance and procedures required, and obtain confirmation that the insurance covers the risk involved.

10.5.4   When private cars are used, it is advisable to establish procedures to ensure that an adult is never on his/her own with a single child (other than his/her own child), apart from in an emergency.

Further reading

- Croner CCH Group Ltd (2004) **The head's legal guide**. Kingston upon Thames, Croner CCH Group Ltd. Ref no: HLG[1]

- DfEE (1998) **Health and safety of pupils on educational visits**. London, DfEE. Ref no: HSPV2

- DfES (2003) **Insurance: a guide for schools**. London, DfES Publications. Ref no: DfES/0256/2003

- Specific LEA guidelines

Risk management

People

- All those involved in the delivery of physical education should be informed about whether they have, or need, personal injury, public liability, professional indemnity and transport insurances, plus any additional insurance for special events.

- Parents should be informed about the scope and type of insurance provided for pupils, and also about any exceptions.

Organisation

- All those involved in the delivery of physical education should clarify who is responsible for providing insurance cover.

- Anyone working with pupils outside the normal school context (eg schools sports associations) should clarify who provides appropriate insurance cover.

▶▶ See *Chapter two: Risk management* for more detailed, general guidance on risk management issues.

1   This manual and related updates are available via a subscription service (tel 020-8247 1630).

Questions and answers

People

Qu 1   **Is a volunteer parent, who is not qualified but who referees football matches at school, covered while refereeing on school premises? Does it matter if he is officiating at another venue other than the school?**

Ans   You should check with your employer, as they will set the limits of insurance provision. If not covered by your employer, it would be wise for the parent to take out some form of personal injury and professional indemnity insurance. Many national governing bodies now offer such insurance to those qualified to officiate.

Organisation

Qu 2   **I am organising a primary school adventure residential visit. How do I check whether the insurance provided by my school and the residential centre is adequate? With whom should I check and who can advise on the total value of cover provided?**

Ans   You should consult your employer, your head teacher and the head of the residential centre you plan to visit. Obtain a copy of the insurance cover provided by the residential centre and distribute this to the parents of the pupils who will be taking part in the visit.

Chapter eleven

Accidents, incidents and first aid management

11.1 Accidents

11.1.1 Whenever risk is present, accidents are a possibility. To attempt to eliminate accidents entirely would involve reducing the physical education activities in which pupils take part to an unacceptable extent. In addition, some accidents may not be foreseeable and would therefore be difficult to prevent. The guidance provided in this handbook is intended to minimise accidents in physical education. However, it is important to acknowledge that, no matter how carefully programmes are planned and implemented, and risks assessed and managed, accidents will inevitably occur from time to time.

11.1.2 The severity of accidents will vary, ranging from the trivial to the life-threatening. Procedures must be established and implemented in all schools to ensure that all reasonable measures are taken to deal promptly and effectively with any accidents that may occur. This also applies to accidents during activities which take place away from the main school premises, but which are school-initiated or -related.

Managing

11.1.3 Schools are expected to have realistic first aid systems, which are readily available and efficient for dealing with any injuries that may occur. Managing injury means being able to call urgently on skilled medical assistance and hospital transport when required, and arranging for the parents of injured pupils to be summoned as soon as is reasonably possible.

11.1.4 Procedures to address the needs of an injured pupil and the remainder of the group should be anticipated in order to fulfil duty of care. Special care should be taken when planning educational visits away from the school premises, particularly in relation to adult/pupil ratios and group sizes in general.

11.1.5 It is essential that all responsible adults and pupils are aware of the standard accident procedures adopted by their school. This will help to ensure that they all respond to an emergency in the same way, thus minimising the time spent between the accident occurring and the injured pupil(s) receiving qualified first aid assistance.

▶▶ Sample standard accident procedures are provided in Appendix 5. These may be adapted if necessary to suit the needs of individual schools.

11.1.6 Standard accident procedures should be adapted to suit out-of-school-hour learning (OSHL) activities (eg lunchtime, twilight and weekend, away fixtures, educational visits, detached facilities).

11.1.7 Managing accidents (both during curriculum time and OSHL activities) should be included in generic physical education risk assessments.

Recording

11.1.8   It is important that all accidents are recorded on the employer's official accident report form as soon as is reasonably possible. This aids the reporting process and is also useful in the event of a liability claim.

11.1.9   An official accident report form invariably provides a brief report of an accident. It may not contain all the information that a school may be required to submit in the event of a liability claim. Schools may therefore wish to design their own accident report form, which prompts the user to provide all the details of an accident. It is advisable for this form to be completed for all accidents that result in hospital or medical treatment.

▶▶ A sample school accident report form is provided in Appendix 6.

11.1.10   Schools may be required to provide relevant information several years after an accident occurred. Procedures for the storage and retrieval of such information should therefore be established.

Reporting

> The guidance in this section has been written with reference to the Health and Safety Executive (HSE) Guidance to the Health and Safety (First Aid) Regulations 1981 and the Revised Approved Code of Practice 1997.

11.1.11   School staff should submit an official accident report form to their employer as soon as is reasonably possible. This is essential in order that the employer can comply with the Reporting of Injuries, Diseases and Dangerous Occurrences Regulations 1995 (RIDDOR).

11.1.12   RIDDOR regulations apply when major injuries or death are caused by accidents. They cover workplace or work-related accidents (both on- and off-site) involving pupils and employees. Brief descriptions of the key terms referred to in the title of the Regulations are provided below:

a   A reportable accident is defined as any resulting in death or injury requiring hospital treatment for any length of time.

b   Major injuries include fractures (other than to the bones of the hands and feet), unconsciousness resulting from electric shock or lack of oxygen, and acute illness caused by a pathogen, a substance or infected material.

c   The list of reportable diseases is unlikely to apply in schools, other than possibly hepatitis caused by exposure to human blood or secretions, and occupational asthma resulting from work with epoxy resins or animals.

d   Dangerous occurrences may be the result of the unintentional collapsing or fall of structures (eg walls, floors or equipment), pressurised vessels exploding, or the accidental release of substances or pathogens which severely threaten health.

11.1.13   RIDDOR requires that notifiable accidents be reported to the HSE by phone and, within seven days, in writing using the appropriate form. Some local education authorities may do this on behalf of the schools for which they are responsible but, in many cases, individual schools will be responsible for fulfilling RIDDOR requirements themselves

11.1.14   The following details should be reported:

a   Location of accident

b   Time of accident

c   Name and status of injured party

d   Nature and site of injury

e   Names of those involved

f   Names of witnesses

g   Activity during which the accident was sustained by the injured party

h   Circumstances of the accident, including any environmental factors

i   Protective measures in operation (if applicable)

j   Training of the injured person for the activity

k   Supervision at the time

l   Any design or facility fault which may have contributed to the accident.

11.1.15   Failure to comply with RIDDOR requirements may result in prosecution.

▶▶   See *Chapter one: Physical education and the law* for further information about RIDDOR requirements.

11.1.16   In order to develop safe practice in schools, it is essential that all accidents be discussed by school staff (and pupils if appropriate) in order to inform future practice.

11.2   Incidents

11.2.1   An incident (or *near miss*) is an occurrence that could have developed into an accident resulting in an injury to a pupil or adult.

11.2.2   Schools should develop a standard system for recording incidents, similar to that for accidents, which describes, in some detail, the sequence of events leading up to the incident.

11.2.3   In order to develop safe practice in schools, it is important that all incidents are recorded and subsequently discussed by school staff (and pupils if appropriate) in order to inform future practice.

11.3   First aid management

11.3.1   First aid in schools is subject to the Health and Safety (First Aid) Regulations 1981 and Guidance, and to subsequent revisions as approved by the Health and Safety Commission.

11.3.2   First aid is defined as the immediate attention required to prevent minor injuries becoming major. It excludes giving tablets or medicines to treat illness.

11.3.3   First aid regulations state that every school should appoint a facilitator for first aid. This *appointed person* (not necessarily a first aider) is responsible for overseeing first aid in the school.

11.3.4   The level of first aid requirements should be determined by risk assessment. These requirements will vary from a basic need at school level to specialist provision in high-risk situations (eg leading groups in remote areas).

11.3.5   The appointed person is required to carry out a risk assessment to determine the number of first aiders his/her school requires. He/she is also responsible for arranging any necessary training and for ensuring that all first aiders have the materials and equipment required to carry out their roles.

11.3.6   Schools are deemed to be low-risk areas of work by the Health and Safety Commission. The guidance provided for low-risk areas includes recommended first aid personnel/employee ratios. Schools should bear in mind that pupils are classed as visitors to the school, not employees. Typically, one person qualified to emergency aid level may be available when there are less than 50 employees, at least one first aider when there are 50 to 100 employees and an additional first aider for every additional 100 employees.

11.3.7   Provision for those working off-site should also be made. A travelling first aid kit[1] and clear, effective procedures for contacting the emergency services would be deemed as the minimum requirement.

11.3.8   Schools are advised to ensure that their employer provides insurance cover for its school staff in the event of any claims made against them as a result of fulfilling their first aid duties.

11.3.9   It is good practice to keep records of incidents which required first aid to be provided.

First aid training

11.3.10   Employers are responsible for arranging first aid training and retraining as required.

11.3.11   First aiders should be appropriately trained in techniques relevant to the circumstances in which physical education activities will take place.

---

1   See page 121 for further details.

11.3.12   First aiders should be trained to a level recognised by the HSE. The following subjects should be included in the syllabus for those appointed as first aiders:

     a   Resuscitation

     b   Treatment and control of bleeding

     c   Treatment of shock

     d   Management of unconscious casualties

     e   Contents of first aid kits and their use

     f   Purchasing of first aid supplies

     g   Transport of casualties

     h   Recognition of illness

     i   Treatment of injuries to bones, muscles and joints

     j   Treatment of minor injuries

     k   Treatment of burns and scalds

     l   Eye irrigation

     m   Poisons

     n   Simple record-keeping

     o   Personal hygiene in treating wounds – reference to hepatitis B and human immuno-deficiency virus (HIV) with regard to first aiders

     p   Communication and delegation in the event of an emergency.

11.3.13   Additional training should be arranged for adults involved in activities in which specific hazards are possible (eg training on how to treat hypothermia during activities which take place in mountainous areas or in, or on, water).

11.3.14   First aid qualifications are valid for the period of time specified by the HSE[1], after which time a refresher course and examination are required to obtain re-certification.

First aid kits

11.3.15   First aid kits should be made of suitable material designed to protect the contents from damp and dust. They should be clearly identified in accordance with the Safety Signs Regulations 1980 (ie white cross on a green background).

11.3.16   A risk assessment should be carried out to determine the contents of a school's permanent first aid kit.

11.3.17   Sufficient quantities of each item should always be available in every first aid kit, with nothing else besides. Most first aid kits will include the following items:

     a   One card providing general first aid guidance

     b   20 individually wrapped, sterile adhesive dressings (assorted sizes) appropriate to the work environment

     c   Two sterile eye pads (with attachment)

     d   Four individually wrapped triangular bandages

---

1   Currently three years.

e   Six safety pins

f   Six medium-sized, individually wrapped, sterile unmedicated wound dressings
     (approx 10 cm x 8 cm)

g   Two large, individually wrapped, sterile unmedicated wound dressings
     (approx 13 cm x 9 cm)

h   One pair of sterile disposable gloves.

11.3.18   Sterile first aid dressings should be packaged in such a way as to allow the user
           to apply the dressing to a wound without touching the part which is to come into
           direct contact with the wound.

11.3.19   The part of the dressing which comes into contact with the wound should be
           absorbent. A bandage or other similar fixture should be attached to the dressing
           to hold it in place. The design and type of dressings available (including
           adhesive ones) should be appropriate for their intended use.

11.3.20   When mains tap water is not readily available for eye irrigation, at least 900
           millilitres of sterile water or sterile normal saline (0.9%) should be provided in
           sealed disposable containers. Each container should hold at least 300 millilitres
           and should not be re-used once the sterile seal is broken. Eye baths, eye cups
           or refillable containers should not be used for eye irrigation.

11.3.21   Soap and water, and disposable drying materials, should be provided for first aid
           purposes. Alternatively, wrapped, moist cleaning wipes, which are not
           impregnated with alcohol, may be used.

11.3.22   The contents of first aid kits should be replenished as soon as possible after use
           in order to ensure that there is always an adequate supply of materials. Items
           should not be used beyond the expiry date shown on the packets. It is therefore
           essential that first aid kits are checked frequently to make sure there are
           sufficient quantities and that all items are still usable.

11.3.23   If an employee has received additional training in the treatment of specific
           hazards which require the use of special antidotes or special equipment, these
           may be stored near the hazard area or may be kept in the first aid kit.

Supplementary equipment

11.3.24   The following items may be stored alongside first aid kits:

a   Blunt-ended stainless steel scissors (minimum length 12.7 cm) – when used,
     consideration should be given to avoiding cross-contamination.

b   Disposable plastic gloves and aprons, suitable protective equipment, and
     appropriate protection against hypothermia – these should be properly stored
     and regularly checked to ensure that they remain in good condition.

c   Plastic disposable bags for soiled or used first aid dressings – employers
     should ensure that systems are in place for the safe disposal of items such as
     used dressings. They should be contacted for guidance on disposal
     procedures.

d   Blankets – it is recommended that these are stored in such a way as to keep
     them free from dust and damp.

e Suitable carrying equipment for transporting casualties – this is recommended if a school covers a large area or is divided into a number of separate and self-contained working areas.

Travelling first aid kits

11.3.25 The contents of travelling first aid kits should be appropriate for the circumstances in which they are to be used. At least the following items should be included:

a One card providing general first aid guidance

b Six individually wrapped, sterile adhesive dressings

c One large sterile unmedicated dressing

d Two triangular bandages

e Two safety pins

f Individually wrapped moist cleaning wipes.

11.3.26 School staff undertaking ventures with pupils in remote areas should consider attending a relevant mountain first aid course, which includes practice in the use of inflatable splints.

11.4   HIV and AIDS

The guidance in this section has been written in accordance with advice from the Department for Education and Skills (DfES).

11.4.1 The following extract outlines the view of DfES on children with HIV or acquired immuno-deficiency syndrome (AIDS) attending school:

Children with HIV and AIDS

Since on all present evidence, the risk of transmitting HIV in the school setting is minimal, and since the benefits to a child with HIV or AIDS of attending school and enjoying normal social relationships far outweigh the risks of him or her acquiring harmful infections, such children should be allowed to attend school freely and be treated in the same way as other pupils.

It follows from this that the fact of HIV infection or AIDS should not, in the Department's view, be a factor taken into account by local education authorities, governing bodies and head teachers in discharging either their various duties concerning school admissions, transfers and attendance (in respect of an infected child or otherwise), or their powers of exclusion from school.

HIV and AIDS: A Guide for the Education Service (DFE, 1991)[1]

1   See page 122 for full reference details.

11.4.2   School staff should consider the following points in relation to pupils with HIV or AIDS:

a   Pupils may take part in physical education, sport and outdoor and adventurous activities, providing they do not have any other medical condition that prevents them from participating.

b   Swimming pools and splash pools should be chlorinated or suitably treated according to standard practice. Normal precautions should be taken.

c   Barefoot work presents no risks.

d   Bleeding resulting from accidents should be dealt with immediately. First aiders should wear disposable waterproof gloves and rinse wounds with water only.

e   No cases have been recorded of HIV being transmitted as a result of direct mouth-to-mouth resuscitation, although there is a theoretical risk when there are bleeding cuts or sores in the mouth. In an emergency, direct mouth-to-mouth resuscitation should not, therefore, be withheld. Rigid airways for resuscitation may only be used by first aiders who have received appropriate specialist training.

Further reading

- DFE (1991) **HIV and AIDS: a guide for the Education Service.** London, DFE. Ref no: IB/94/0032/056A

- DfEE (1998) **Guidance on first aid for schools**. London, DfEE. Ref no: GFAS98

- Health and Safety Commission (1997) **First aid at work: The Health and Safety (First Aid) Regulations 1981 – approved code of practice and guidance.** Sudbury, HSE Books. ISBN 0 7176 1050 0

Questions and answers

People

Qu 1   **Are all school staff who teach physical education expected to have a first aid qualification?**

Ans   No. All school staff should understand what is required of them to manage the initial stages of a first aid situation, to prevent circumstances becoming worse and more complex. Nominated first aiders may gain particular qualifications. They must have a full first aid certificate if there are more than 50 employees.

Qu 2   **My job description as Subject Leader for Physical Education includes the post of *Appointed Person for First Aid*. Could you please list what duties will be expected of me?**

Ans   The post of *Appointed Person for First Aid* was designated in the DfEE publication *Guidance on First Aid for Schools* (1998)[1]. The job involves the *administration* of first aid, not the *performing* of first aid. Key duties include:

   a   ensuring that the school has efficient standard accident procedures

   b   checking that knowledge of the procedures is included in:

   - parental guidance

   - the staff handbook

   - the system of induction for newly qualified teachers and volunteers and paid coaches

   - pupils' safety education.

   c   taking charge of the situation when someone is injured or becomes ill

   d   ensuring that professional medical help is summoned when appropriate

   e   overseeing and maintaining first aid equipment.

Context

Qu 3   **Is there a legal requirement to record incidents (ie near misses)? It seems to me that this is yet another time-consuming activity that has no relevance!**

Ans   There is no legal requirement to record incidents (ie near misses). However, you should check your employer's *Safe Practice Policy* to determine if incident recording is included. If it is, you should ensure that all recording requirements are met.

   Even though there is no legal requirement, schools are recommended to develop an incident recording system which exemplifies good practice. Reporting, recording and discussion by the school staff involved can identify issues such as:

   a   a fault in the initial risk management of the environment or task

   b   insufficient preparation

   c   incorrect teaching techniques

   d   a gap in standard procedures

   e   a lack of *match* between task and pupil.

   ---

   1   See page 122 for full reference details.

Appropriate action to resolve issues like these could prevent a particular incident developing into an accident (ie an injury occurring) when the associated activity is repeated.

Qu 4 **Now that the HSE has lifted restrictions on the content of first aid kits, what patent medicines would you recommend be stored in first aid kits based in school and those taken on school fixtures and visits?**

Ans School staff should not prescribe or administer any patent medicines. Therefore, none should be stored in any first aid kit.

Organisation

Qu 5 **During a recent professional development course, I was informed that because of my *duty of care* to my pupils, I need to be aware of, and consider, their inherent health problems (eg asthma, diabetes) when teaching physical education. What are the implications of this statement?**

Ans You were correctly informed and your school should therefore determine a policy that lays down procedures which conform to this statement.

Those procedures should include:

a informing parents about the need and reasons for up-to-date information about their children's health and any medications that have been prescribed

b devising a system to collect and collate this information from parents

c ensuring that up-to-date information is passed to all adults who will have a duty of care for these *at risk* pupils

d identifying any members of school staff who may not teach the pupils, but who have a responsibility for first aid

e ensuring that all school staff involved are aware of the correct treatment if a pupil reacts to their health problem

f ensuring that the process for accessing immediate medical assistance is included in standard accident procedures

g checking, via risk assessment, that the activities presented to pupils with medical conditions are deemed as reasonable.

Head teachers should ensure that their employer's insurance policy covers both school staff who administer first aid and those who supervise and administer prescription drugs to pupils with medical conditions.

Part two
Specific guidance

People

Appropriate
challenge

▲

PHYSICAL
EDUCATION

▼

Acceptable risk

Context   Organisation

Chapter twelve

Athletic activities

> Please read the general guidance provided in *Part one* of this handbook[1] before reading this chapter. This will help to ensure that you have a comprehensive awareness of safe practice issues affecting athletic activities and physical education in general.

12.1   General guidance

12.1.1   Athletics embraces a range of both track and field events. It is an activity in which constant and maximum effort is used by individual participants, sometimes under the pressure of competition, and in which a variety of separate running, jumping and throwing events may take place at the same time.

12.1.2   Throwing events present the greatest hazard, although all aspects of athletics require careful planning and supervision. Sound management and vigilance are necessary to avoid the dangers that can arise during teaching, training or competition.

12.1.3   This section contains general guidance that applies to all athletic activities. Subsequent sections focus on additional considerations relating to specific activities. In all cases, the specific guidance provided must be read in conjunction with the general guidance in this section and all the chapters in *Part one* of this handbook[1].

People

12.1.4   Responsibility for safety is a matter for all involved in athletic activities. This includes:

     a   those involved in planning the layout of athletics facilities

     b   grounds staff

     c   organising officials

     d   school staff, volunteers and paid coaches

     e   pupils.

12.1.5   Clear written guidelines and established routines based on good practice will help to ensure that all those in positions of authority or leadership are aware of their roles in relation to safety issues.

---

1   See pages 1–124.

12.1.6   All pupils must learn to be safe participants and spectators. It is essential that they develop a sense of responsibility and self-discipline. School staff/coaches must ensure that pupils are able to exercise such control before introducing the more hazardous athletic activities (eg throwing).

12.1.7   Pupils must be sufficiently mature, fit and skilled to tackle each new athletics event.

12.1.8   Pupils taking part in athletics competitions should always be suitably prepared and should have reached the appropriate standard required for the competition.

12.1.9   Pupils should share in the assessment and management of the risks associated with athletic activities. This is an essential part of the learning process. Due to different abilities, the risk management process should be applied to individual pupils, to pupil groups and to the class as a whole.

Context

12.1.10   Athletics facilities should be maintained in good condition. Maintenance checks should be carried out on a regular basis, particularly prior to and during the athletics season. In addition, school staff should check the condition of athletics facilities before they are used to ensure that the intended activities can take place safely.

12.1.11   Training areas should be level and free from danger zones (eg areas in which activities may overlap or into which pupils may inadvertently wander).

12.1.12   There should be adequate space overall for the intended activities.

12.1.13   Throwing zones must be positioned in a defined area specifically set aside for that purpose.

12.1.14   Care must be taken in all events when the ground is wet. Throwing and hurdling are particularly hazardous in wet weather.

12.1.15   The chewing of food, sweets or gum immediately before or during athletic activities should never be allowed. Chewing can result in choking, which can have serious, even fatal, consequences.

Organisation

12.1.16   The secondary school environment presents the greatest potential for danger. Teaching athletic activities to a mixed ability class on a school playing field is potentially more hazardous than coaching specialist athletes using properly prepared facilities with full back-up resources at an athletics stadium.

12.1.17   Teaching athletic activities safely requires good control, organisation and supervision. Safe methods must be taught from the outset and school staff/coaches must ensure that the training provided follows a carefully graduated programme.

12.1.18 National governing bodies (NGBs) sometimes issue directives concerning the safe management of athletics. When a competition takes place under the remit of an NGB (eg affiliated competitions), any relevant directives should be considered as rules, which need to be followed. However, NGBs have no authoritative remit in the context of the National Curriculum, out-of-school-hours learning activities or friendly competitions. In these circumstances, their directives have the same status as that of this handbook – well intentioned guidance which managing staff should consider in relation to their particular situation. School staff/coaches are advised to use NGB recommendations as a guide to events and distances that are suitable for pupils at different ages and stages of development.

12.1.19 Particular care should be taken when teaching athletic activities to pre-pubescent pupils. The emphasis should be on developing basic, safe working techniques associated with running, jumping and throwing. For example:

a sprint racing should be limited to 100 metres for older pupils in primary school and much less for younger pupils

b repeated jumps in a horizontal plane should be limited

c a variety of light implements may be used with Key Stage 2/3 pupils to develop sound throwing technique.

12.1.20 School staff/coaches should remain in direct control of group events involving beginners. They should anticipate, and allow for, mistakes and a wide variation in standards.

12.1.21 Particular vigilance and control are required when standards are being recorded (eg judging, measuring, time-keeping, photographing). Spectators should be allocated specific safe zones and should be appropriately supervised. They should never crowd around the edges of the track or field event areas.

12.1.22 During a multi-event athletics session, it is recommended that a maximum of four events take place at a time, only one of which should be a throwing event.

12.1.23 For external competitions, the regulations and recommendations of the body under whose rules the competition will run should be carefully studied and followed.

12.2 Field events

12.2.1 All field events, especially throwing, involve obvious hazards. They must be introduced gradually into an athletics programme, one event at a time. They must only take place under the direct control of competent school staff or qualified coaches.

Throwing activities

General guidance

> Please read the general guidance provided in *Part one* of this handbook[1] and in paragraphs 12.1.1 to 12.1.23[2] before reading this section. This will help to ensure that you have a comprehensive awareness of safe practice issues affecting throwing activities, other athletic activities and physical education in general.

12.2.2   Good preliminary work can be done under class instruction and by using demonstration and practice. However, more intensive coaching requires smaller groups. Whatever the circumstances, working space must be adequate at all times. School staff/coaches must judge when pupils are ready to work on their own.

12.2.3   The following routine of lining up, throwing and retrieving must be strictly enforced:

   a   Throwers waiting to throw should stand well behind the circle or scratch line until ready to move forward. They should be well spaced and all eyes should be on the thrower(s) in action.

   b   School staff/coaches and the thrower(s) must always check that the predicted line(s) of flight and the adjacent area are clear of pupils. A wide margin of error should be anticipated.

   c   The thrower(s) must always remain behind the circle or scratch line after throwing. They must only retrieve their implement when school staff/coaches instruct them to do so. They must walk back to the circle or scratch line, carrying their implements according to the taught method. On no account should implements ever be thrown back.

   d   Care should be taken to accommodate left-handed throwers. They should be suitably positioned to ensure that throwing activities remain free of risk.

   e   Where space is limited, only one pupil at a time should be allowed to throw.

   f   Implements should never be used if they are cracked or damaged in any way. They should be dried off after each throw if necessary.

   g   Footwear must provide a firm foothold.

Discus

> Please read the general guidance provided in paragraphs 12.2.2 to 12.2.3 before reading this section. This will help to ensure that you have a comprehensive awareness of safe practice issues affecting throwing activities.

1   See pages 1–124.

2   See pages 127–29.

12.2.4 Younger pupils or beginners should be introduced to discus throwing using a foam or small rubber practice discus. This is lighter, less hazardous and easier to control than the metal-rimmed version. However, it is essential that the same level of care be taken whichever version is used.

12.2.5 Control should be developed by initially teaching standing throws. Once these have been accomplished, movement can be introduced to add momentum. Turning should only be introduced once these progressions have been learned and consolidated.

12.2.6 Discuses with cracks, worn rims or projecting rivet heads should never be used.

12.2.7 Discuses should be carried from the store room to the practice or competition area in a basket.

12.2.8 Throwing should always be confined to a safe area in which no other activities are taking place.

12.2.9 In restricted areas and for higher level competitions, safety nets or cages should always be provided.

12.2.10 Throwers waiting to throw should stand well back from the throw line.

12.2.11 Retrieved discuses should be held firmly and carried back to the throw line. Under no circumstances should they ever be rolled or thrown.

Hammer

> Please read the general guidance provided in paragraphs 12.2.2 to 12.2.3[1] before reading this section. This will help to ensure that you have a comprehensive awareness of safe practice issues affecting throwing activities.

12.2.12 Hammer throwing is arguably the most hazardous and physically demanding of all the throwing events. It requires great technical skill and coordination. Younger pupils or beginners should be introduced to the event using a quoit and rope, or a tennis ball inside a nylon tight or stocking.

12.2.13 Hammer throwing must always be strictly controlled in accordance with rules and procedures, which are clearly understood and applied by all involved.

12.2.14 Only purpose-made hammers should be used. The spindle must be free to rotate. Bent, worn or rusty wires are dangerous.

12.2.15 Protective cages are essential and should conform to NGB standards. The frame must be fixed firmly in the ground. The cage may be of wire mesh or suspended fibre netting, which must not be rigid.

12.2.16 The throwing sector must be roped off, at a wider angle than the sector itself, to prevent access to the landing area and its immediate surrounds.

12.2.17 A system of auditory and visual ready and response signalling should be used when preparing for throws.

12.2.18 Retrieved hammers must be carried back to the throwing circle.

1 See page 130.

Javelin

> Please read the general guidance provided in paragraphs 12.2.2 to 12.2.3[1] before reading this section. This will help to ensure that you have a comprehensive awareness of safe practice issues affecting throwing activities.

12.2.19   Younger pupils or beginners should be introduced to throwing for technique, control, accuracy and distance using balls and/or foam javelin shapes.

12.2.20   The metal javelin is potentially lethal and should only be used in secondary schools and, even then, only when basic throwing skills have been mastered.

12.2.21   If possible, javelins should be carried in portable storage stands, which can be taken from the store room to the practice or competition area. When a single javelin is being moved, both ends should be covered with a block of cork or some other protective material.

12.2.22   No-one (neither throwers nor carriers) should ever run with a javelin except when throwing.

12.2.23   Javelins should never be stuck in the ground at a dangerous angle. At the throwing assembly point, they should be kept in a vertical position, either in the ground or in storage racks.

12.2.24   Before a thrown javelin is removed from the ground, it should first be levered into a vertical position. It should then be carried in the same vertical position with the point as near to the ground as possible.

12.2.25   Whenever possible, a surfaced area should be used for the javelin run-up, as this provides a firmer foothold than grass.

Shot put

> Please read the general guidance provided in paragraphs 12.2.2 to 12.2.3[1] before reading this section. This will help to ensure that you have a comprehensive awareness of safe practice issues affecting throwing activities.

12.2.26   Younger pupils or beginners should be introduced to the shot put using foam shot shapes and/or cricket and rounders balls. All of these provide some weight against which to push and are good for developing technique.

12.2.27   The put should be learned from a side-on, standing position. An approach should only be introduced when the standing put has been successfully accomplished.

1   See page 130.

12.2.28   Rotational methods should be introduced at a later stage and only when very good control and technique have been achieved during prior stages.

12.2.29   Shots should be carried securely in two hands, held close to the body and placed carefully on the ground (never dropped) on arrival at the shot put area.

Jumping activities

General guidance

> Please read the general guidance provided in *Part one* of this handbook[1] and in paragraphs 12.1.1 to 12.1.23[2] before reading this section. This will help to ensure that you have a comprehensive awareness of safe practice issues affecting jumping activities, other athletic activities and physical education in general.

12.2.30   Sandpit landing areas for the high jump and pole vault are only safe for low heights where jumpers land on their feet. For more advanced training and competitions, a landing module is required[3].

12.2.31   If the edges of the sandpit landing area are lined with wood or concrete, they should be flush with the ground and covered at places where jumpers are liable to make contact with them. A convenient and adequate cover can be made from small sacks loosely filled with cork or granular rubber chips.

12.2.32   The sand used in jumping areas should be *sharp* (ie non-caking) and deep enough to absorb the impact of any landing without jarring. It must be free from hard or sharp objects (eg metal, wire, broken glass) and hazardous substances, and must fill the pit to the level of the runway.

12.2.33   The sand should be dug and raked over frequently, both during training and competition. Jumping must never take place while this is being done.

12.2.34   Digging and raking implements should never be left lying near the landing area, or with the teeth or prongs pointing upwards. They should be stored at least three metres away from the pit when not in use.

High jump and pole vault

> Please read the general guidance provided in paragraphs 12.2.30 to 12.2.34 before reading this section. This will help to ensure that you have a comprehensive awareness of safe practice issues affecting jumping activities.

12.2.35   Round bars are recommended, especially for *flop* styles of jumping. If flexi-bars are used, the supporting stands must be secured so that they do not collapse on the jumpers.

1 See pages 1–124.

2 See pages 127–29.

3 See paragraph 8.3.27 on page 97 for further information.

12.2.36   Flexi-bars should be colourful and strong, so that they are clearly visible to, and remain still for, the jumpers.

12.2.37   Soft, multi-unit landing areas are essential when jumpers use styles which involve feet to other body part landings. These should conform to the following minimum requirements:

   a For training and competition purposes, the landing area must be large enough to allow safe use by all pupils, irrespective of jumping style.

   b For competitive jumping, the size of the landing area should conform to NGB recommendations for the level and age range of the competition.

12.2.38   Cushioning material must be deep and dense enough to prevent *bottoming out* (ie the weight of the landing must be completely absorbed by the material). Suppliers should be asked to provide relevant data on absorbency, which may be checked against NGB reference tables.

12.2.39   Fitted coverall sheets for landing areas enable units to be held firmly together to give an even cushioning effect. They must be all-weather, low-friction and resistant to wear from spikes. They should be used during both practice and competitions.

12.2.40   Soft landing areas deteriorate over time. They should therefore be inspected regularly and maintained and/or repaired as appropriate.

12.2.41   Depending on their level of experience, pupils should take some responsibility for checking that the landing area is safe and suitable.

12.2.42   When teaching the high jump, pupils must be taught that the angle of approach and take-off point largely determines the landing position.

12.2.43   Fibre poles used for pole vaulting:

   a can deteriorate and snap after extensive use

   b should be examined regularly and discarded if they are cracked or spiked

   c should be treated with care

   d should be stored in a box or covered when not in use

   e should never be used in planting boxes which have a vertical back plate, as these do not allow the pole to achieve its full bend.

Long jump and triple jump

> Please read the general guidance provided in paragraphs 12.2.30 to 12.2.34[1] before reading this section. This will help to ensure that you have a comprehensive awareness of safe practice issues affecting jumping activities.

12.2.44   Ideally, separate runways and landing areas should be provided for long jump and triple jump. If only one runway is available, it should be long enough for staggered boards.

---

1   See page 133.

12.2.45   Runways should be repacked and rolled when they become so worn that the edge of the take-off board is no longer level with the surface of the runway.

12.2.46   If grass is used as an approach surface, spikes are recommended.

12.2.47   It is advisable to place a coloured cane on the runway when pupils are not allowed to jump.

12.2.48   Take-off boards should be:

   a of regulation size

   b painted in a distinguishing colour

   c firmly embedded in the runway[1]

   d kept clean and dry.

12.2.49   If there is only one board for the triple jump, it may not be suitably positioned for all abilities. If this is the case, additional boards may be inserted level with the runway at distances of 7 metres, 9 metres, 11 metres and 13 metres from the landing area. Whatever method is used, it is essential that all pupils complete the triple jump in the sand pit.

12.2.50   Gymnastics/composition mats may be used as a landing area for standing or one-step jumping indoors. However, under no circumstances should weight-absorbing mattresses be used for this purpose.

Competitive field events[2]

> Please read the general guidance provided in *Part one* of this handbook[3] and in paragraphs 12.1.1 to 12.1.23[4] before reading this section. This will help to ensure that you have a comprehensive awareness of safe practice issues affecting competitive field events, other athletic activities and physical education in general.

12.2.51   The planned programme should limit the number of events taking place at any one time to a safe and manageable level.

12.2.52   Throwing areas should be clearly identifiable and should be roped off well away from the throwing sector lines marked on the ground to prevent casual access.

12.2.53   Where a throwing circle and cage is situated within a running area, no hammer throwing should take place while a track event is in progress.

12.2.54   Circle and scratch lines must be sited so that implements thrown fairly (or otherwise) will not land in the vicinity of spectators or the judges and officials of other events.

12.2.55   Implements must only be thrown from their respective circles or scratch lines. This applies during both practice and competition.

---

1   A loose board can cause serious injury to the instep of the take-off foot.
2   For example, school sports days or inter-school competitions.
3   See pages 1–124.
4   See pages 127–29.

12.2.56   Careful instructions should be given on the methods to be used for the retrieval and return of implements. They must always be carried back to the starting area.

12.2.57   Written advice and rules should be provided on the back of clipboards issued to officials for recording purposes.

12.2.58   Officials should stand so that each successive throw or jump point is blocked until measurement and recording of the previous throw or jump has been completed.

12.2.59   Planned auditory and visual signals should be used by all involved in the events to ensure effective communication.

12.3   Track events

> Please read the general guidance provided in *Part one* of this handbook[1] and in paragraphs 12.1.1 to 12.1.23[2] before reading this section. This will help to ensure that you have a comprehensive awareness of safe practice issues affecting track events, other athletic activities and physical education in general.

12.3.1   Track events may seem relatively safe compared to field events. However, it cannot be assumed that they are hazard-free, particularly during competitions.

12.3.2   All races of one lap or less should be run in lanes. This is particularly important for relay races.

12.3.3   Starting blocks and any other materials must be removed from the track immediately after use.

12.3.4   Hurdles should be rigid, smooth and free from sharp or protruding edges. Their weight and resistance must conform to NGB requirements. Their legs and feet must be at right angles to the top bar. Hurdles must be positioned so as to allow them to fall forwards if pupils hit them while running.

12.3.5   Finishing tapes should be made from worsted (or similar material which breaks easily) and should be held at no higher than the chest height of the pupils involved.

12.3.6   Officials, competitors and spectators must ensure that the track remains clear for runners at all times.

Spikes

12.3.7   Self-discipline and control are necessary when using spikes to prevent accidents and injuries. Pupils should be taught how to use them correctly at the earliest possible opportunity.

12.3.8   When spikes are worn, the pupils participating in a track event should be limited to a safe and manageable number.

1   See pages 1–124.
2   See pages 127–29.

12.3.9   When spikes are not being used, they should be placed with the spikes facing
          down.

Starting pistols

12.3.10   There is no such thing as a safe firearm.

12.3.11   Current legislation prohibits the possession and use of a *firearm* above, and
          including, .22 calibre by any individual not duly licensed by the police. A firearm
          is interpreted as any pistol or revolver that can, or can be converted to, fire a live
          round of ammunition.

12.3.12   School staff/coaches are strongly recommended not to use, attempt to use or
          procure such a firearm to use as a starting pistol at athletics events. However,
          very small calibre *cap* firing pistols are acceptable.

12.3.13   If in any doubt about their position, school staff/coaches should contact their
          local police authority.

12.3.14   For training and basic competition purposes, a clapperboard provides a safe,
          acceptable alternative to a starting pistol.

12.3.15   If a starting pistol is used, following the guidelines below will promote safe
          practice:

          a Starting pistols should always be fired at arm's length above the head.

          b Starting pistols should never be left loaded after use. The slide or magazine
             should be taken out, the ammunition removed and the pistol, firing
             mechanism and ammunition locked away securely and separately.

          c For reasons of security, all starting pistols should be marked with the name of
             the owner or school.

          d The loss of a starting pistol or ammunition should be reported immediately to
             the police.

12.4   Indoor athletics

> Please read the general guidance provided in *Part one* of this
> handbook[1] and in paragraphs 12.1.1 to 12.1.23[2] before reading this
> section. This will help to ensure that you have a comprehensive
> awareness of safe practice issues affecting both indoor and outdoor
> athletic activities, and physical education in general.

12.4.1   Most of the safe practice guidance provided in Sections 12.1 to 12.3 of this
          chapter[3] also applies to indoor athletics. However, because of the more confined
          environment involved, there are some specific considerations which need to be
          taken into account to ensure that pupils are not exposed to unnecessary risk.

---

1   See pages 1–124.

2   See pages 127–29.

3   See pages 127–37.

12.4.2 As with outdoor athletics, a level surface, adequate space and clearly designated training areas are essential, particularly for high-speed running activities.

12.4.3 Athletic activities should take place well away from projections and walls.

12.4.4 Rebound boards can be useful for sustaining fast running in a confined space, providing pupils have been taught how to use them correctly. Otherwise, running events should be organised as *run-around* activities, using skittles or suitable markers.

12.4.5 Approach runs should be kept to a minimum (eg four strides) when jumping for height and distance.

12.4.6 Composition mats should be used to cushion landings when jumping for distance.

12.4.7 Weight-absorbing mattresses should be avoided. The teaching of sound landing technique will do much to avoid potential injury where space is limited and no specialist facilities are available.

12.4.8 Throwing implements made from foam or rubber should be used. Although these are less hazardous than their conventional equivalents, it is just as important to follow strict throwing routines[1].

12.4.9 Equipment should be stored safely and securely when not in use, well away from working areas.

12.5 Cross-country running

Please read the general guidance provided in *Part one* of this handbook[2] and in paragraphs 12.1.1 to 12.1.23[3] before reading this section. This will help to ensure that you have a comprehensive awareness of safe practice issues affecting cross-country running, other athletic activities and physical education in general.

Competitions

12.5.1 Cross-country courses should be graded for different abilities. The slowest runner should be tailed throughout the race, so that runners injured or in distress can be located and escorted back for treatment.

12.5.2 Runners should be counted at the start, during the run and at the finish. Short cuts should not be permitted.

12.5.3 The start should be sufficiently wide to accommodate the number of runners safely.

12.5.4 There should be a long, clear approach to the first obstacle to enable the competitors to thin out. The obstacle should be sufficiently wide to prevent queues or bunching.

1   See paragraph 12.2.3 on page 130.
2   See pages 1–124.
3   See pages 127–29.

safe practice in physical education and school sport

12.5.5   First aid and casualty transport should be provided at various points on the course.

12.5.6   Wherever possible, basic amenities should be provided, including hot drinks, showers and washing and changing facilities.

Training in schools

12.5.7   Cross-country courses should be chosen with care and should avoid busy roads.

12.5.8   Distances should be appropriate to the age and fitness levels of the pupils.

12.5.9   Hazardous sections (eg ditches) should be marshalled or kept in view.

12.5.10   A supervisory presence throughout the course is essential.

12.5.11   Pupils should be counted out and back in. A back marker should be nominated.

12.5.12   Advice on all aspects of cross-country training or competition in schools can be obtained from the English/Northern Ireland/Scottish/Welsh Schools' Athletic Association.

Risk management

People

- **Pupils should share in the assessment and management of the risks involved**.
- Pupils should receive an induction on safe procedures when participating in track and field events.
- Supervisory staff should attend relevant training courses offered by their local education authority and NGBs to ensure that their knowledge of technique and safety is up to date.

Context

- Clearly designated training areas should be provided, particularly for throwing activities.
- Athletics facilities should be well maintained.
- Athletics equipment should be well maintained and appropriate to the developmental stage of the pupils involved.

Organisation

- Running, throwing and jumping activities should be appropriate to the capabilities of the pupils involved.
- Athletic activities should take place within an effective, progressive scheme of work, which will develop pupils' competence.

▸▸ See *Chapter two: Risk management* for more detailed, general guidance on risk management issues.

Questions and answers

Organisation

Qu 1   **How can I ensure complete safety when teaching throwing activities?**

Ans   The constant reinforcement and consolidation of pupils' knowledge and understanding of safe procedures when participating in throwing activities is absolutely critical. It is good practice to provide opportunities for pupils to actively explore the effectiveness of different throwing techniques involving a range of different implements. However, safety procedures should be applied at all times, even when throwing relatively safe implements, such as foam discuses and javelins. The organisation and supervision of throwing activities should be such that no-one is permitted to enter the throwing area while throwing is under way.

Qu 2   **Should all track and field events be included within my athletics curriculum?**

Ans   No – good practice is safe practice. Pupils at different stages of development will demonstrate different needs and capabilities. To simply impose the ten Olympic athletics events on them will not be appropriate or meaningful for many pupils. Suitable athletic challenges relating to basic running, jumping and throwing techniques need not necessarily involve Olympic implements. Similarly, a progressive athletics scheme of work should not attempt to cover all ten events every year or even over a Key Stage. Providing athletic teaching units, which allow for sufficient practice and improvement, will enable pupils to learn more effectively and achieve more.

Qu 3   **What are the essential safety requirements for a school sports day?**

Ans   There are two key safety requirements for school sports days:

a **The safe layout and sequencing of the activities involved (applies to both primary and secondary schools)**

- Careful consideration should be given to the relative positioning and timing of running, throwing and jumping events, to ensure that neither competitors nor spectators are exposed to risk.

- There should be clearly designated spectator zones.

- Adequate space should be allowed for each event.

- Throwing areas should be clearly marked and have sufficient warning notices.

- Strict rules on crossing the track should be enforced as competitors move between events.

- There should be clearly designated marshalling areas for competitors awaiting the start of events.

b **The availability of informed and experienced judges and officials (particularly for secondary school events)**

- It may not be necessary for all judges and officials to hold NGB awards. However, it is essential for event organisers to ensure that they are given appropriate inductions and training, so that their allocated events proceed in a safe and responsible manner.

- It is a good idea to remind judges of key safe practice points relating to their specific event by noting these on the recording sheets issued to them.

Chapter thirteen

Combat activities

> Please read the general guidance provided in *Part one* of this handbook[1] before reading this chapter. This will help to ensure that you have a comprehensive awareness of safe practice issues affecting combat activities and physical education in general.

13.1 General guidance

13.1.1 Combat activities involve overcoming an opponent, often through physical contact. They include:

    a boxing

    b fencing

    c judo

    d martial arts

    e self-defence

    f wrestling.

13.1.2 This section contains general guidance that applies to all combat activities. Subsequent sections focus on additional considerations relating to specific activities. In all cases, the specific guidance provided must be read in conjunction with the general guidance in this section and all the chapters in *Part one* of this handbook[1].

People

13.1.3 Supervising adults should have a sound knowledge of the combat activity they intend to teach and be capable of officiating in accordance with rules with which pupils are familiar.

13.1.4 Combat activities in schools are often delivered by coaches. As the potential for injury is high, great care should be taken to appoint competent coaches, who hold relevant national governing body (NGB) coaching qualifications and who are experienced in working with young people. If necessary, school staff should contact relevant national, regional and county agencies to check coaches' suitability to deliver combat activities in schools.

13.1.5 Pupils should be adequately prepared for all activities and made aware of their personal responsibilities for their own safety and that of others.

13.1.6 Pupils should be taught to participate according to the rules and to respect the decisions of officials.

1   See pages 1–124.

13.1.7 Pupils should understand that excessive and over-zealous competitiveness, loss of temper and inappropriate language will not be tolerated. Supervising adults should always take appropriate action in the event of pupils displaying such behaviour. If necessary, the combat activity should be stopped.

13.1.8 Pupils should share in the assessment and management of the risks associated with combat activities. This is an essential part of the learning process. Due to different abilities, the risk management process should be applied to individual pupils, to pupil groups and to the class as a whole.

Context

13.1.9 Combat activities may take place in:

a gymnasia

b sports halls

c dojos[1]

d specialist rings for boxing and wrestling

e specialist pistes for fencing.

13.1.10 Care should be taken to ensure that practice arenas used for combat activities:

a are sited away from walls and other obstructions, and are surrounded by a clear safety area

b are large enough to allow safe play without overcrowding

c are reasonably level, non-slip and clean

d are free of obstructions and the potential for tripping

e provide secure footing.

▶▶ See *Chapter eight: Environment and equipment* and *Chapter twenty-one: Play in the school environment* for further information about play areas and surfaces.

13.1.11 All school staff and coaches should be fully aware of current British Standards European Norm (BS EN) requirements relating to the use of combat mats. Phased compliance when combat mats are replaced is strongly advised.

13.1.12 Arrangements should be made for the regular inspection, repair and maintenance of equipment.

13.1.13 Faulty equipment (eg mats, boxing gloves, fencing foils) should be clearly marked and removed from use (and access by pupils) until repaired or replaced.

13.1.14 Potentially hazardous items of equipment (eg fencing foils) should be stored in a safe place where pupils cannot access them.

13.1.15 Pupils should wear appropriate clothing, footwear and protective equipment for the intended activity, whether this takes place in a teaching situation or match play. This should be checked before the activity commences.

13.1.16 Long hair should be tied back, nails cut short and all potentially hazardous personal effects removed or made safe prior to taking part in any combat activity.

---

1 A place in which judo and other martial arts take place.

13.1.17   The chewing of food, sweets or gum immediately before or during combat activities should never be allowed. Chewing can result in choking, which can have serious, even fatal, consequences.

Organisation

13.1.18   Parental consent should always be sought before pupils take part in combat activities.

13.1.19   If combat activities are taught within the context of the National Curriculum/GCSE syllabus, school staff should ensure that the relevant requirements are met.

13.1.20   All combat activities undertaken should match the age, experience, stamina and ability of the pupils involved. Pupils should only be exposed to challenges for which they have the mental ability and physical skills and fitness required to respond.

13.1.21   The number of pupils should be appropriate for the space available. Group sizes may need to be reduced if the working environment demands it.

13.1.22   Care should be taken to *match* pupils by size, weight, age, experience and ability, particularly in teaching situations and activities involving body contact, and when mixed gender practice is permitted.

13.1.23   Mixed gender competition is not permitted. Pupils should only compete against other pupils of the same gender.

13.1.24   An adequate warm-up session should be provided prior to all combat activities.

13.1.25   The importance of self-discipline and sound techniques should be emphasised. Attitudes and discipline should be set and controlled jointly by school staff and coaches, both for active and non-active participants.

13.1.26   School staff/coaches should maintain continuous observation of all combat activities.

13.1.27   School staff/coaches must not demonstrate or compete with pupils during combat activities. This includes *King of the Castle* type games, in which school staff/coaches take on pupils at the end of a session.

13.1.28   Before competitive combat begins, pupils should be taught the basic skills and rules involved in the intended activity. School staff/coaches should apply the rules fully and consistently.

13.1.29   The teaching of all combat activities should follow a carefully planned and graduated progression, which helps to ensure that all pupils master the necessary skills at any given level of competence before progressing to the next stage.

13.1.30   NGBs sometimes issue directives concerning the safe management of combat activities. When a competition takes place under the remit of an NGB (eg affiliated competitions), any relevant directives should be considered as rules, which need to be followed. However, NGBs have no authoritative remit in the context of the National Curriculum, out-of-school-hours learning activities or friendly competitions. In these circumstances, their directives have the same status as that of this handbook – well intentioned guidance which managing staff should consider in relation to their particular situation.

13.2 Boxing

> Please read the general guidance provided in *Part one* of this handbook[1] and in paragraphs 13.1.1 to 13.1.30[2] before reading this section. This will help to ensure that you have a comprehensive awareness of safe practice issues affecting all combat activities and physical education in general.

13.2.1 Some medical authorities believe that, if delivered with force and frequency, blows to the head in boxing can cause damage to the brain, eyes, ears, mouth and hands. The physical education profession is constantly striving to minimise the risk of accidents and injuries to all participants of boxing, and to exercise the control necessary to achieve this objective.

People

13.2.2 The following points should be considered in relation to the people involved in boxing activities:

a Schools have a duty to ensure that coaching is provided by responsible and qualified coaches in a safe environment. Only qualified and experienced coaches should be employed to teach, coach or officiate boxing in schools.

b Schools that choose to offer boxing should ensure that all parents and pupils involved are aware of, and accept, the inherent and obvious risks.

Context

13.2.3 Mandatory headgear, footwear and gloves must be used, and must meet national requirements and guidelines.

Organisation

13.2.4 The following points should be considered in relation to the organisation of boxing activities:

a The Schools Amateur Boxing Association's Standard Scheme provides national guidance on the safe delivery of boxing activities.

b In order to reduce the potential for injury, schools are advised to consider running the Amateur Boxing Association of England Ltd's *Kid Gloves Scheme* (or other similar schemes), which focuses on the development of non-contact boxing skills.

13.3   Fencing

> Please read the general guidance provided in *Part one* of this handbook[1] and in paragraphs 13.1.1 to 13.1.30[2] before reading this section. This will help to ensure that you have a comprehensive awareness of safe practice issues affecting all combat activities and physical education in general.

13.3.1   The three common forms of fencing are épée, foil and sabre. Safety measures must be thoroughly addressed in order to minimise the risks involved in these potentially lethal activities. Full personal protection must be worn at all times, both for practice and competition. British Fencing rules must be strictly observed.

People

13.3.2   The following points should be considered in relation to the people involved in fencing activities:

a   All fencing coaches used by schools must be experienced in working with young people and hold relevant and up-to-date British Fencing coaching qualifications.

b   School staff must be qualified in fencing to lead the activity.

Context

13.3.3   The following points should be considered in relation to the context in which fencing activities take place:

a   The fencing environment should meet British Fencing safety requirements.

b   Pistes (both competition and practice) should be well spaced out at least 1.5 metres apart.

c   Practice pistes should meet national recommendations.

d   There should be a clear run-off at both ends of a piste for the safety of participants and/or spectators.

e   Only swords which are in good condition should be used; others should be condemned or taken out of use for repair.

f   The points of swords should be covered with purpose-made protective tips.

g   All swords must be checked regularly by knowledgeable school staff/coaches.

h   Any electrical equipment used for scoring should be stored safely and observed carefully while in use.

1   See pages 1–124.
2   See pages 141–43.

i   Adequate body protection is essential. Pupils must only be allowed to participate in fencing activities if they are wearing the following items of protective clothing/equipment:

   • A plastron

   • A mask complete with bib and an effective head clip which fits correctly (substandard masks are unacceptable)

   • A jacket long enough to cover the waistband of the trousers (the official requirement is a 10 cm overlap when in the *en garde* position)

   • Gloves with a gauntlet to cover the cuff of the jacket sleeve and protect the wrist and arm (the gauntlet must extend halfway up the forearm to ensure a safe overlap)

   • Breeches (optional during practice, mandatory during competitions).

j   Right-handed fencers must wear right-handed garments which have openings on the left-hand side. The opposite applies for left-handed fencers.

13.4   Judo

> Please read the general guidance provided in *Part one* of this handbook[1] and in paragraphs 13.1.1 to 13.1.30[2] before reading this section. This will help to ensure that you have a comprehensive awareness of safe practice issues affecting all combat activities and physical education in general.

13.4.1   Judo involves two participants, one of whom *throws* or *takes* his/her opponent to the *ground*. The sport is underpinned by a strong code of conduct from its roots in Eastern culture, which should be understood and implemented by all concerned (ie school staff, coaches and pupils).

People

13.4.2   The following points should be considered in relation to the people involved in judo activities:

a   Judo should be taught by a coach of 1st Dan grade (British Judo Association) who has also attended a sports coach UK *How to Coach Children in Sport* workshop.

b   Judo could be taught by a qualified teacher (recognised by the Department for Education and Skills) who has a minimum of 2nd KYU grade (British Judo Association).

---

1   See pages 1–124.

2   See pages 141–43.

Context

13.4.3   The following points should be considered in relation to the context in which judo activities take place:

a   The ceiling should be at least three metres high.

b   During free practice (randoori), it is reasonable to allow 11 square metres for each pair of pupils. This could be increased if the total mat area and number of pupils allow it.

c   A wide range of judo mats is available from recognised manufacturers. Phased compliance with current BS EN requirements is advised as mats are replaced.

d   The density of judo mats is such that they minimise the risk of injury from high impact falls/throws. Gymnastic mats should not be used as a substitute, as their density is inadequate for the purposes of judo.

e   The edge of the mat area should be at least two metres away from any walls, projections or open doors.

f   For competitions, the mat area (excluding safety area) should measure 5.5 metres x 5.5 metres or 7 metres x 5 metres.

g   Canvas covers should not be used to cover or secure mats. Frames can be constructed to secure mat areas permanently, but they should be covered if they present a hazard.

h   The thickness of the mats may need to be increased if the floor has little resilience. The manufacturer's guidelines should be followed.

i   Pupils should wear mandatory judo clothing. This should be a generous fit, as ill-fitting clothing can cause injury.

Organisation

13.4.4   The following points should be considered in relation to the organisation of judo activities:

a   GCSE syllabuses provide a useful guidance tool for the organisation of judo activities.

b   Mixed gender practice is permitted. It is therefore particularly important to *match* pupils by size, weight, age, experience and ability. However, mixed gender competition is not permitted.

c   Pupils should not practise throwing techniques while others are practising groundwork skills.

13.5 Martial arts

> Please read the general guidance provided in *Part one* of this handbook[1] and in paragraphs 13.1.1 to 13.1.30[2] before reading this section. This will help to ensure that you have a comprehensive awareness of safe practice issues affecting all combat activities and physical education in general.

13.5.1 The following points should be considered in relation to the people involved in martial arts activities:

a A qualification in one martial art is not transferable to another.

b All coaches must hold a licence which provides appropriate indemnity insurance to complement the third party liability insurance provided by schools.

Aikido

> Please read the general guidance provided in paragraph 13.5.1 before reading this section. This will help to ensure that you have a comprehensive awareness of safe practice issues affecting martial arts in general.

13.5.2 Aikido is a weaponless martial art which has been described as being *as active as tumbling and as elegant and dramatic as fencing*. It involves holds and locks which are usually taught by modern/practical or classical/ceremonial methods.

Context

13.5.3 The following points should be considered in relation to the context in which aikido activities take place:

a The mats used should meet the same requirements as judo mats[3] or other comparable health and safety guidelines.

b Pupils should wear a loose tunic and, preferably, the recommended trousers.

1   See pages 1–124.
2   See pages 141–43.
3   See paragraph 13.4.3 on page 147 for further information.

Organisation

13.5.4 The following points should be considered in relation to the organisation of aikido activities:

a Dangerous locks, holds or movements must not be taught or practised.

b Pupils should understand that they should not apply their aikido skills outside the class.

Karate

> Please read the general guidance provided in paragraph 13.5.1[1] before reading this section. This will help to ensure that you have a comprehensive awareness of safe practice issues affecting martial arts in general.

13.5.5 Karate is a Japanese weaponless martial art based on scientific principles which encompass physical culture, character development, self-defence and sport.

People

13.5.6 The following points should be considered in relation to the people involved in karate activities:

a There are many different karate organisations in the UK. It is essential that only coaches from approved organisations be appointed to lead karate sessions in schools. Details of approved organisations can be obtained from the sports councils for England, Scotland, Northern Ireland and Wales.

b Karate coaches should hold at least a 1st Dan Black Belt qualification.

c The procedures taught during karate activities should develop pupils' respect for their peers, coaches and environment.

Context

13.5.7 The following points should be considered in relation to the context in which karate activities take place:

a Three square metres per pupil are required when practising fundamental techniques (Kihon) and four square metres per pupil when practising formal exercises (Kata).

b Coaches and pupils should wear appropriate karate clothing. This should be laundered on a regular basis.

1 See page 148.

Organisation

13.5.8   The following points should be considered in relation to the organisation of karate activities:

a   GCSE/A Level syllabuses provide a useful guidance tool for the organisation of karate activities.

b   Karate sessions which take place during curriculum time should last for no more than one hour. It should consist of a warm-up and the three major components of karate:

- Fundamental techniques (Kihon)
- Formal exercise (Kata)
- Sparring (Kumite).

c   Out-of-school-hours karate sessions should last for no more than one and a half hours.

d   All Kihon, Kata and Kumite activities should be appropriate for the ability and experience of the pupils involved.

e   The importance of developing technical competence should be emphasised.

f   There are many forms of Kihon, Kata and Kumite. Pupils should successfully master each grade before progressing to more advanced techniques and skills.

Kendo, Kung Fu and Ju Jitsu

> Please read the general guidance provided in paragraph 13.5.1[1] before reading this section. This will help to ensure that you have a comprehensive awareness of safe practice issues affecting martial arts in general.

13.5.9   As the potential for harm in these activities is high, school staff are recommended to seek guidance from appropriate organisations (eg local education authority (LEA) advisory support services, NGBs) before appointing coaches to deliver these activities in their schools.

Tae kwondo

> Please read the general guidance provided in paragraph 13.5.1[1] before reading this section. This will help to ensure that you have a comprehensive awareness of safe practice issues affecting martial arts in general.

13.5.10   The Korean martial art of tae kwondo appeals to young people as it is characterised by high kicks and energetic movements, often in sequence. In addition, participants learn to apply powerful hand and joint-locking techniques. The risk of injury is high; to minimise this to an acceptable level, great care should be taken to ensure sound discipline and respect among pupils.

---

1   See page 148.

safe practice in physical education and school sport

People

13.5.11   Supervising adults who deliver tae kwondo sessions should be experienced Black Belts.

Context

13.5.12   The following points should be considered in relation to the context in which tae kwondo activities take place:

a   If mats are used, they should be joined together securely, so that they do not move apart.

b   Particular care should be taken to minimise risks if tae kwondo activities take place outdoors.

c   Pupils should wear appropriate equipment (eg headgear, knee pads) which meets recommended standards. This should be the correct size and be washed on a regular basis.

Organisation

13.5.13   The following points should be considered in relation to the organisation of tae kwondo activities:

a   When grouping pupils for sparring (especially freestyle), particular care should be taken to *match* pupils by gender, size, weight, age, experience and ability.

b   Pupils should be made aware of the potential for injury when performing holds and locks, and should be taught to perform them safely.

c   Pupils should strive for technical competence and avoid posing or showing off.

13.6   Self-defence

> Please read the general guidance provided in *Part one* of this handbook[1] and in paragraphs 13.1.1 to 13.1.30[2] before reading this section. This will help to ensure that you have a comprehensive awareness of safe practice issues affecting all combat activities and physical education in general.

13.6.1   Self-defence classes are becoming increasingly popular and, in schools, are mainly targeted at teenage girls in Key Stage 4. Self-defence involves control and restraint, self-protection, and elements of judo and some martial arts.

People

13.6.2   Self-defence coaches should be experienced in working with young people in the context of formal classes and hold a relevant coaching qualification in judo and/or one or more martial arts (eg tae kwondo, karate).

---

1   See pages 1–124.

2   See pages 141–43.

Organisation

13.6.3   Coaches should provide an in-depth syllabus of what will be taught.

13.7   Wrestling

> Please read the general guidance provided in *Part one* of this handbook[1] and in paragraphs 13.1.1 to 13.1.30[2] before reading this section. This will help to ensure that you have a comprehensive awareness of safe practice issues affecting all combat activities and physical education in general.

13.7.1   The rules and philosophy of the internationally agreed freestyle form of wrestling (ie Olympic Style Wrestling) are formulated so that two wrestlers can engage in hard physical combat without pain and/or injury. This should be the philosophy of all taking part in wrestling activities in schools (ie school staff, coaches and pupils).

People

13.7.2   The following points should be considered in relation to the people involved in wrestling activities:

a   Wrestling activities should always be supervised and refereed by competent, trained and qualified people.

b   Advice on training and qualifications for school staff wishing to deliver wrestling activities can be obtained from relevant wrestling organisations (eg British Amateur Wrestling Association).

Context

13.7.3   The following points should be considered in relation to the context in which wrestling activities take place:

a   The ceiling should be at least three metres high.

b   Any potentially hazardous walls should be padded.

c   The wrestling area should measure at least three square metres.

d   Mats should meet British Amateur Wrestling Association requirements.

e   Clothing should be close-fitting without being too restrictive (eg swimming costumes are ideal for training). Shorts are unsuitable and should not be worn.

f   Specifically designed wrestling costumes should be worn during competitions. There should be no loose parts which could trap an opponent's fingers. Tracksuits (or other similar clothing) should be worn over wrestling costumes to keep warm while waiting to compete.

chapter thirteen

1   See pages 1–124.
2   See pages 141–43.

g Footwear for beginners should be free of metal lace tags or eyelets, and have smooth soles.

h Protective arm and knee pads should be worn.

i Suitable support protection (in line with wrestling rules) should always be worn by both male and female pupils.

Organisation

13.7.4　The following points should be considered in relation to the organisation of wrestling activities:

a A trained and experienced mat chairperson should be positioned at the edge of the mat during competitions. He/she must intervene immediately if any move or hold performed is likely to cause pain.

b School staff/coaches should adopt the role of mat chairperson during practice sessions.

c Moves which put pressure on, or twist, the neck are extremely hazardous.

d Wrestlers in the Under 17, Under 15 and Under 13 age categories are not allowed to execute any form of full-nelson or half-nelson which involves holding the chin with the other hand.

e Pupils under the age of 11 are not allowed to use any form of nelson or bridging.

Further reading

- Perkins, J, Ridenhour, A and Kovsky, M (2000) **Attack proof – the ultimate guide to personal protection**. Champaign IL, Human Kinetics. ISBN 0 736003 51 7

- Skipp, A (1999) **Handbook of foil fencing**. Leeds, Coachwise Solutions. ISBN 1 902523 27 X

- Thompson, G (1998) **The fence – the art of protection**. Summersdale Publishers Ltd. ISBN 1 840240 84 9

Risk management

People

- **Pupils should share in the assessment and management of the risks involved**.

- Pupils should be adequately prepared and possess the necessary fitness and skills required.

- School staff responsible for groups of pupils should have a sound knowledge of the intended combat activity.

- Great care should be taken to appoint competent coaches, who hold relevant NGB coaching qualifications and who are experienced in working with young people

Context

- Any relevant NGB and/or LEA recommendations should be taken into account.

- The combat area and surface should be appropriate.

- Equipment should be appropriate for the pupils involved and be maintained in good condition.

- Pupils should wear appropriate clothing, footwear and protective equipment.

Organisation

- Parental consent should always be sought for pupils to take part in combat activities.

- Care should be taken to *match* pupils by size, weight, age, experience and ability.

- School staff/coaches must not demonstrate or compete with pupils during combat activities.

- The teaching of all combat activities should follow a carefully planned and graduated progression.

▶▶ See *Chapter two: Risk management* for more detailed, general guidance on risk management issues.

Questions and answers

Organisation

Qu 1   **Should pupils of different genders practise judo against each other?**

Ans   Only during ground work and kata demonstrations. Strict supervision is essential.

Qu 2   **I teach an outstanding wrestler who has achieved success in county competitions outside the school programme. Can and should I select him for our senior wrestling team? He is only 14 and most of the team and the opposition will be over 17.**

Ans   You should consult the British Amateur Wrestling Association and any relevant national schools' associations for guidelines on fighting out of an age category, even if the weight of the pupil in question matches that of his teammates and opponents. Ensure that you consult the pupil's parents and your head teacher, with a view to making a joint decision about the pupil's selection for the senior wrestling team, particularly in relation to insurance issues.

Chapter fourteen

Dance activities

> Please read the general guidance provided in *Part one* of this handbook[1] before reading this chapter. This will help to ensure that you have a comprehensive awareness of safe practice issues affecting dance activities and physical education in general.

14.1 Introduction

14.1.1   Dance may generally be considered as one of the safest physical education activities. It takes many forms, ranging from specific to more creative dance styles.

14.2 People

14.2.1   School staff should be appropriately qualified or experienced, and should be knowledgeable about the structure and function of the human body.

14.2.2   Pupils should be given opportunities to think about safe practice in relation to themselves and others when involved in holding, lifting and supporting techniques.

14.2.3   Pupils should share in the assessment and management of the risks associated with dance activities. This is an essential part of the learning process. Due to different abilities, the risk management process should be applied to individual pupils, to pupil groups and to the class as a whole.

14.3 Context

14.3.1   Dance activities are often taught in facilities which are not designed for that purpose. In these circumstances, great care should be taken to ensure that any modifications or adaptations meet satisfactory safety standards.

14.3.2   Facilities should be maintained in good order.

14.3.3   Floors should be non-slip and obstructions to the dance activity should be removed.

14.3.4   Heating and lighting should be appropriate for the dance activity.

14.3.5   Dance equipment should be maintained in good order. All risks associated with its use should be properly assessed and managed.

---

1   See pages 1–124.

14.3.6   Pupils should work in bare feet whenever safe to do so. Any clothing or footwear worn should be appropriate for the dance activity.

▶▶   See *Chapter nine: Cothing, personal effects and protection for further information about clothing and footwear.*

14.3.7   All personal effects should be removed or made safe before the dance activity starts.

14.4   Organisation

14.4.1   An adequate warm-up is essential before strenuous exercise. School staff should ensure that pupils are properly prepared for the physical demands of the dance activity.

14.4.2   Health-related dance styles (eg aerobics, step, and slide) may involve moderate to vigorous intensity exercise. Correct technique should be emphasised in order to maximise the associated benefits and minimise any risks.

14.4.3   In the context of dance, care should be taken to ensure that the following movements/exercises are carried out in an informed and controlled way:

a   Vigorous rotation of the neck

b   Maximal and loaded arching of the spine

c   Exercises which extend the spine under stress loads

d   Movements which flex the hips while seeking to over-extend straightened legs.

14.4.4   School staff should observe pupils carefully to check that they do not over-stress themselves.

14.4.5   When working in pairs or small groups on exercises involving lifting or supporting, extra care should be taken to ensure that pupils have worked through progressive practices.

Risk management

People

- **Pupils should share in the assessment and management of the risks involved.**
- Dance activities should be appropriate to the age and development of the pupils involved.
- Supervising adults should be appropriately qualified or experienced, and should be knowledgeable about the structure and function of the human body.

Context

- Supervising adults should ensure that pupils' clothing and footwear are appropriate for the environment in which a dance activity takes place.

Organisation

- The nature and requirements of individual dance forms should be considered when organising dance activities.
- All school staff (and pupils where appropriate) should be aware of the action to take if dance facilities become unsafe.
- ▶▶ See *Chapter two: Risk management* for more detailed, general guidance on risk management issues.

Questions and answers

People

Qu 1   **Is it acceptable to work with dance agencies in schools?**

Ans   Working with a dance agency can enhance pupil experiences and make a valuable contribution to learning. However, school staff need to be satisfied that agency staff are suitable to work with pupils and should ensure that all necessary checks are carried out. It is also good practice for school staff to inform parents about any activities involving external agencies.

▶▶ Refer to *The Use of Volunteers and Paid Coaches (Contractors) in Physical Education and School Sport* by BAALPE and DfES for further related guidance[1].

1   Visit the BAALPE website (www.baalpe.org) or DfES website (www.dfes.gov.uk) for further details.

Chapter fifteen

Games activities

> Please read the general guidance provided in *Part one* of this handbook[1] before reading this chapter. This will help to ensure that you have a comprehensive awareness of safe practice issues affecting games activities and physical education in general.

15.1 General guidance

15.1.1 This chapter provides guidance on safe practice in the following types of games activities:

 a Invasion games

 b Net/wall and racket games

 c Striking/fielding games

 d Target games

 e Other games.

15.1.2 This section contains general guidance that applies to all games activities. Subsequent sections focus on additional considerations relating to the specific types of games activities listed above. In all cases, the specific guidance provided must be read in conjunction with the general guidance in this section and all the chapters in *Part one* of this handbook[1].

People

15.1.3 Supervising adults should have a sound knowledge and understanding of the games activity they intend to teach, and of how to conduct sessions safely. They should be capable of officiating in accordance with rules with which pupils are familiar.

15.1.4 Supervising adults should be aware of the risks associated with personal participation while teaching or coaching games activities, particularly those which are likely to involve physical contact with pupils or in which hard missiles (eg cricket balls) are used. Participation by adults should be restricted to demonstrations in a controlled setting and to keeping games moving. It should not adversely affect their ability to maintain overall control of the games activity. Adults should not participate as team members alongside pupils during games or practices.

15.1.5 All coaches used by schools should be experienced in working with young people and hold relevant and up-to-date national governing body (NGB) coaching qualifications.

15.1.6 Supervising adults should ensure the safety of pupils at all times.

15.1.7 Supervising adults should have knowledge of first aid and resuscitation techniques, and understand the procedures for treating neck and spinal injuries.

---

1   See pages 1–124.

15.1.8 In all competitive situations, match officials should be competent and should apply the rules. When NGBs stipulate that they should hold a specific qualification, this requirement should be met.

15.1.9 Pupils should be suitably fit and adequately prepared for all activities and made aware of their personal responsibilities for their own safety and that of others.

15.1.10 Pupils should be taught to play according to the rules and to respect the decisions of officials.

15.1.11 Pupils should understand that excessive and over-zealous competitiveness, loss of temper and inappropriate language is wholly unacceptable. Supervising adults should always take appropriate action in the event of pupils displaying such behaviour. If necessary, the games activity should be stopped.

15.1.12 Pupils should share in the assessment and management of the risks associated with games activities. This is an essential part of the learning process. Due to different abilities, the risk management process should be applied to individual pupils, to pupil groups and to the class as a whole.

Context

Playing areas

15.1.13 Playing areas include:

a gymnasia

b sports halls

c grass and synthetic pitches (including cricket wickets)

d tennis courts

e hard play areas such as playgrounds.

15.1.14 Care should be taken to ensure that playing areas used for games activities:

a are large enough to allow safe play without overcrowding

b are reasonably level

c are clean and free from avoidable hazards or obstructions (eg removed clothing, stones, tins, glass, dog faeces)

d have lines marked with safe (ie non-toxic/non-corrosive) substances

e provide adequate distances between the boundaries of the playing area and surrounding obstacles (eg fences, hedges, posts)

f provide secure footing

g are accessible to the emergency services should the need arise (when off-site, it is advisable for a mobile phone and/or emergency numbers to be readily available).

▶▶ See *Chapter eight: Environment and equipment* and *Chapter twenty-one: Play in the school environment* for further information about play areas and surfaces.

Equipment and clothing

15.1.15   All equipment used should be suitable for the age, size, strength, ability and experience of the pupils involved.

15.1.16   Potentially hazardous items of equipment (eg hard balls) should be stored in a safe place where pupils cannot access them.

15.1.17   Equipment not being used should be removed from the playing area.

15.1.18   Games posts should conform to current BS EN requirements, be kept in good condition and be regularly painted. Lighter portable goals should be secured to prevent them tipping over. Free-standing posts should be secured, both when in use and when stored. All games posts should be checked regularly.

> ▶▶   See *Chapter eight: Environment and equipment* for further information about free-standing goalposts.

15.1.19   When using games posts as markers, care should be taken to ensure that pupils are not at risk from collision or impalement.

15.1.20   Corner flags should be tall enough and sufficiently pliable to avoid injury to pupils on impact.

15.1.21   Balls that inflate should be maintained at the correct pressure.

15.1.22   All equipment should be in good condition. Arrangements should be made for it to be inspected, repaired and maintained on a regular basis.

15.1.23   Faulty equipment should be clearly marked and removed from use (and access by pupils) until repaired or replaced.

15.1.24   Pupils should wear appropriate clothing, footwear and protective equipment for the intended activity, whether this takes place in a teaching situation or match play. This should be checked before the activity commences.

15.1.25   Pupils should wear appropriate footwear for the playing surface. Footwear should be checked on a regular basis to ensure it is safe. Studs should conform to current BS EN requirements and should be examined regularly.

15.1.26   Pupils are recommended to wear tracksuit trousers and long-sleeved tops when playing on artificial surfaces to prevent friction injuries occurring if they fall.

15.1.27   Long hair should be tied back, nails kept short and all potentially hazardous personal effects removed or made safe prior to taking part in any games activity.

15.1.28   The chewing of food, sweets or gum immediately before or during games activities should never be allowed. Chewing can result in choking, which can have serious, even fatal, consequences.

Organisation

15.1.29   GCSE/A Level syllabuses provide a useful guidance tool for the organisation of games activities.

15.1.30   Care should be taken to *match* pupils by size, weight, age, experience and ability, particularly in teaching situations and activities involving body contact, and when mixed gender practice is permitted.

15.1.31   Key considerations include team size, pitch size and duration of the activity. Pupils should only be exposed to challenges for which they have the mental ability and physical skills and fitness required to respond.

15.1.32   Supervising adults should clearly explain the rules and arrangements for games activities. All pupils should be made fully aware of acceptable routines and safe practice.

15.1.33   An adequate warm-up session should be provided prior to all games activities.

15.1.34   The rules and etiquette of the game (including any self-determined conditions) should be known and applied by all involved (ie school staff, coaches, volunteers and pupils).

15.1.35   The spirit of the game should be considered as important as playing to the rules. The competitive element should be kept in perspective. Completing a task successfully should be stressed as important and merits praise.

15.1.36   Supervising adults should use appropriate intervention and advice to ensure the safety of pupils, while accepting that a reasonable level of robust play is inevitable and an appealing part of many games.

15.1.37   Refereeing or umpiring matches in schools will often involve an element of teaching and learning as well as officiating, especially when safety issues arise.

15.1.38   Conditioned or modified versions of games activities promote safe participation and are particularly appropriate for beginners, groups of varying abilities, or where any lack of personal kit or protection may have safety implications. However, care should be taken to ensure that improvised rules, skills, tactics and equipment are used in an appropriate way that promotes safe practice.

15.1.39   Before competitive play begins, pupils should be taught the basic skills and rules involved in the intended activity.

15.1.40   The teaching of all games activities should follow a carefully planned and graduated progression, which ensures that all pupils master the necessary skills at any given level of competence before progressing to the next stage.

15.1.41   NGBs sometimes issue directives concerning the safe management of sport. When a match or competition takes place under the remit of an NGB (eg affiliated matches), any relevant directives should be considered as rules, which need to be followed. However, NGBs have no authoritative remit in the context of the National Curriculum, out-of-school-hours learning activities or friendly matches. In these circumstances, their directives have the same status as that of this handbook – well intentioned guidance which managing staff should consider in relation to their particular situation.

15.2   Invasion games

15.2.1   Invasion games is a collective term used to describe games involving two teams of players in which the objective is to attack/defend territory with the aim of scoring (eg a goal, a basket or a try). They include:

a   association football

b   basketball

c   Gaelic games

d   handball

e   hockey

f   ice hockey

g   lacrosse

h   netball

i   roller hockey

j   rugby league

k   rugby union.

Association football

> Please read the general guidance provided in *Part one* of this handbook[1] and in paragraphs 15.1.1 to 15.1.41[2] before reading this section. This will help to ensure that you have a comprehensive awareness of safe practice issues affecting games activities and physical education in general.

15.2.2   Association football is a very popular game which is played in many schools. As physical contact is involved and the risk of injury is therefore high, it must be played in accordance with the rules by pupils who are familiar with the skills of the game.

Context

15.2.3   The following points should be considered in relation to the context in which football activities take place:

a   Halls with unprotected windows or low-level mirrors should never be used for indoor football.

b   Plastic marker cones are suitable for use as improvised goals. Cricket stumps, stakes or the like should not be used for this purpose.

c   Pupils should wear appropriate footwear for the playing surface to ensure control and prevent slipping.

d   Pupils should carry studded boots to and from grass playing areas if this involves walking on hard surfaces.

---

1   See pages 1–124.

2   See pages 161–64.

e NGB[1] advice should be sought on the use of appropriate footwear for synthetic pitches. Boots with suitable traction should be worn to minimise the risk of stress injury.

f Shin pads should be worn in competitive matches.

Organisation

15.2.4 The techniques of tackling and legitimate body contact should be introduced very carefully at appropriate stages of maturity and ability.

Basketball

> Please read the general guidance provided in *Part one* of this handbook[2] and in paragraphs 15.1.1 to 15.1.41[3] before reading this section. This will help to ensure that you have a comprehensive awareness of safe practice issues affecting games activities and physical education in general.

15.2.5 Basketball is a game played at speed in a confined space and on a hard surface, often on a court surrounded by obstacles. It must be played as a non-contact game from the very early stages of learning.

People

15.2.6 The following points should be considered in relation to the people involved in basketball activities:

a Pupils should have good peripheral spatial awareness.

b Pupils should be capable of playing without (or with minimal) physical contact.

Context

15.2.7 The following points should be considered in relation to the context in which basketball activities take place:

a The court surface should be even, firm, clean, dry and non-slip.

b Any protruding obstructions within one metre of the side or end lines of the court should be removed or padded, particularly if behind and in line with the backboards.

c Any gymnastics apparatus or other equipment stored around the perimeter of the court should not protrude into the one metre *safe zone* around the court.

d It is recommended that any posts or backboards used outdoors be permanently fixed into the ground.

e Schools purchasing new basketball (and mini-basketball) equipment should ensure that it meets the appropriate British Standards European Norm (BS EN) requirements.

f Where possible, backboards should have an overhang of 1.25 metres on match courts and 0.75 metres on practice courts.

---

1 Football Association, Irish Football Association, Scottish Football Association and Football Association of Wales as appropriate.

2 See pages 1–124.

3 See pages 161–64.

g Backboards should be fitted and maintained by specialist contractors.

h Regulation pattern rings and nets should be used.

i Basketballs should not be over-inflated. They should be regularly inspected for splits or other damage, and removed from use if necessary.

j Specially designed basketball boots are preferable. Pupils should not play in socks or stockinged feet.

k Vests and other clothing should be reasonably close-fitting.

Gaelic games

> Please read the general guidance provided in *Part one* of this handbook[1] and in paragraphs 15.1.1 to 15.1.41[2] before reading this section. This will help to ensure that you have a comprehensive awareness of safe practice issues affecting games activities and physical education in general.

15.2.8   Gaelic football, hurling and camogie are fast-moving contact sports. As the potential for harm is high, school staff are recommended to seek guidance from the Gaelic Athletic Association before delivering these activities in their schools.

Handball

> Please read the general guidance provided in *Part one* of this handbook[1] and in paragraphs 15.1.1 to 15.1.41[2], 15.2.5 to 15.2.7[3] and 15.2.22 to 15.2.24[4] before reading this section. This will help to ensure that you have a comprehensive awareness of safe practice issues affecting hand passing games and physical education in general.

15.2.9   Handball is a non-contact game similar to other hand passing games (eg basketball, netball).

Context

15.2.10   The following points should be considered in relation to the context in which handball activities take place:

a Attacking areas may become slippery during play due to perspiration from pupils who have made contact with the ground. Appropriate action should be taken to maintain a safe floor surface.

b Balls should be soft to the touch and not over-inflated, to avoid stinging the hands when caught.

c A water-resistant ball is required when handball is played outdoors.

---

1   See pages 1–124.

2   See pages 161–64.

3   See pages 166–67.

4   See pages 171–72.

Hockey

Please read the general guidance provided in *Part one* of this handbook[1] and in paragraphs 15.1.1 to 15.1.41[2] before reading this section. This will help to ensure that you have a comprehensive awareness of safe practice issues affecting games activities and physical education in general.

15.2.11   Hockey is a fast-moving game that can be played on a variety of surfaces, both indoor and outdoor. The development of synthetic surfaces (eg sand-filled and water-based) has done much to improve the safety of the game. In addition to the 11-a-side game, mini hockey is suitable for younger pupils and zone hockey for disabled pupils. Further information can be obtained from the relevant NGB[3].

Context

15.2.12   The following points should be considered in relation to the context in which hockey activities take place:

a   Grass pitches should be cut and rolled regularly to ensure that the ball runs true.

b   Synthetic surfaces should be maintained in accordance with the manufacturer's advice.

c   Surface damage and/or wear and tear may render pitches unsafe.

d   Care should be taken when using artificial surfaces which are not specifically designed for hockey.

e   Inclement weather (eg excessive rain, wind or frost) may affect playing conditions and particular care should be taken to ensure pupil safety.

f   Corner flags should be between 1.2 metres and 1.5 metres high, and should be smoothly rounded at the top.

g   Hockey sticks must be maintained in good condition. They should never be used if they become dangerous due to wear and tear, roughness, splinters or other faults.

h   A variety of types of hockey balls are available for different playing surfaces. Care should be taken to ensure that the correct type of ball is used. Lighter balls may be more suitable for younger pupils.

i   If hockey is played on a playground (or other similar tarmac surface), the game should be modified to suit the playing surface and a softer pudding ball should be used.

j   During match play practices and competitive matches, pupils are strongly recommended to wear shin pads, knuckle protectors and personally designed mouthguards.

k   When playing on synthetic surfaces, pupils are strongly recommended to wear knee, elbow and hand protection.

1   See pages 1–124.

2   See pages 161–64.

3   England Hockey, Irish Hockey Association, Scottish Hockey Union and Welsh Hockey Union as appropriate.

safe practice in physical education and school sport

l Goalkeepers must always be well equipped and protected. During match play practices and competitive matches, they should wear:

- pads and kickers
- gauntlet gloves
- body and abdominal protectors
- a full helmet and throat guard.

Organisation

15.2.13   The following points should be considered in relation to the organisation of hockey activities:

a Particular emphasis should be placed on rules relating to potentially dangerous play (eg use of the stick, lifting the ball, body interference and obstruction).

b Pupils should develop and exercise good stick and ball control. The use of hockey sticks should be governed by careful control and intention, with controlled pushing being well established in games before hitting is introduced.

c Goalkeepers should try to remain on their feet.

d Great care should be taken when more than one ball is in use during teaching and pre-match situations.

e Umpires should maintain firm control of matches, but not to the extent that the flow of the game is adversely affected.

f Loss of temper, dangerous play and deliberate body contact should be penalised.

Ice hockey

Please read the general guidance provided in *Part one* of this handbook[1] and in paragraphs 15.1.1 to 15.1.41[2], 15.2.11 to 15.2.13[3] and 18.2.38 to 18.2.40[4] before reading this section. This will help to ensure that you have a comprehensive awareness of safe practice issues affecting ice hockey and physical education in general.

People

15.2.14   Pupils should be competent in the basic skills of ice skating.

1   See pages 1–124.
2   See pages 161–64.
3   See pages 168–69.
4   See page 235.

Context

15.2.15 The following points should be considered in relation to the context in which ice hockey activities take place:

a Ice rinks should be maintained to provide an even, smooth surface for skating.

b Surface damage and/or wear and tear may render rinks unsafe.

c Boots should be well fitted and skates in good condition.

d Specialist padded clothing and knee, elbow and hand protection must be worn.

Organisation

15.2.16 Care must be taken never to overcrowd the rink during practice sessions.

Lacrosse

Please read the general guidance provided in *Part one* of this handbook[1] and in paragraphs 15.1.1 to 15.1.41[2] before reading this section. This will help to ensure that you have a comprehensive awareness of safe practice issues affecting games activities and physical education in general.

Men's lacrosse

15.2.17 Men's lacrosse is a fast-moving contact sport.

Context

15.2.18 The following points should be considered in relation to the context in which men's lacrosse activities take place:

a The extent of protective clothing required in the senior game depends on the level at which the game is played. At junior level, protective clothing is not compulsory, but pupils should be advised to wear as much of it as possible.

b Gauntlets should always be worn and should be well padded on the outside of the hand and wrist.

c A rigid or padded cap is recommended to protect the head and face. It should be fitted with a mask and chin strap, and be properly fastened on both sides.

d Goalkeepers should wear chest protection, stomach and thigh pads, and an abdominal protector.

e Full protective clothing is mandatory at international level.

1 See pages 1–124.
2 See pages 161–64.

safe practice in physical education and school sport

Women's lacrosse

15.2.19   Women's lacrosse is a non-contact sport. The rules are specifically designed to protect players, especially around the head.

Context

15.2.20   The following points should be considered in relation to the context in which women's lacrosse activities take place:

a   Close-fitting gloves without webbing or excessive padding should be worn.

b   Boots with metal studs must not be worn.

c   Goalkeepers should wear leg pads, a body pad and a helmet. A throat protector may also be worn.

d   International rules require all players to wear mouthguards. Other protection (eg nose guards) may be worn, but field players are not allowed to wear protective headgear or face masks.

Pop lacrosse

15.2.21   Pop lacrosse is an ideal introduction to lacrosse. It incorporates the basic skills and strategies of the game, but has more flexible rules which can be adapted to suit the needs of the pupils, equipment and playing area involved. No body or stick contact is involved.

Netball

> Please read the general guidance provided in *Part one* of this handbook[1] and in paragraphs 15.1.1 to 15.1.41[2] before reading this section. This will help to ensure that you have a comprehensive awareness of safe practice issues affecting games activities and physical education in general.

15.2.22   Netball is a non-contact game. Simplified versions have been developed to introduce netball to younger players (eg *First Step Netball* for children aged nine years and under; *High Five Netball* for children aged 11 years and under).

Context

15.2.23   The following points should be considered in relation to the context in which netball activities take place:

a   The court surface should be even, firm, clean, dry and non-slip.

b   There should be at least one metre of space between the outer lines of the court and any netting, wall, kerb edging or other obstruction.

c   There should be at least two metres of space between adjacent courts.

d   Indoor courts should be free of furniture or other obstructions.

e   Equipment should conform to NGB[3] rules and requirements.

f   Posts must be stable. Free-standing posts should have weighted bases to ensure stability.

1   See pages 1–124.

2   See pages 161–64.

3   England Netball, Northern Ireland Netball Association, Netball Scotland and Welsh Netball Association as appropriate.

g Bases should not project onto the court area.

h Posts and rings should be checked regularly for signs of wear and tear, damage and rust.

i Clothing should allow pupils sufficient freedom to run, jump and throw safely.

j During competitive matches, gloves may only be worn if they are needed for medical reasons. Umpires must be satisfied that gloves do not present a hazard to other players.

Organisation

15.2.24   Official NGB rules, which prohibit physical contact and rough play, should always be enforced.

Roller hockey

> Please read the general guidance provided in *Part one* of this handbook[1] and in paragraphs 15.1.1 to 15.1.41[2], 15.2.11 to 15.2.13[3] and 18.2.38 to 18.2.40[4] before reading this section. This will help to ensure that you have a comprehensive awareness of safe practice issues affecting roller hockey and physical education in general.

People

15.2.25   Pupils should be competent in the basic skills of roller skating.

Context

15.2.26   The following points should be considered in relation to the context in which roller hockey activities take place:

a The playing area should be made of wood, asphalt, concrete or other suitable material. In all cases, it should be even, level and non-slip.

b Sticks should be made of wood or plastic.

c Skates should be maintained in good condition with the wheels running freely.

d Pupils should wear appropriate protective clothing.

15.2.27   Further advice on safety issues can be obtained from the National Roller Hockey Association.

Rugby league

> Please read the general guidance provided in *Part one* of this handbook[1] and in paragraphs 15.1.1 to 15.1.41[2] before reading this section. This will help to ensure that you have a comprehensive awareness of safe practice issues affecting games activities and physical education in general.

---

1   See pages 1–124.
2   See pages 161–64.
3   See pages 168–69.
4   See page 235.

15.2.28   Rugby league is a contact invasion game. At an introductory level, it can be played with modified numbers and simplified rules in both non-contact and contact versions of the game. As with all sports, safe practice is necessary in order to minimise the risk of injury.

Context

15.2.29   The following points should be considered in relation to the context in which rugby league activities take place:

a   A suitable playing surface is critical to safety. It must be soft enough to accommodate falls during tackles and be free from debris, dangerous obstacles and obstructions.

b   Pitch and space markings should take into account the age and size of the pupils taking part, and the kind of game being played.

c   Goal post uprights should be protected by padding.

d   Corner flags must be flexible and sufficiently high so that they are not hazardous to falling players.

e   Although not compulsory, it is good practice for pupils to wear mouthguards to protect their mouth and headguards to protect against concussion.

f   Shoulder padding is permitted but is not compulsory.

Organisation

15.2.30   The following points should be considered in relation to the organisation of rugby league activities:

a   Pupils should not take part in the contact version of rugby until they have accomplished the basics of the game and are proficient in tackling and scrummaging.

b   Tackling should be introduced gradually with sound technique. Pupils should also receive training in effective ways of taking a tackle – for example, how to fall with the ball and the legitimate use of the fend (hand off), as referred to in the *Rugby League Safe Play Code*.

c   Mixed gender competition may be suitable for primary age pupils but is not appropriate for older pupils (ie secondary age and above).

d   Pupils who experience concussion should always receive medical treatment. Guidance relating to clearance to play should be strictly applied.

e   Teaching should be progressive and should build on existing skills. Guidance on suitable progression is provided in RLCEP resources.

Rugby union

Please read the general guidance provided in *Part one* of this handbook[1] and in paragraphs 15.1.1 to 15.1.41[2] before reading this section. This will help to ensure that you have a comprehensive awareness of safe practice issues affecting games activities and physical education in general.

1   See pages 1–124.
2   See pages 161–64.

Context

15.2.31   The following points should be considered in relation to the context in which rugby union activities take place:

   a Corner flags should be smooth and flexible, and have rounded ends.

   b Goal posts should be padded in accordance with NGB[1] recommendations for both matches and practices.

   c Scrummaging machines should be inspected and maintained on a regular basis.

   d All types of body protection should conform to the recommendations of the International Rugby Board (IRB) and the National Schools Rugby Football Union of England, Ireland, Scotland and Wales.

   e Pupils who play in the front row are advised to wear shin guards which are preferably strapped in position.

   f Pupils are strongly recommended to wear personally designed mouthguards as a valuable means of protection. Professional advice should be sought on fitting them correctly.

   g The requirements of IRB and constituent body safety pamphlets should be fully met.

Organisation

15.2.32   The following points should be considered in relation to the organisation of rugby union activities:

   a The national RFU *continuum* should be followed as a nationally accepted method of progressive learning (eg numbers relating to the age of pupils should be strictly followed in competitions).

   b County schools unions are regularly sent risk assessment guidelines and individual schools are now required to carry out a risk assessment of the playing area every time it is used.

   c School staff should take particular care to avoid risks when working with pupils who are not yet ready to play competitively (eg those with inadequate experience or progressive coaching to play in the first row of the scrum).

   d The full-sided game may not be appropriate for pupils who lack coordination or confidence. Differentiation of the game should be considered to accommodate their needs.

   e Pupils should be suitably trained and experienced for key competitive situations in accordance with IRB laws and pupil variations (ie ages and key positions).

   f Pupils who experience concussion must take a three-week break from playing rugby

---

1   Rugby Football Union (RFU), Irish Rugby Football Union, Scottish Rugby Union and Welsh Rugby Union as appropriate.

safe practice in physical education and school sport

15.3 Net/wall and racket games

General guidance

15.3.1 Net/wall and racket games include:

a badminton

b squash and racketball

c tennis

d volleyball.

15.3.2 The mini or short versions of the games promote safe participation and are particularly appropriate for beginners or groups of varying abilities.

15.3.3 Net/wall and racket games are comparatively safe, although injuries (including eye damage) can occur. Many safe practice issues are common or adaptable across the range of games. It is therefore advisable to read the whole of this section (in conjunction with the general guidance provided in *Part one* of this handbook[1] and in paragraphs 15.1.1 to 15.1.41[2]) in order to ensure a comprehensive awareness of safe practice issues affecting net/wall and racket games in general. This is particularly important if guidance is sought for any games not specifically included in this section (eg fives, table tennis).

People

15.3.4 The following points should be considered in relation to the people involved in net/wall and racket games:

a Although net/wall and racket games are relatively low-risk, school staff should either be qualified in coaching them or be experienced players in order to control them safely.

b The most common causes of accidents include:

- Being struck by a racket, ball or shuttle

- Tripping or slipping

- Wearing unsuitable, damaged or improperly fitting footwear

- Colliding with walls or equipment in the vicinity of the playing area.

c Pupils should be aware of the rules and the special conditions and etiquette relating to the different games.

Context

15.3.5 The following points should be considered in relation to the context in which net/wall and racket games take place:

a The court surface should be even, clean, dry and non-slip.

b Any protrusion from the walls or equipment not being used should be well clear of the court boundary.

c Equipment left lying on the floor presents a safety hazard.

d Nets should be in good condition, pulled tight and secured flush with the posts so that there are no holes or gaps through which a shuttle or ball can pass.

1 See pages 1–124.
2 See pages 161–64.

Organisation

15.3.6 Pupils should be alerted to potential hazards (eg permanent columns or pillars, radiators) and explain appropriate procedures to ensure safe practice.

15.3.7 Everyone should avoid crossing a court which is in use.

Badminton

> Please read the general guidance provided in *Part one* of this handbook[1] and in paragraphs 15.1.1 to 15.1.41[2] and 15.3.1 to 15.3.7[3] before reading this section. This will help to ensure that you have a comprehensive awareness of safe practice issues affecting games activities and physical education in general.

Context

15.3.8 The following points should be considered in relation to the context in which badminton activities take place:

a There should be sufficient space on court to accommodate group practices and to avoid pupils playing over post bases between courts.

b Background lighting should permit clear visibility of the shuttle in flight.

c Lighter rackets and slow-flight shuttles may be more suitable for younger pupils and beginners.

d Rackets with broken strings should not be used.

e Posts (preferably wheel-away push or pull) should be positioned and stored appropriately and handled with care.

Organisation

15.3.9 Pupils should never attempt to hit the shuttle if there is a risk of colliding with, or hitting, another pupil.

Squash and racketball

> Please read the general guidance provided in *Part one* of this handbook[1] and in paragraphs 15.1.1 to 15.1.41[2] and 15.3.1 to 15.3.7[3] before reading this section. This will help to ensure that you have a comprehensive awareness of safe practice issues affecting games activities and physical education in general.

15.3.10 Squash is played in a confined area and particular care is therefore required to ensure the safety of the pupils involved.

15.3.11 Racketball is suitable for young pupils and beginners, both as an introduction to squash and as a game in its own right.

1 See pages 1–124.
2 See pages 161–64.
3 See pages 175–76.

Context

15.3.12   The following points should be considered in relation to the context in which squash and racketball activities take place:

a Short-lever rackets are recommended for beginners. Long-lever rackets are not only a hindrance to skill learning, but are also a hazard during play.

b Due to the potential for eye injury, it is advisable for pupils to wear protective eye shields.

c Footwear should be non-marking and provide a good grip.

Organisation

15.3.13   The following points should be considered in relation to the organisation of squash and racketball activities:

a The supervisory problem posed by court separation – discipline needs to be maintained even though constant observation is not possible.

b As squash is played in a confined area, the number of pupils per court should vary according to the age and ability of the group. A maximum of six pupils per court is recommended.

c Pupils should be made aware of the danger of opening squash court doors while play is in progress. They should be taught to knock and wait to be admitted.

d Pupils should also be made aware of the danger of attempting to hit the ball when it is in close proximity to another player.

e Pupils should be taught never to intentionally impede an opponent.

f Doubles play requires good playing techniques and a sound understanding of the game. Pupils should only progress to doubles when a high standard of singles play has been achieved.

Tennis

> Please read the general guidance provided in *Part one* of this handbook[1] and in paragraphs 15.1.1 to 15.1.41[2] and 15.3.1 to 15.3.7[3] before reading this section. This will help to ensure that you have a comprehensive awareness of safe practice issues affecting games activities and physical education in general.

15.3.14   Short tennis is a suitable introduction to the game of tennis and should be used to develop basic safe court craft.

---

1   See pages 1–124.
2   See pages 161–64.
3   See pages 175–76.

Context

15.3.15 The following points should be considered in relation to the context in which tennis activities take place:

a Line markings on the court surface should be flat, level and securely fixed.

b *Redgra* or similar material court surfaces should be watered and rolled regularly to maintain a firm, level surface.

c When rain or frost has made outdoor courts hazardous, play or practice should be delayed until the surface reverts to its normal state.

d Broken wire-surround fencing can be particularly hazardous and should be repaired as soon as possible. Pupils should be kept away from the area until the repair is complete.

e When posts are removed, caps should be used to cover the holes. This is particularly important on multi-use play areas.

f Portable equipment should be removed from the playing area after use.

g Lighter, shorter rackets are more suitable for younger pupils and beginners, and in areas where space is limited.

h The use of sponge or other types of soft ball is recommended in areas where space is limited.

Organisation

15.3.16 The following points should be considered in relation to the organisation of tennis activities:

a A court may be used safely by two groups for rallying purposes, each group using half the available space across the court.

b When pupils are practising serving, smashing or lobbing, a routine drill is required to prevent accidents. During service practice, there should be a maximum of six pupils behind the baseline. For smashing practice, feeders of the ball should never be positioned directly in front of pupils practising the smash. Pupils should wait their turn off the court, well spaced and alert, so that, if necessary, they can move quickly to avoid being hit.

c Group formations should be designed to ensure that players moving backwards do not collide with other players or with the wall, fencing or any other restricting barrier.

d Sufficient space must be allowed for the stroke that is being played, including allowance for any follow-through. Pupils should not play a stroke if they think another player is likely to get hit by the racket or ball.

e Pupils should be constantly reminded never to:

- attempt to play strokes outside their own playing area

- look round at a partner who is serving

- jump over, climb over or duck under the net when changing ends

- use an exaggerated back swing or follow-through.

Volleyball

> Please read the general guidance provided in *Part one* of this handbook[1] and in paragraphs 15.1.1 to 15.1.41[2] and 15.3.1 to 15.3.7[3] before reading this section. This will help to ensure that you have a comprehensive awareness of safe practice issues affecting games activities and physical education in general.

15.3.17 Volleyball is a court team game which can be played indoors or outdoors. It involves constant movement and quick reactions by players. Players generally remain on their feet during volleyball games. However, when playing at a high level, they may roll on the floor to return to position after striking a low ball.

Context

15.3.18 The following points should be considered in relation to the context in which volleyball activities take place:

a All lights above the court should be guarded.

b Weighted posts should be tied back to the wall and should not be allowed to stand freely. Tie wires should be positioned well above head height. Bases should not protrude into the court.

c Badminton posts should not be used.

d Free-standing or weighted posts are not permitted in competitive matches.

e Ropes used as nets should be clearly visible to all players. Practice nets are recommended.

f Trainer (soft) balls should be used by beginners to avoid injury.

Organisation

15.3.19 The following points should be considered in relation to the organisation of volleyball activities:

a If space is limited, the numbers of players should be reduced accordingly.

b The rules of the game should be strictly enforced, especially those covering play at the net, which involves smashing, blocking and possible physical contact.

c Players practising smashes or serves should be well spaced out. When practising smashes, players should aim the ball at an empty part of the court.

d During match play where only one ball is used, the ball should be rolled back to the other half of the court. In practice situations where both halves of the court are in use, balls should be carried back to the other half of the court, not rolled.

e Deliberate falling and rolling should not be practised until pupils are experienced and competent at the game.

1 See pages 1–124.
2 See pages 161–64.
3 See pages 175–76.

15.4   Striking and fielding games

15.4.1   In striking and fielding games, a ball is bowled (or otherwise delivered), struck by an implement, fielded and returned for the procedure to be repeated. Games are normally played by two teams, each taking turns at batting and fielding. The games most commonly played in schools are:

a   cricket

b   rounders

c   softball

d   baseball

e   stoolball.

15.4.2   Many safe practice issues are common or adaptable across the range of striking and fielding games.

Cricket

> Please read the general guidance provided in *Part one* of this handbook[1] and in paragraphs 15.1.1 to 15.1.41[2] before reading this section. This will help to ensure that you have a comprehensive awareness of safe practice issues affecting games activities and physical education in general.

15.4.3   When played with a soft ball, cricket should present supervising adults with few difficulties. *Softball cricket* and *kwik cricket* are now nationally recognised games with flexible rules that are simple to adapt, understand and implement. They are relatively safe ways to introduce the skills of cricket.

15.4.4   The potential risk is increased when cricket is played with a hard ball. Safe practice is therefore essential.

Context

15.4.5   The following points should be considered in relation to the context in which cricket activities take place:

a   The wicket (batting and bowling ends) should be reasonably true.

b   A level synthetic wicket is an acceptable alternative to a grass wicket and is preferable to a grass surface that cannot be adequately maintained.

c   Synthetic wickets should be maintained in good condition. They must be securely fastened and any tears in the material should be repaired before further use.

d   Netting should be inspected frequently and maintained in good condition.

e   Boots or shoes with a grip on the soles are suitable for both grass and artificial wickets.

f   Batters and wicketkeepers should wear appropriate protective equipment.

g   NGB[3] advice on the wearing of helmets should be followed.

1   See pages 1–124.
2   See pages 161–64.
3   England and Wales Cricket Board, Northern Ireland Cricket Association, Scottish Cricket Union and Welsh Cricket Association as appropriate.

Organisation

15.4.6   The following points should be considered in relation to the organisation of nets practice:

a   Nets should be positioned so that users of adjacent areas are not at risk from balls hit from the nets. A roof net is desirable to contain balls within the nets.

b   Bowlers in nets should bowl in a controlled order and ensure that batters are fully ready before each delivery.

c   Balls coming to rest in a net should be collected only after all bowlers have completed their deliveries and when it is safe to do so.

d   If a ball comes to rest in an adjacent net, it should only be retrieved when bowling in the other net is halted. The batter should retrieve it by reaching with his/her bat under the net, keeping his/her head well away from the net. Alternatively, the ball can be retrieved by the bowler, but only when all bowlers have bowled.

e   Pupils waiting to bat should observe from a safe position at all times. This applies in all situations, including class teaching, net practice or games.

15.4.7   The following points should be considered in relation to the organisation of games of cricket:

a   Wickets should be sited to provide a reasonable boundary and avoid the risk of balls being hit onto paths, roadways or gardens.

b   The laws of the game should be understood, observed and implemented as appropriate.

c   Pupils under the age of 15 should not be allowed to field closer than 7.3 metres (8 yards) from the middle stump until the batter has struck the ball. The only exceptions are fielders behind the stumps and on the offside (eg slip and gully). This distance should be increased to 10 metres (11 yards) for pupils under the age of 13. These distances apply even if the fielders wear helmets. The game or practice should not be allowed to continue if fielders encroach within the stated distances.

d   Pupils under the age of 18 must wear a helmet (and for boys, a box) when fielding within 5.5 metres (6 yards) of the bat, except when fielding behind the wicket on the offside.

e   Pupils waiting to bat should observe from a safe position at all times. This applies in all situations, including class teaching, net practice or games.

Rounders, softball, baseball and stoolball

> Please read the general guidance provided in *Part one* of this handbook[1] and in paragraphs 15.1.1 to 15.1.41[2] and 15.4.3 to 15.4.7[3] before reading this section. This will help to ensure that you have a comprehensive awareness of safe practice issues affecting striking and fielding games, and physical education in general.

1   See pages 1–124.
2   See pages 161–64.
3   See pages 180–81.

Context

15.4.8   The following points should be considered in relation to the context in which rounders, softball, baseball and stoolball activities take place:

   a Running areas should be free from hazards and moved as required to avoid worn and uneven patches developing near bases.

   b To reduce the risk of damage to fingers, softer and/or larger balls should be used when introducing the game to younger pupils whose hand-eye coordination is not fully developed.

   c Catching mitts/gloves should be worn as appropriate for softball and baseball.

Organisation

15.4.9   The following points should be considered in relation to the organisation of rounders, softball, baseball and stoolball activities:

   a The ball should not be pitched unless and until all pupils, especially the batter, are fully prepared and ready to play.

   b Rounders bats should always be carried when running between bases. It is dangerous to throw the bat away after striking the ball and beginning to run.

   c Pupils waiting their turn to bat should be positioned at a safe distance from the striker.

   d Backstops/catchers should be positioned at a safe distance behind the hitter to avoid being struck by a back swing.

15.5   Target games

15.5.1   This section covers archery and golf. However, the guidance provided can be applied to other target games.

Archery

> Please read the general guidance provided in *Part one* of this handbook[1] and in paragraphs 15.1.1 to 15.1.41[2] before reading this section. This will help to ensure that you have a comprehensive awareness of safe practice issues affecting games activities and physical education in general.

People

15.5.2   The following points should be considered in relation to the people involved in archery activities:

   a Archery in schools should always be organised and supervised by competent and qualified personnel. Advice on appropriate training and qualifications can be obtained from the Grand National Archery Society.

---

1   See pages 1–124.
2   See pages 161–64.

safe practice in physical education and school sport

b Pupils must understand that arrows can be lethal and that safe practice is therefore vital.

Context

15.5.3 The following points should be considered when archery activities take place on indoor ranges:

a The hall in which archery takes place must be large enough to enable shooting at ranges of not less than nine metres.

b Purpose-made archery backstop curtains should be positioned behind the targets. These should be at least 3.5 metres high and should extend the full width of the hall (or at least six metres on either side of the target).

c The entrance doors to the hall in which archery takes place should be kept locked, with the key on the inside, throughout the archery session.

d Removable shutters should be used to cover all glass panes in any doors which may be in the target area.

15.5.4 The following points should be considered when archery activities take place on outdoor ranges:

a The range should be positioned so that it does not lie on the route to other playing areas and is away from buildings, walls, hedges or fences, from behind which a person may emerge without warning.

b The width of the range should be such that no target is positioned less than 27 metres from a public road, right of way or any areas over which school staff have no control.

c The whole range area should be clearly marked and roped off, with warning notices displayed.

d If there is no bank or slope behind the target, the range should be limited to 135 metres and the target should be positioned inside this area with at least 45 metres clear behind it.

e If there is a bank or slope of adequate height behind the target, the clear area may be reduced, but care must be taken to ensure that no-one is able to walk into any part of the area where an arrow might land, including the area behind the bank/slope.

f A shooting line should be clearly marked and a waiting line (behind which those who are not actually shooting should wait) should be positioned at least 4.5 metres behind it. These lines should remain fixed, while targets should be moved as appropriate.

g Grass should be cut short and there should be no bushes or undergrowth within the range area. This will ensure that stray arrows fall safely and can be easily seen and retrieved.

h Further guidance on the layout of an archery field can be obtained from the Grand National Archery Society.

15.5.5 The following points should be considered in relation to the equipment used during archery activities:

a Target supports should be padded to reduce the risk of rebound or ricochet. The use of drawing pins (or other similar objects) to attach additional targets to the boss is forbidden.

b Younger pupils should use bows of a suitable size and draw weight to ensure they can handle them comfortably and safely.

c When fully drawn back, arrows should project no less than five centimetres in front of the arrow rest.

d Pupils should wear bracers while shooting. These will keep sleeves out of the way of strings and provide some measure of arm protection in the event of a bad shot.

e Tabs are advisable in order to perform a clean loose of the arrow and to protect the shooting fingers.

f Loose clothing may foul the string and should not be worn. Neckties should be removed prior to the start of archery activities.

Organisation

15.5.6   The following points should be considered in relation to the organisation of archery activities:

a Archery should only be practised on an archery range.

b An appropriate adult/pupil ratio should be determined by a risk assessment. In all cases, the number of pupils per qualified supervising adult should not exceed 12, with no more than four pupils at a target at any one time.

c Spectators should remain at least 4.5 metres behind the shooting line.

d The target area and range must be clear before shooting begins.

e Archers must be in position on the shooting line and should only load their bows following a given signal from the supervising adult. Archers must point their bows at the target as soon as loading begins.

f A drawn bow must never be pointed at anyone.

g Targets should be at least 3.5 metres apart and archers should stand at least 1.5 metres apart when on the shooting line.

h Only when all archers have completed their shooting, should the signal be given to advance to the target to retrieve the arrows. Archers should walk to the side of the range to retrieve arrows.

i When arrows are being withdrawn from the target, the archer and any others present should stand at the side of the target, so that there is no possibility of anyone being struck as the arrow is pulled out.

j Archers should understand, and respond immediately to, archery commands:

  • *Fast!* means that everybody should stop shooting.

  • *Comedown!* is used to instruct a specific archer who may be having difficulties.

k Shooting must not take place when the wind strength is such that arrows may be dangerously deflected. Shooting directly into wind should be avoided.

Golf

Please read the general guidance provided in *Part one* of this handbook[1] and in paragraphs 15.1.1 to 15.1.41[2] before reading this section. This will help to ensure that you have a comprehensive awareness of safe practice issues affecting games activities and physical education in general.

People

15.5.7 Golf requires discipline and great care. Golf activities in schools should always be organised and supervised by competent and experienced school staff, volunteers or coaches.

Context

15.5.8 The following general points should be considered in relation to the context in which golf activities take place:

a Golf activities should ideally take place on a golf course or driving range.

b Pupils should understand the importance of maintaining golf equipment in good condition, checking regularly for worn grips and badly cut golf balls, which could contribute to lack of control.

15.5.9 The following additional points should be considered when a net is used for practice:

a A special golf net with a fine mesh should be used. It should be at least 2.5 metres high and should hang clear of any supports.

b If pupils are using both sides of the net at the same time, only airflow or similar type light, short-flight balls should be used.

c The mesh of the net should be examined regularly for signs of damage.

15.5.10 The following additional points should be considered when golf activities take place indoors without a net:

a Airflow plastic or similar type light, short-flight balls should be used.

b Suitable protective mats should be used on the floor.

Organisation

15.5.11 The following points should be considered in relation to the organisation of golf activities:

a Acceptable layouts for practising strokes or playing shots include:

- a straight line of pupils facing the same direction
- two straight lines of pupils at least six metres apart and facing away from each other
- a semi-circle of pupils facing outwards.

b Pupils driving at a net should remain strictly in line.

---

1 See pages 1–124.
2 See pages 161–64.

c Pupils should be at least three metres apart at all times when handling golf clubs. During demonstrations, this distance should also be maintained between the demonstrator and the observers.

d When playing or practising, pupils must ensure that the immediate space in front, around and behind them is clear of any person before they swing a golf club or drive a ball.

e Pupils should not advance to retrieve balls (or for any other purpose) until all the balls have been struck by the other pupils. Balls should only be retrieved on a given signal.

f Pupils should not walk up to each other during play or practice.

15.6 Other games

Relay races and tag games

> Please read the general guidance provided in *Part one* of this handbook[1] and in paragraphs 15.1.1 to 15.1.41[2] before reading this section. This will help to ensure that you have a comprehensive awareness of safe practice issues affecting games activities and physical education in general.

15.6.1 Relay races and tag games often form part of games sessions, particularly in primary schools. They are reasonably straightforward to organise, pupils enjoy them and they promote active participation in physical education. However, these games usually involve an element of competition. Supervising adults should ensure that this does not place any pupils at risk.

Context

15.6.2 The following points should be considered in relation to the context in which relay races and tag games take place:

a The surface used should be conducive to safe practice.

b Walls should not be used as turning points in races. Lines marked on the floor or marker cones should be used instead.

c Tag games should be contained within clear boundary markings.

d Footwear and floor surfaces should provide good traction.

e Any equipment used should be appropriate for the activity.

Organisation

15.6.3 The following points should be considered in relation to the organisation of relay races and tag games:

a Practice should take place in a non-competitive context, so that pupils are well versed in the skills involved before applying them in a relay race or tag game.

b Highly challenging skills, where it is foreseeable that pupils might fall (eg running backwards, carrying a partner), should not be used in races.

---

1 See pages 1–124.

2 See pages 161–64.

safe practice in physical education and school sport

Tug-of-war

> Please read the general guidance provided in *Part one* of this handbook[1] and in paragraphs 15.1.1 to 15.1.41[2] before reading this section. This will help to ensure that you have a comprehensive awareness of safe practice issues affecting games activities and physical education in general.

15.6.4   Tug-of-war is a popular activity in schools, particularly during sports days. The potential for injury is high and great care should be taken to ensure the safety of the pupils involved. Guidance on all aspects of tug-of-war activities can be obtained from the Tug-of-War Association.

People

15.6.5   Tug-of-war activities are not recommended for pupils under the age of eight.

Context

15.6.6   The following points should be considered in relation to the context in which tug-of-war activities take place:

a   The tug-of-war arena should be sited on short grass, not concrete. Flooded/marshy ground should be avoided.

b   An area of 60 metres x 6 metres is required for one rope. This should be cordoned off with rope or fencing to protect participants and spectators. The centre point should be clearly marked.

c   The arena surface should be level and free from obstructions (eg glass, stones).

d   Particular care should be taken when tug-of-war activities take place in extreme weather conditions.

e   Tug-of-war ropes should preferably be made of dry sisal. They should be approximately 35 metres long and ideally have a diameter of 10 centimetres (under 15s) or 12.5 centimetres (maximum for under 19s).

f   The centre of the rope should be marked with red tape. White and blue tape markers should also be positioned at the following distances from the centre of the rope:

- **Under 11 years** – white tape: two metres; blue tape: three metres
- **Under 15 years** – white tape: three metres; blue tape: four metres
- **Under 19 years** – white tape: four metres; blue tape: five metres.

g   Ropes should be checked regularly for signs of wear and tear (eg splits, tears, fraying).

h   Pupils should wear at least two layers of clothes on their upper body, including a short-sleeved protective shirt (preferably cotton, definitely not nylon), which covers the waist. Weight training belts may be worn on top of shirts.

i   Pupils may wear shorts or tracksuit/jogging bottoms on their lower body.

1   See pages 1–124.
2   See pages 161–64.

j *Anchors* may require extra layers of clothing.

k No items of clothing worn should contain any zips.

l Boots (not studded or spiked, no steel toe caps) or trainers with a good grip may be worn. All footwear should be tied up tightly to offer maximum support.

m Gloves should not be worn.

Organisation

15.6.7 The following points should be considered in relation to the organisation of tug-of-war activities:

a Tug-of-war teams should contain a similar number of pullers. Numbers can be adjusted to allow for weight differences. Mixed gender teams are allowed. However, it is not recommended that all-girl teams pull against all-boy teams.

b The centre of the rope (red marker) should be aligned with the centre of the tug-of-war arena.

c The first puller should hold the rope at the blue marker.

d The rope should go from the front of the anchor's body under his/her right arm, around the back, over his/her left shoulder and back under his/her left armpit. Care must be taken to ensure that the rope does not go round his/her neck.

e Pulling should only start on the instruction of the judge using the following commands:

- *Pick up the rope* (pullers pick up the rope)
- *Take the strain* (pullers pull the rope tight)
- *Steady* (judge checks rope is central, pullers lean back)
- *Pull* (pulling begins).

f When pulling, pupils should:

- stand to the left of the rope, facing towards the centre
- keep their backs and arms straight
- push with their legs
- try to ensure that their feet remain in front of their hands to avoid bending their backs
- pull in a straight line (if the rope starts to snake towards spectators, the pull should be stopped and restarted)
- keep both hands on the rope
- not sit or let go of the rope during the pull.

g The length of pulls varies according to the age of the pupils involved:

- **Under 11 years** – two metres from the centre or 30 seconds maximum
- **Under 15 years** – three metres from the centre or 60 seconds maximum
- **Under 19 years** – four metres from the centre.

Risk management

People

- **Pupils should share in the assessment and management of the risks involved**.

- Pupils should be adequately prepared and possess the necessary fitness and skills required.

- Supervising adults should have a sound knowledge and understanding of the intended games activity, and of how to conduct it safely.

Context

- Any relevant NGB and/or LEA recommendations should be taken into account.

- The playing area and surface should be level, clean and free from avoidable hazards and obstructions.

- Equipment should be appropriate for the pupils involved and be maintained in good condition.

- Pupils should wear appropriate clothing, footwear and protective equipment.

- Adequate first aid equipment should be available.

Organisation

- Care should be taken to *match* pupils by size, weight, age, experience and ability.

- The teaching of all games activities should follow a carefully planned and graduated progression.

▶▶ See *Chapter two: Risk management* for more detailed, general guidance on risk management issues.

Questions and answers

People

Qu 1 If an exchange teacher from another country is invited to coach/teach football while spending a year at my school, what steps should I take to ensure that he/she is competent?

Ans Seek advice from an external, county level referee. The lead member of school staff should arrange school-based training and assess the teaching competences of the exchange teacher on behalf of the head teacher.

Qu 2 The engagement sequence of *crouch*, *pause*, *touch*, *engage* in rugby always causes me management problems at this potential flashpoint. How can I improve my performance/skills?

Ans If you are already familiar with refereeing qualifications/competences, you should try to attend a specialist clinic/seminar on front row play. Rugby academies often provide these for all teachers/coaches/players.

Qu 3 A few of my more capable pupils are not extended by the quality of bowling provided by fellow pupils in cricket sessions. Is it reasonable for a member of school staff, or other supervising adult, to bowl to these pupils?

Ans Cricket is a game in which a hard missile is aimed towards another player. In the vast majority of cases, it is inadvisable for an adult to use his/her greater skill, strength or experience in a situation where their actions could cause injury to pupils. Fast bowling by an adult would certainly fall into this category where the age, skill or experience of the pupil batting is known to be limited.

An adult might consider bowling to a pupil who bats to a good standard and is known to play with, and against, adults on a regular basis, but only if the playing surface is level and affords even bounce. Even in these circumstances, great care is needed and the pace of bowling must often be adapted to ensure that the pupil is given the opportunity to improve his/her batting skills. In most cases, it is better to devise a practice in which the ball can be delivered in a controlled manner (eg feeding the ball from an agreed distance and the pupil batting is aware of the ball's expected length and direction). Excellent practices can be devised using a soft ball, and can often be used without the need for full protective clothing and equipment. In all circumstances, the advice provided in this chapter[1] on the use of helmets and fielding positions must be strictly observed.

It should be remembered that some pupils can also bowl fast enough to cause injury and that not all pupils will have the necessary skill and control to bowl accurately. Care should be taken to ensure that the ability of pupils is fairly matched. Again, the advice on helmets and fielding positions must be observed. Bowling by a teacher (or other adult) in a match situation and school staff/parents versus pupil games are not recommended.

---

1   See paragraph 15.4.7 on page 181.

safe practice in physical education and school sport

Context

Qu 4   **Should pupils be allowed to wear fingerless gloves in certain positions on the rugby field?**

Ans   Yes – fingerless gloves can assist pupils when catching, distributing clearly and throwing in to a lineout, particularly in inclement weather.

Qu 5   **To obtain a more true bounce of the ball, I would like to teach short tennis on the playground rather than on the school field and have been granted the funding required to paint the courts. Does this follow approved practice?**

Ans   You should carry out a thorough risk assessment to ensure that your playground and its surrounds do not contain any hazards. The surface should be level and free from accumulation of loose grit. You should also ensure that building features do not project onto the playing area.

    You should ensure that the courts are well separated and that playground features, seats, climbing apparatus etc are not immediately adjacent to the playing area.

Qu 6   **Our tennis courts are also used as the school playground and we have a major problem with litter. It has been suggested that a number of litter bins be purchased and attached to the surround netting of the courts. Do you have any comments?**

Ans   It would be unwise to take up this suggestion. Due to financial constraints, school tennis courts are usually constructed with minimal run-back behind the back line and minimal distance between the side lines and the surround netting. It could be argued that placing an obstruction, such as a litter bin, in this area would create a hazard in what was previously a hazard-free area.

Organisation

Qu 7   **How should I stop pupils lifting their hockey sticks too high when they hit the ball?**

Ans   For safety reasons, it is essential that pupils maintain full control of their hockey sticks. Before allowing pupils to hit the ball at all, it is good practice to introduce conditioned hockey in which the ball can only be pushed with the stick. This will enable pupils to develop sound stick control without lifting their sticks too high. Pushing and hitting skills should be practised and well consolidated using the correct techniques before being applied in a game situation.

Qu 8   **Is mixed gender practice/competition acceptable in rugby?**

Ans   Mixed gender non-contact rugby (ie touch or tag rugby) is suitable for all age groups. However, mixed gender contact rugby (ie tackle) is not recommended for any school pupils.

Qu 9 **After watching a volleyball match on TV, my pupils have started to imitate the players they saw by diving to retrieve a difficult return. Would you include this technique in future teaching sessions?**

Ans Diving for the ball is an advanced technique used by experienced players. Careful consideration should be given as to whether it should be included in your teaching programme. It is advisable for the technique only to be taught when coaching competent players in a club situation. In normal teaching and play situations, you should emphasise that diving for the ball is against your rules.

Qu 10 **Is there a recommended distance at which pupils should stand while waiting to bat in a game of rounders or associated practices?**

Ans It is essential that pupils waiting their turn should be at a distance that enables them not only to see the bat as it is used, but also to take evasive action if necessary. It should be remembered that the bat may either slip from the grasp of, or be thrown by, the striker. Claiming that pupils had been instructed not to throw away the bat after striking or attempting to strike the ball, is unlikely to be an adequate defence. School staff should be aware that not all pupils have the ability to react at the same speed and that they may not be paying full attention.

Qu 11 **Can pupils go to a golf course and play as part of a planned activity programme?**

Ans Younger Key Stage 2 pupils will benefit from the mini/try-golf activities that schools/LEAs can access through NGBs of golf[1].

It may be appropriate for schools to arrange for Key Stage 4 pupils, who are junior members of a golf club, to play at their club during physical education sessions. Pupils, who are not members of a golf club, could play in a group session at a public or private golf course/practice ground managed by school staff and appropriately qualified and experienced coaches.

---

1   English Golf Union, Irish Golf, Scottish Golf Union and Welsh Golfing Union as appropriate.

Chapter sixteen

Gymnastic and trampolining activities

16.1 Gymnastic activities

> Please read the general guidance provided in *Part one* of this handbook[1] before reading this section. This will help to ensure that you have a comprehensive awareness of safe practice issues affecting gymnastic activities and physical education in general.

16.1.1 Gymnastic activities involve developing body movement skills (eg rocking, rolling, climbing, descending, hanging, swinging, inverting and balancing), which in turn contribute to the development of pupils' muscular strength, suppleness, endurance and coordination. Gymnastic activities also help pupils to learn about their personal capabilities and to evaluate individual differences in performance.

16.1.2 Some skills may be specifically taught, while others may be developed through the setting of tasks within defined parameters, which provide the opportunity for pupils to respond individually and which produce a variety of outcomes. The aim of gymnastic activities is to develop and refine, over time, a range of controlled movements across recognised skill areas, which may be performed separately, in combination or in sequence, using the floor and apparatus.

16.1.3 Competitive gymnastics is a developed sport involving grading and competition, using a more formal and prescriptive approach to which some (generally more gymnastically able) pupils may be suited. Recognised forms include artistic, rhythmic and acrobatic gymnastics. In a school context, it is generally limited by provision to vaulting, floor work and basic acrobatics. It is frequently offered at secondary level as an out-of-school-hours learning (OSHL) activity in which pupils take part by choice.

16.1.4 Training is essential for the safe teaching and coaching of all forms of gymnastics. Fundamental techniques need to be understood and sound principles of progression in the learning of skills applied. Without this knowledge on the part of those teaching or coaching gymnastic activities, pupils may be placed at foreseeable risk of injury.

16.1.5 The learning and consolidation of basic gymnastic skills over time is very important and provides the foundations for future progress. Progression which is too rapid, sometimes as a result of pupil enthusiasm, is neither safe nor conducive to quality performance.

1   See pages 1–124.

People

16.1.6   School staff/coaches involved in teaching or coaching any form of gymnastics must be appropriately trained, either through initial teacher training (ITT) or continuing professional development (CPD) opportunities. Otherwise, pupils will be placed at greater risk.

16.1.7   Specialist physical education teachers in secondary schools will normally have received training in curriculum gymnastics as part of their ITT. Where this is not the case, compensatory professional development will need to be provided.

16.1.8   Primary school teachers are not physical education specialists and are likely to have received varying levels of training in gymnastics and in physical education in general. Again, CPD opportunities will need to be provided to compensate for any shortfall in ITT.

16.1.9   In addition to adequate ITT in curriculum gymnastics, teachers should receive appropriate professional development from time to time, to reinforce and consolidate their knowledge and to learn about new developments. School staff/coaches should regularly assess and, if necessary modify, their practice in the light of their own and colleagues' experiences.

16.1.10   If school staff are assisted by volunteers and paid coaches, overall responsibility always rests with the teacher. The level of supervision should be commensurate with the assessed abilities of those present.

16.1.11   School staff and coaches of the sport of gymnastics should attend courses specific to the activities they plan to deliver to pupils. British Gymnastics provides relevant courses and guidance.

16.1.12   Pupils should share in the assessment and management of the risks associated with gymnastic activities. This is an essential part of the learning process. Due to different abilities, the risk management process should be applied to individual pupils, to pupil groups and to the class as a whole.

Context

Facility

16.1.13   Gymnastics usually takes place in a gymnasium (secondary school) or hall (primary school). In all cases, the working surface should be clean and non-slip, and ideally provide the level of resilience associated with a sprung wooden floor.

16.1.14   The space and equipment available should be sufficient to accommodate a whole class activity. If it is not, either the number of pupils should be reduced proportionally, or the activities modified to ensure safe participation (eg half the class work while the other half observe and evaluate). This should be regarded as a temporary measure pending the provision of a suitable indoor space.

Procedure

16.1.15   The chewing of food, sweets or gum immediately before or during gymnastics sessions should never be allowed. Chewing can result in choking, which can have serious, even fatal, consequences.

Equipment

16.1.16 Gymnastics apparatus should conform to the appropriate British Standards European Norm (BS EN) requirements. It should be stored consistently and safely, and be readily accessible for use during sessions. It should always be checked (by school staff/coaches and pupils) each time it is used before any activities start.

16.1.17 All gymnastics apparatus should be subject to an annual inspection and repaired or replaced as appropriate. All maintenance work should be carried out by suitably qualified contractors. The most cost-effective and efficient way to do this is for employers to contract suitable service providers and to manage the maintenance of equipment on behalf of schools.

16.1.18 Defective equipment should be marked accordingly and placed out of use until specialist repair work can be carried out. Equipment which is deemed beyond economical repair should be clearly labelled, removed and disposed of. Schools should resist the temptation to keep it *just in case it may come in useful*.

16.1.19 Particular care must be taken when using mats during gymnastics sessions.

▶▶ See *Chapter eight: Environment and equipment* for detailed guidance on gymnastics apparatus and mats.

Clothing and personal effects

16.1.20 Pupils should change out of their normal school clothes into clothing which allows free, unrestricted movement without being loose (eg leotards, shorts and t-shirts). Very loose clothing may snag on equipment and cause injury. Extra clothing (eg tracksuits) may be worn during warm-up activities.

16.1.21 Pupils may either wear gymnastics slippers or work in bare feet. Taking part in gymnastic activities in bare feet exercises the feet and ankles, improves the aesthetic quality of movements and provides safe traction and positional awareness when in contact with the floor and apparatus. Plimsolls are acceptable in primary schools where floor surfaces may not be conducive to working in bare feet.

16.1.22 Footwear may be considered appropriate for activities that involve high-momentum landings or rope climbing. When worn, it should be flexible and close-fitting, with soles that provide good traction and *feel* for the apparatus. Training shoes with thick, inflexible soles are not suitable. Pupils must never work in socks or stockinged feet, which can reduce traction friction and present an unacceptable risk of slipping.

16.1.23 Before gymnastics sessions start, long hair should be tied back and all personal effects (eg jewellery, watches) should be removed or the situation made safe if they cannot be removed[1]. Injuries (some serious) have occurred in the past when these requirements have not been met.

Record-keeping

16.1.24 A record of attendance should be kept, together with a record of the skills and tasks covered, and the levels of performance attained. This will enable effective progression in gymnastics, especially if someone else is likely to take over the class.

1   See Section 9.3 on page 105 for further information.

Accidents

16.1.25   In the event of an accident during a gymnastics session, the person in charge should stop all activities and follow the school's emergency procedures. Priority must be given to a nominated first aider dealing with the injured pupil, and to providing effective supervision for the rest of the class. If a head injury or spinal damage (ie tingling or loss of sensation in an arm or leg) is suspected, the pupil involved should be kept as still as possible and not moved, and expert medical attention summoned to the scene. The accident should be recorded on an accident report form as soon as possible, together with relevant supporting notes.

16.1.26   An analysis of incidents (near misses) can provide useful information on measures which should be taken to prevent a recurrence. For this reason, near misses should be recorded and shared with colleagues and pupils.

▶▶   See *Chapter eleven: Accidents, incidents and first aid management* for further guidance.

Organisation

16.1.27   Written schemes of work from which session plans are drawn should provide the basis for all gymnastics teaching in schools. Such schemes should incorporate risk management as part of the teaching and learning process. Particular attention should be given to movements which have the potential for higher risk, with measures identified to ensure that these risks are reduced to an acceptable level.

16.1.28   Schemes of work should be reviewed and updated from time to time, to take account of changes in practice that will inevitably occur. This should happen via consultative exercises involving all relevant parties, so that awareness of changes, and the reasons for them, are fully understood.

16.1.29   Training schedules associated with competitive gymnastics must not exceed reasonable limits on frequency, intensity and time. Pressures leading up to a competition have, on some occasions, involved pupils in excessive training, which has resulted in injury from loss of concentration and fatigue.

16.1.30   Subject to employers' requirements, school staff/coaches with suitable gymnastics qualifications or expertise must always be present when gymnastic activities take place in schools, whether during curriculum time or as an OSHL activity. On no account should pupils ever be left unsupervised. If this person is called away from the session for any urgent reason, all gymnastic activities must stop immediately and alternative competent supervision provided before the activities continue.

16.1.31   Good communication between school staff, coaches and pupils is essential. All parties involved should have a clear understanding of their respective responsibilities.

16.1.32   Pupils should be taught (commensurate with the key stages of learning) how to handle gymnastics apparatus safely, including lifting, carrying, lowering, assembling, disassembling, checking and storing.

16.1.33   A disciplined and structured approach should be taken to gymnastics sessions. Establishing consistent session routines, with which pupils are thoroughly familiar and accustomed, will significantly contribute to safe practice.

16.1.34   Gymnastics sessions should typically involve four phases:

      a Warm-up (whole class activity)

      b Development based on a focused skill or task (whole class activity)

      c Application of the focused skill or task (together with previously learned skills or tasks) on apparatus (in groups)

      d Warm-down (whole class activity).

16.1.35   Warm-ups using jogging and muscle-stretching exercises will prepare the body for the activities to be undertaken in the main part of the session. This will reduce the likelihood of injury to muscles, joints or tendons during the two main activity phases.

16.1.36   The skill or task focused on during the main part of the session should continue on from previous sessions and take account of the varied abilities of pupils by allowing for differentiated responses. This will ensure that pupils are challenged appropriately as individuals, at neither too high (which may result in injury), nor too low, a level.

16.1.37   Pupils learning a new skill, or presented with a new task, should have the necessary strength, flexibility and body awareness to be capable of the activity requirements. They should also have experienced the appropriate progressive stages leading up to that new skill or task. Pupils will achieve success at different rates during the progressive stages of learning. It is essential that each pupil accomplishes each stage successfully before the next is attempted, regardless of the time taken.

16.1.38   In the case of prescribed movements, school staff/coaches must fully understand the mechanics and techniques of every action and the progressive stages leading up to it. They must be able to assess the mental and physical readiness of pupils for each new skill to be taught. They must also be aware of the symptoms of physiological and psychological fatigue, and be prepared to stop activities if pupils display them.

16.1.39   Skills already learned may have to be revisited and relearned after periods of inactivity (eg school holidays). Relearning and consolidating skills is particularly important at times of significant physiological change which occurs during adolescence and growth spurts. Great care should be taken when reintroducing pupils to gymnastics following prolonged absence through illness.

16.1.40   Cooling down at the end of sessions should include the gentle stretching of muscle groups used during the activities undertaken. This will help to relax the muscles and prevent tension or involuntary contraction, which may otherwise occur after vigorous activity has taken place.

16.1.41   There may be occasions when pupils require physical support in order to carry out movements safely. This can be the case for some vaulting activities, especially those which involve rotation. School staff/coaches should provide assistance in such a way that pupils land on their feet and that the support compensates effectively for any under- or over-rotation.

16.1.42   School staff/coaches who give support should continue to provide adequate assistance for successive vaults until pupils are able to consistently generate the correct amount of rotation to land in control on their feet, without being held. At this stage, support can be reduced to *standing by* by appropriately trained adults or pupils. *Standing by* can later be withdrawn.

16.1.43 Whenever physical support is considered, it is essential that school staff/coaches and pupils involved discuss and agree on how this should be done. There must be no surprises for either party. Care must be taken to ensure that support is provided in accordance with common and accepted good practice.

16.1.44 National governing bodies (NGBs) sometimes issue directives concerning the safe management of gymnastic activities. When a competition takes place under the remit of an NGB (eg affiliated competitions), any relevant directives should be considered as rules, which need to be followed. However, NGBs have no authoritative remit in the context of the National Curriculum, OSHL activities or friendly competitions. In these circumstances, their directives have the same status as that of this handbook – well intentioned guidance which managing staff should consider in relation to their particular situation.

16.2 Trampolining activities

> Please read the general guidance provided in *Part one*[1] of this handbook and paragraphs 16.1.1 to 16.1.44[2] before reading this section. This will help to ensure that you have a comprehensive awareness of safe practice issues affecting gymnastic and trampolining activities, and physical education in general.

16.2.1 Trampolining involves performing consecutive jumps on a rebound bed, with movements performed in free flight between contacts with the bed. It offers a popular and exciting experience to pupils of all abilities. As well as challenging the more gymnastically able, under well controlled circumstances supervised by appropriately qualified staff, it can also stimulate movement in pupils with special educational needs.

16.2.2 Whatever the purpose served, great care must be taken to ensure the safety and well-being of all pupils. Serious accidents can occur on both trampolines and their smaller counterparts, trampettes, if pupils are not able to exercise full control of their bodies when using this equipment.

16.2.3 Because of the specialist nature of the activity and the potential risks associated with rebound jumping, trampolines and trampettes are not recommended for use in primary schools.

People

16.2.4 School staff/coaches involved in teaching or coaching trampolining must be appropriately trained. They should be knowledgeable about the basic skills and techniques of jumping, and understand the biomechanics of the moves they teach. Even the basic skill of feet-to-feet jumping involves a number of fundamental requirements which must be understood, taught and learned so that full control of the body can be maintained.

---

1   See pages 1–124.

2   See pages 193–98.

16.2.5   School staff/coaches who wish to teach or coach trampolining at a more advanced level, or to enter pupils in competitions, should attend courses organised or approved by British Gymnastics, and be appropriately qualified.

16.2.6   Pupils should share in the assessment and management of the risks associated with trampolining activities. This is an essential part of the learning process. Due to differentiation in abilities, the risk management process should be applied to individual pupils, to pupil groups and to the class as a whole.

Context

Facility

16.2.7   Trampolining usually takes place in sports halls or gymnasiums in secondary schools.

16.2.8   Trampolining equipment should be sited well away from walls, fire exits and overhead obstructions. In sports halls, it should generally be separated by drawn netting from any other activities taking place.

16.2.9   The ceiling should be at least five metres high (higher for competition).

Equipment

16.2.10   The procedure for positioning, assembling and folding trampolines must be systematic and deliberate. It requires closely coordinated teamwork in which the roles of individual pupils are clearly understood and implemented. Injuries have occurred during this exercise, mainly when the end of the trampoline frame has been opened or folded, but has not been held with sufficient force to counter the tension caused by the springs.

> ▶▶ See *Chapter eight: Environment and equipment* for detailed guidance on positioning, folding/unfolding and checking trampolines.

16.2.11   Two trampolines may be positioned end to end, with a large weight-absorbing mattress covering the frames and frame pads at the adjoining ends. Adequate supervision must be ensured when more than one trampoline is being used.

16.2.12   The metal frame and springs/cables of trampolines should be covered by fixed coverall pads.

16.2.13   Spotters should be positioned one or two at each side, plus one at each end, unless end weight-absorbing mattresses are provided, in which case spotters will only be needed at the sides. It is accepted practice for weight-absorbing mattresses to be placed on the ends of trampolines, providing they are suitably supported beyond the frame to keep them level.

16.2.14   An overhead support rig may be used to teach pupils movements involving rotations or twists on the trampoline. The supporter (usually an adult) must be competent in using the rig and must be capable of holding the weight, and controlling the descent, of a pupil. Care should be taken to ensure that the centre of the trampoline is vertically aligned with the centre of the rig.

16.2.15   Damaged trampolines and trampettes should not be used until they have been repaired or replaced.

Clothing and personal effects

16.2.16   Clothing for trampolining is similar to that worn for gymnastics[1], except that non-slip socks or trampolining slippers are necessary to prevent pupils slipping and to prevent their toes entering gaps in the webbing when they make contact with the trampoline bed. Cotton and wool socks are suitable but nylon socks on a webbed nylon bed are unlikely to provide adequate traction. A long-sleeved top is advisable to prevent friction burns to the forearms when performing front drops.

16.2.17   It is advisable to wear training shoes to protect the feet when erecting and folding away trampolines.

16.2.18   Before trampolining sessions start, long hair should be tied back and nails trimmed. All personal effects (eg jewellery, watches) should be removed or the situation made safe if they cannot be removed[2]. Injuries, some serious, have occurred in the past when these requirements have not been met.

Record-keeping

16.2.19   A record of attendance could be kept, together with a record of the skills and tasks covered, and the levels of performance attained. This will enable effective progression in trampolining, especially if someone else is likely to take over the class.

Accidents

16.2.20   Trampolining accidents should be very rare if the activity is taught well and pupils learn sound techniques which enable them to exercise good control. However, accidents do occasionally happen, usually as a result of:

   a   unfolding or folding the trampoline (resulting in arms or fingers getting trapped)

   b   landing awkwardly on the trampoline bed and placing a hand down ahead of the body (resulting in a broken arm).

16.2.21   Falling from trampolines does not happen very often and is unlikely if competent spotters and weight-absorbing mattresses are in place. Very serious injuries can result from landing inverted during an attempted rotating movement, so that the head strikes the bed and the neck is either hyper-flexed or hyper-extended on impact (causing a potential neck fracture and/or spinal damage).

16.2.22   The procedure in the event of an accident is the same as for gymnastics[3]. In the case of a suspected spinal injury, the injured pupil should be kept as still as possible on the trampoline bed until expert medical help arrives, since any movement may exacerbate the damage caused.

▶▶   See Chapter eleven: Accidents, incidents and first aid management for further guidance.

Organisation

16.2.23   As for gymnastics, written schemes of work are necessary to ensure that skills are taught in a logical sequence, using appropriate progressions.

---

1   See paragraph 16.1.20 on page 195 for further information.
2   See Section 9.3 on page 105 for further information.
3   See paragraphs 16.1.25 and 16.1.26 on page 196 for further information.

16.2.24   Subject to employers' requirements, school staff/coaches with suitable trampolining qualifications must always be present when trampolining activities take place in schools, whether during curriculum time or as an OSHL activity. On no account should pupils ever be left unsupervised. If this person is called away from the session for any urgent reason, all trampolining activities must stop immediately, the trampoline(s) must be folded to prevent unauthorised jumping and an alternative supervised activity should be provided.

16.2.25   With suitable qualifications and experience, it is possible to supervise several trampolines at once. When this is the case, it is important to observe all the activities taking place, so that intervention and advice may be provided when necessary. At such times, pupils should only practise and consolidate skills which they can already perform correctly and confidently unless they are working under the direct supervision of a member of school staff/coach.

16.2.26   Beginners with little or no previous experience, or pupils who are learning new skills, should always be directly supervised.

16.2.27   Appropriate warm-up exercises, similar to those for gymnastics[1], should be carried out at the start of trampolining sessions. Initial jumping should also contribute to body warm-up.

16.2.28   Only one pupil at a time should normally be allowed on the trampoline. Work should only begin when everyone is appropriately positioned and ready. The pupil should rebound in a position as near to the centre of the bed as possible, at a height at which he/she is able to maintain complete control.

16.2.29   If loss of control is experienced, the pupil performing should flex at the knee and hip joints during the very next contact of the feet with the bed. This will effectively deaden the jumping. Following discussion on how and why control was lost, and what measures should be taken to address the problem, the pupil should return to the centre of the bed and recommence work.

16.2.30   Beginners should work for periods of around thirty seconds. This time can be gradually extended (up to one minute), but pupils must stop jumping immediately if they begin to tire or lose concentration.

16.2.31   It is good practice to provide support for pupils who need it when learning movements on the trampoline. School staff/coaches should be suitably trained and skilled in accepted support methods (eg overhead support rigs, throw-in mattresses).

16.2.32   Pupils should understand, and be constantly reminded of, the disciplined approach required when trampolining. Pupils must remain vigilant at all times, regardless of whether they are jumping on the trampoline or spotting for others.

16.2.33   Trampolining skills are very specific and must be taught correctly from the very start. Basic straight jumping may appear simple and straightforward, but this is deceptive, as anyone mounting a trampoline for the first time will verify. There is little room for trial and error in teaching and learning trampolining skills. Pupils must be taught how to jump correctly and what to do by way of immediate remedial action if they begin to move away from the centre of the bed. This will nearly always mean stopping, returning to the middle, and recommencing jumping.

1   See paragraph 16.1.35 on page 197 for further information.

16.2.34   Pupils must appreciate the importance of using the correct techniques in order to maintain control when jumping, and must understand that loss of control can result in injury. Total concentration is necessary when jumping and spotting for others, since incidents tend to happen very suddenly and require a swift response. The important role of spotters in preventing jumpers, who move too close to the edge of the trampoline, from falling to the floor cannot be too strongly emphasised.

16.2.35   Pupils acting as spotters may sometimes be tempted to give vocal encouragement to the pupil jumping. This can be distracting for the jumper, affecting their concentration and causing loss of control, and must not be permitted. Discussions should only take place between phases of jumping.

16.2.36   *Tag on* type games, in which pupils in turn add a movement to the sequence or routine of the previous pupil, are not recommended. They may encourage pupils to jump beyond their abilities.

16.2.37   Pupils should be constantly monitored for signs of fatigue. Those displaying any symptoms (eg deterioration in the quality of performance and/or loss of concentration or persistent travel) must stop immediately and rest.

16.2.38   Basic skills should be learned and consolidated in isolation before being combined into sequences. Charts should be used to record individual progress.

16.2.39   Gradual, step-by-step progression over time should be provided, with the emphasis on basic skills, correct techniques and quality of movement. Pupils should be dissuaded from making over-rapid progress and taking unnecessary risks.

16.2.40   Some pupils may wish to progress beyond basic jumping to more exciting moves involving rotation (eg back drops, front drops and somersaults). Not all pupils will be capable of doing so; those that are should first demonstrate that their basic straight jumps are well consolidated. Trampolining accidents frequently occur when pupils try to progress too quickly before they have mastered basic skills. It is important to resist pressure from pupils to move on to the next stage before they are ready to do so.

16.2.41   During competitions or displays, pupils should only perform movements which they have successfully practised and consolidated during training. It is not acceptable for pupils to be put at risk by changing their sequences in a bid for higher marks during a competition.

16.2.42   NGBs sometimes issue directives concerning the safe management of trampolining activities. When a competition takes place under the remit of an NGB (eg affiliated competitions), any relevant directives should be considered as rules, which need to be followed. However, NGBs have no authoritative remit in the context of the National Curriculum, OSHL activities or friendly competitions. In these circumstances, their directives have the same status as that of this handbook – well intentioned guidance which managing staff should consider in relation to their particular situation.

Trampettes

Please read the general guidance provided in *Part one*[1] of this handbook and paragraphs 16.1.1 to 16.1.44[2] and 16.2.1 to 16.2.42[3] before reading this section. This will help to ensure that you have a comprehensive awareness of safe practice issues affecting gymnastic and trampolining activities, and physical education in general.

16.2.43 Because of the specialist nature of the activity and the potential risks associated with rebound jumping, trampolines and trampettes are not recommended for use in primary schools.

16.2.44 Particular care must be taken when using trampettes in secondary schools. Basic trampette skills are the same as those for trampolining, except that forward travel occurs and landing takes place on a thick weight-absorbing mattress (or mattresses). Following the guidance below will promote safe practice:

a Appropriate footwear should be worn when using trampettes with webbed beds.

b Basic jumping skills are best learned on a trampoline before being applied to a trampette.

c Beginners should approach a trampette in an unhurried and controlled manner using just a few paces.

d When a trampette is used as one activity within a gymnastics session, close attention should be paid to the performance of basic trampette skills. Observation and control of the class as a whole should be maintained.

e Each trampette skill should be thoroughly practised, learned and consolidated before progressing to the next.

f Support may be provided and should be appropriate to the skill being practised. It should provide a physical check for pupils as they land, preventing them from pitching forwards or falling backwards. Responsible, mature pupils may be trained to provide support.

g Rotational skills during flight from a trampette are potentially dangerous and must never be attempted by beginners. The same applies to forward rolls after landing.

h Special care must be taken when teaching somersault actions, which should only be undertaken by pupils who are judged to have the potential ability and who have mastered basic skills. Direct supervision is required.

i Somersault actions are most safely taught on a trampoline using an overhead support rig. When transferred to a trampette, competent support to counter possible under-rotation or over-rotation must always be provided until the movements have been thoroughly consolidated.

j The use of standard single trampettes is recommended. The use of double trampettes (where two or more jumps precede the final action of flight and landing) is more suitable with advanced performers in specialist trampolining clubs.

---

1 See pages 1–124.
2 See pages 193–98.
3 See pages 198–202.

Risk management

People

- **Pupils should share in the assessment and management of the risks involved.**

- School staff/coaches should be appropriately trained and knowledgeable about skills and progression.

- School staff/coaches should be able to assess pupil ability and match this to suitable activities.

- A disciplined and systematic approach should be adopted by all those involved in gymnastic and trampolining activities.

Context

- Equipment should be checked each time it is used. It should also be subject to an annual inspection and be repaired or replaced as appropriate.

- Appropriate clothing and footwear should be worn.

- All accidents and near misses should be recorded and communicated to others for future reference.

Organisation

- Written schemes of work and session plans are necessary.

- All sessions should start/finish with a thorough warm-up/cool-down.

- School staff/coaches should ensure that the skills/tasks undertaken are appropriate for the pupils involved.

- Spotters should be positioned as appropriate around trampolines.

- Special care is required when undertaking rotational activities and when using rebound equipment.

- Adequate support should be provided where necessary.

▶▶ See *Chapter two: Risk management* for more detailed, general guidance on risk management issues.

Questions and answers

People

Qu 1 **As a secondary specialist teacher of physical education, am I able to use rebound equipment in my school without an NGB award?**

Ans Trampolines and trampettes add an exciting dimension to gymnastics programmes in many secondary schools, but the potential for serious injury is high. To minimise the risks involved, you should have specialist knowledge about rebound equipment (including correct techniques and safe practice measures) and should take great care when using it. You should also ensure that the progressive stages of learning are fully implemented.

Because of the hazardous nature of rebound activities, you are recommended to attend appropriate courses from time to time, to keep up to date with current developments and recommendations. Some LEAs arrange and validate their own professional development courses; others rely on courses provided by British Gymnastics. It is important to find out what your employer's policy on training is and to ensure that you follow it. If you have gained acceptable or approved experience through attending relevant courses such as these, this may enable you to teach rebound activities without holding an NGB award.

Qu 2 **A pupil in my Year 4 class has difficulty controlling his behaviour and will often interfere with, or impede, other pupils when working on gymnastics apparatus. What action should be taken?**

Ans It is clearly unacceptable for any pupil to put themselves or others at risk through unsociable behaviour. The following preventative measures could be taken:

a Monitor the pupil very closely and guide him/her positively during physical education and other sessions.

b Restrict the activities of the pupil until a positive behavioural response can be anticipated.

c Obtain the services of a support assistant to work on a one-to-one basis with the pupil until satisfactory behaviour is developed.

d Develop a code of conduct in conjunction with the pupil and his/her parents to foster acceptable behaviour in school and at home. Review the agreement periodically.

If the problem persists, expert professional guidance could be sought.

▶▶ See also Qu 3 in *Chapter three: Qualifications, competence and supervision* (pages 35–36).

Context

Qu 3   **Due to a lack of storage space, the large apparatus that we use for gymnastics in the hall of my primary school has to be stored around the perimeter of the hall. Is this acceptable?**

Ans   It is common and accepted practice in many primary schools to store large apparatus in the school hall. Care should be taken to ensure that the apparatus is well spaced, stable and readily accessible for use in gymnastics sessions, while leaving passageways and emergency exits unblocked. Large and heavier items should be sited so that the distances over which they need to be moved for use and storage purposes are minimised. It is good practice for equipment to always be returned to the same place after use.

Qu 4   **The primary school in which I work is very well equipped for gymnastics but the hall isn't big enough to allow all the available apparatus to be used at the same time. How could this problem be resolved?**

Ans   It is desirable for primary schools to have a sufficient variety and quantity of gymnastics apparatus to enable pupils to experience and develop a broad range of body management skills. However, it is most unlikely that all the available apparatus will be appropriate for use in a single session. You should relate the apparatus to be used to the theme or task(s) of the session (or preferably to a related series of sessions) and select individual/combinations of items which best support the skills to be developed during the session.

To ensure that gymnastics activities take place safely, apparatus should be sited well away from walls (or equipment stored at the sides) and there should be sufficient space between individual items. This requirement will determine the total number of individual/combinations of items which can be used at any one time.

Qu 5   **Some pupils in my Year 6 class take unacceptable risks when working on climbing apparatus during gymnastics sessions, to such an extent that they are likely to fall. Would it be appropriate to provide thick weight-absorbing mattresses in case this should happen?**

Ans   All pupils should receive, and be able to understand, guidance on the safe use and management of mats. A mat(s) should normally be provided where planned landings are intended.

If you think a pupil is likely to fall while performing a specific task, you should modify the task to reduce the risk to an acceptable level. If a pupil is performing a task which is at, or near to, the threshold of his/her movement ability and he/she has experienced the progressive stages leading up to it, you may provide physical support to enable him/her to perform the task safely. This support may be reduced, and eventually removed altogether, as the pupil develops the ability and confidence to perform the task correctly and unaided.

Qu 6   **I understand that thick weight-absorbing mattresses may be used in trampolining in two ways: (a) as a learning aid for certain activities by being pushed onto the bed for a performer to land on (b) as an alternative to spotters when two trampolines are placed end to end, the mattress being positioned across the adjoining frames and coverall pads. Are these measures acceptable?**

Ans   Developments in trampolining are happening all the time and the use of thick weight-absorbing mattresses in the ways you describe are just two innovations that have taken place. In addition to this, end deck spotting platforms with mats have been introduced, which can be positioned at either, or both, ends of a trampoline. Mats for throwing onto the bed are now produced with strap handles to facilitate this action.

It is important to keep abreast of new equipment and associated practices, and of how to incorporate them safely into your own procedures. This will almost certainly require additional training to ensure that your trampolining activities take place in accordance with commonly accepted good practice.

Organisation

Qu 7   **I supervise an out-of-school-hours trampolining club at my school. The club is popular and is attended on a voluntary basis by approximately 20 pupils (girls and boys) aged 11 to 16 years. As only one trampoline is available, pupils spend a considerable amount of time as spotters between opportunities to jump. They tend to get bored and their attention wanders. What measures would you suggest to overcome this problem?**

Ans   It is important that trampolining is conducted safely, in accordance with regular procedures to which all involved must be prepared to conform. Pupils spotting and waiting their turn to jump must concentrate on what is happening, and be prepared to act to prevent a jumper falling from the trampoline.

Given that only one trampoline is available, the number of pupils attending your club is too large and will need to be reduced. You could manage this by arranging a second session during the week, splitting the pupils equally between the two sessions. Alternatively, pupils could attend your weekly session once a fortnight. In the longer term, perhaps your school could consider buying a second trampoline, particularly if it is likely to be used during curriculum time.

Qu 8   **When should support or *standing by* be provided in gymnastics sessions?**

Ans   In order to successfully perform certain gymnastic movements and associated progressive lead-up practices, physical support is often required. This can either be provided by trained and competent adults or pupils. Performers and supporters should always have a clear understanding of, and agree on, the activity to be undertaken and the type of support to be provided.

Support should gradually be reduced over time until pupils are able to perform the movements confidently and correctly without assistance. At this stage, the supporters should *stand by* sufficiently close in case performers make mistakes and require support.

The ultimate aim should be for pupils to feel so sure and safe that they opt to perform the movements freely and unaided. It is important to agree when this stage has been reached – pupils should never be allowed to make this decision on their own. There is no set number of successful *stand by* attempts required before movements can be performed unaided – this will vary from pupil to pupil.

Before embarking on movements requiring the provision of support, school staff/coaches must ensure that they have a sound knowledge of the movements and associated techniques, and be confident that the pupils have the ability to learn them.

Qu 9 **In gymnastics, is it reasonable to allow pupils learning a recognised rotational vault to perform unassisted, providing a thick weight-absorbing mattress is provided to receive their landing?**

Ans The aim of any formal rotational vault, or other formal rotational action involving flight, is to develop the orientation and motion necessary to complete the action correctly by landing under control on the feet. The stages leading up to this level of performance may require physical support as described in the answer to Question 8 above.

When the action has been practised and consolidated successfully to the extent that a feet-first landing under control by the performer can be confidently expected at each attempt, support may be reduced to *standing by* and eventually removed.

A thick weight-absorbing mattress may be the most suitable means for receiving the body momentum generated by the action but it cannot, and must not, replace the provision of physical support during the learning phase; neither can it be guaranteed to prevent injury. Care should be taken to ensure that the weight-absorbing mattress provides a relatively firm dismount surface. If the mat gives too much, the risk of injury to the lower leg will be higher.

Chapter seventeen

Health-related exercise

> Please read the general guidance provided in *Part one* of this handbook[1] before reading this chapter. This will help to ensure that you have a comprehensive awareness of safe practice issues affecting health-related exercise and physical education in general.

17.1 General guidance

17.1.1 The Health Education Authority defines health-related exercise as *exercise of the appropriate type, intensity and duration to improve and/or maintain health*. In the context of physical education, it can:

a enhance participation in a wide range of physical activities

b provide a good basis of fitness for participating in these activities

c encourage commitment to a physically active lifestyle

d develop the knowledge and experience required to take part in physical activity safely.

17.1.2 This section contains general guidance that applies to all health-related exercises. Subsequent sections focus on additional considerations relating to specific activities. In all cases, the specific guidance provided must be read in conjunction with the general guidance in this section and all the chapters in *Part one* of this handbook[1].

People

17.1.3 It is essential that school staff have the necessary skills, experience and training to supervise specific aspects of health-related exercise.

17.1.4 School staff should be aware of pupils at risk from strenuous activity and know what alternative challenges are appropriate for such pupils.

17.1.5 Pupils who have recently had a viral infection, including the common cold or high temperature illness, should avoid exercise until they have recovered to the stage where they feel well in themselves.

17.1.6 Pupils should share in the assessment and management of the risks associated with health-related exercise. This is an essential part of the learning process. Due to different abilities, the risk management process should be applied to individual pupils, to pupil groups and to the class as a whole.

---

1   See pages 1–124.

Context

17.1.7   Fitness facilities (eg fitness rooms, gymnasiums) should be hazard-free with sufficient space for pupils to exercise safely and move freely from activity to activity.

17.1.8   Fitness facilities should be secure. Systems should be in place to guard against inappropriate access and usage.

17.1.9   Fitness equipment should be stored safely. This is particularly important when free weights are being used.

17.1.10   Fitness equipment should be checked regularly and repaired or replaced as appropriate. Maintenance should always be carried out by suitably qualified contractors.

▶▶ See *Chapter eight: Environment and equipment* for further information about fitness equipment.

17.1.11   Clothing should be appropriate. It should allow free, unrestricted movement and should not be too loose.

17.1.12   The chewing of food, sweets or gum immediately before or during health-related exercise sessions should never be allowed. Chewing can result in choking, which can have serious, even fatal, consequences.

Organisation

17.1.13   Exercises designed to enhance and maintain mobility and flexibility may be undertaken on a regular basis and should form part of the warm-up and cool-down sections of physical education sessions.

17.1.14   Pupils should be encouraged to participate in safe and effective resistance exercise at least twice a week. Resistance exercise should be part of a balanced exercise and physical education programme.

17.1.15   Careful thought should be given to the frequency, intensity and duration of exercise, particularly when working with pre-pubescent pupils. Factors associated with physiological immaturity and spurts of rapid body growth place limits on training overload.

17.1.16   Pupils should never work unsupervised in fitness facilities.

17.1.17   Pupils should understand the importance of warming up thoroughly before vigorous exercise. All sessions designed to promote health-related exercise should start with a thorough warm-up and end with a recovery cool-down.

17.1.18 School staff should be well informed about the appropriateness of certain activities. Research has indicated that some traditional exercises, which are designed to improve suppleness and strength using the body's own resistance, may be contraindicated for both children and adults. These include:

a straight-legged sit-ups

b V-sits

c burpees

d standing side bends

e full head circles

f sit and reach with legs locked

g hurdle stretches

h deep knee bends.

Such exercises may expose the lower back or other major joints to unnecessary risk and suitable alternative exercises should therefore be used.

17.1.19 Advice relating to diet should be handled sensitively and should take account of body image problems often experienced by adolescents. A healthy diet should be actively encouraged.

17.1.20 School staff should keep a readily available progress record for all pupils, particularly when the exercises pupils take part in involve progressive resistance and repetition.

17.2 Circuit training

> Please read the general guidance provided in *Part one* of this handbook[1] and in paragraphs 17.1.1 to 17.1.20[2] before reading this section. This will help to ensure that you have a comprehensive awareness of safe practice issues affecting health-related exercise and physical education in general.

17.2.1 Circuit training is a popular method of providing vigorous indoor training with an emphasis on muscular endurance and strength. It is essential that the physical demands made are gradually progressed over time and that they reflect individual proficiency. School staff should emphasise the importance of developing efficient technique and should be aware of the potential dangers resulting from poor technique, progressing too quickly and irregular participation.

1 See pages 1–124.

2 See pages 209–11.

17.3 Fitness testing

Please read the general guidance provided in *Part one* of this handbook[1] and in paragraphs 17.1.1 to 17.1.20[2] before reading this section. This will help to ensure that you have a comprehensive awareness of safe practice issues affecting health-related exercise and physical education in general.

People

17.3.1 Maximal fitness tests which require all-out effort, such as the Multistage Fitness Test (more commonly known as the Bleep Test), requires maximum effort if the test result is to be useful. Pupils with an injury, illness or medical condition should not therefore take part in maximal tests.

17.3.2 Sub-maximal tests (eg step tests, timed curl-ups), which generally require participants to stop before becoming fatigued or exhausted, may be more appropriate for many pupils.

Organisation

17.3.3 It is advisable to perform a thorough warm-up before fitness tests and a cool-down afterwards. A shorter, more gentle warm-up may be appropriate for tests which begin slowly and increase in intensity very gradually.

17.3.4 Care should be taken when involving pupils in fitness testing. The results may not always be reliable and the desire to do well may encourage some pupils to push themselves too far. A competitive environment should be avoided.

17.4 Weightlifting

Please read the general guidance provided in *Part one* of this handbook[1] and in paragraphs 17.1.1 to 17.1.20[2] before reading this section. This will help to ensure that you have a comprehensive awareness of safe practice issues affecting health-related exercise and physical education in general.

17.4.1 Weightlifting is fundamentally a test of strength, usually within a competitive setting, and must not be confused with weight training, which is concerned with the development of muscular strength and endurance in the pursuit of fitness. Weightlifting includes the two Olympic lifts, strength tests and other competitive work with barbells and dumbbells. Mature participants work towards their strength threshold during weightlifting activities.

---

1 See pages 1–124.
2 See pages 209–11.

People

17.4.2   Weightlifting can be hazardous for post-pubescent pupils, as the risk of joint and spine injuries is high. It must therefore only be taught by qualified adults. The minimum requirement for teaching weightlifting in schools is a British Amateur Weight Lifters' Association teaching or coaching award.

Organisation

17.4.3   Class organisation should be similar to that for weight training with free weights[1] but there is a greater need to work in groups with trained and alert spotters.

17.4.4   Early weightlifting sessions should focus on developing good technique.

17.4.5   The risk of overuse injury is high. Overloading must be avoided and competitive lifting should be delayed until skeletal growth is complete.

17.4.6   During weightlifting competitions, post-pubescent pupils should not lift weights which are heavier than their own body weight. Their performance should preferably be judged on the style of lift rather than the amount of weight lifted.

17.5   Weight training

> Please read the general guidance provided in *Part one* of this handbook[2] and in paragraphs 17.1.1 to 17.1.20[3] before reading this section. This will help to ensure that you have a comprehensive awareness of safe practice issues affecting health-related exercise and physical education in general.

People

17.5.1   Resistance training involving free weights can be an effective method for improving the muscular strength and endurance of older pupils (ie Key Stage 4 and Post-16).

17.5.2   Weight training is not appropriate for pupils at Key Stage 3 and below, as it may result in musculo-skeletal injury.

Context

17.5.3   The floor should be suitably matted/covered to avoid damaging the equipment.

17.5.4   Spare weights, collars and bars should be stored safely well away from the performers.

---

1   See paragraphs 17.5.5 to 17.5.8 on page 214.

2   See pages 1–124.

3   See pages 209–11.

Organisation

17.5.5   Weight training sessions should always be supervised – pupils should never be allowed to weight train on their own.

17.5.6   All weights sessions should start with a thorough warm-up. Light to moderate intensity aerobic exercise, followed by gentle stretching of specific muscle groups, will help to prepare the body for the maximal and sub-maximal effort to follow.

17.5.7   All pupils should receive instruction in the application of correct technique. Start by using light, easily manageable weights and progress to heavier ones if necessary.

17.5.8   A long-term, systematic record of performance should be maintained to ensure that progression towards heavier resistance or increased repetitions proceeds at an appropriate incremental rate.

Further reading

- Donovan, C, McNamara, J and Gianoli, P (1989) **Exercise stop danger**. Hampshire, Fitness Leader Network

- Harris, J and Elbourn, J (2002) **Warming up and cooling down**. 2nd edition. Leeds, Human Kinetics Europe Ltd. ISBN 0 73603 878 7

- Harris, J (2000) **Health-related exercise in the National Curriculum: Key Stages 1 to 4**. Leeds, Human Kinetics Europe Ltd. ISBN 0 73600 168 9

- Health Education Authority (1998) **Young and active? policy framework for young people and health-enhancing physical activity**. London, Health Education Authority

- Loughborough University and The National Coaching Foundation (1998) **Multistage fitness test (CD)**. Leeds, Coachwise Solutions. ISBN 0 902523 06 7

- Smith, R (1996) **Flexibility for sport**. The Crowood Press. ISBN 1 85223 985 9

- Stratton, G (2004) **BASES guidelines for resistance exercise in young people (leaflet)**. Leeds, Coachwise Solutions

- Stratton, G (2004) **BASES position statement on guidelines for resistance exercise in young people**. *Journal of Sports Sciences,* No 22, pp 383–390

Risk management

People

- **Pupils should share in the assessment and management of the risks involved.**

- School staff should review medical records to identify any pupils at risk from vigorous activity.

- School staff should be appropriately trained and/or experienced in safe lifting techniques and resistance progression.

- School staff should be familiar with current views on healthy stretching and contraindicated exercise.

- Supervision levels should be adequate to ensure necessary guidance and intervention.

Context

- Fitness facilities should be hazard-free with sufficient space for pupils to exercise safely.

- Fitness equipment, particularly free weights, should be stored safely and securely when not in use.

- Fitness equipment should be checked and maintained on a regular basis.

Organisation

- School staff should ensure that all activities undertaken are appropriate to the developmental stage of the pupils involved.

▶▶ See *Chapter two: Risk management* for more detailed, general guidance on risk management issues.

Questions and answers

Organisation

Qu 1   **How appropriate are fitness circuits for Key Stage 2/3 pupils? Is this type of activity appropriate as a wet weather alternative?**

Ans   It is better if fitness circuits feature within overall planning and progressive schemes of work. Wherever possible, activities should relate to the National Curriculum. Try to include as many physically demanding, but skill-intensive, activities as possible, which reflect ongoing work in games and athletics.

Qu 2   **Would it be appropriate to include weight training within my planned activity programme?**

Ans   Progressive resistance work can be appropriate for older pupils (ie Key Stage 4 and Post-16), providing they are fully informed about the process involved in gaining strength. It is advisable to work with light weights, emphasising the importance of sound technique.

Weight training is not appropriate for pupils at Key Stage 3 and below, as it may result in musculo-skeletal injury.

Chapter eighteen
Outdoor and adventurous activities

> Please read the general guidance provided in *Part one* of this handbook[1] and *Chapter twenty: Educational visits*[2] before reading this chapter. This will help to ensure that you have a comprehensive awareness of safe practice issues affecting outdoor and adventurous activities, and physical education in general.

18.1 General guidance

18.1.1   The range of outdoor and adventurous activities (OAA), and participation levels of pupils, is considerable. The inclusion of OAA in the National Curriculum recognises the potential contribution they can make to pupils' educational development, with the emphasis on adventure and *real life* experiences in the outdoors. Hidden talents and interests are fostered, and personal abilities and limitations become evident. Both independence and teamwork are promoted through activities, which take place in the context of respect and concern for the natural environment.

18.1.2   The spirit of adventure and excitement must at all times be complemented by concern for the well-being and safety of pupils, which is of paramount importance. Planning (incorporating risk management) and progression are very important, as is recognition of the many variable factors which impact on specific ventures or activities. Serious accidents can sometimes occur as a result of an adverse combination of these factors.

18.1.3   This section contains general guidance that applies to all OAA. Subsequent sections focus on additional considerations relating to specific types of OAA. In all cases, the specific guidance provided must be read in conjunction with the general guidance in this section, *Chapter twenty: Educational visits*[2] and all the chapters in *Part one* of this handbook[1].

---

1   See pages 1–124.

2   See pages 277–82.

People

18.1.4   Sound planning is central to safe practice in the outdoors and this requires good leadership. Employers should have policies setting out the competence required of school staff who lead OAA (eg relevant qualifications, recognised training or proven experience in the field).

> ▶▶   See *Chapter three: Qualifications, competence and supervision* for general guidance on the competence required of school staff.

18.1.5   OAA require competent and experienced staff to exercise personal judgement in making and implementing decisions, which are necessary for the safety and well-being of the pupils involved.

18.1.6   Sound judgements are most likely to be made when the group leader[1] has:

a   an understanding of common law[2] *duty of care* and statute law[3] (particularly health and safety legislation)

b   relevant qualifications and skills, including organisational skills

c   first-hand experience or knowledge of the intended location and the activities which he/she will be leading

d   experience of working with pupils in the age range of those involved in the OAA venture

e   a good knowledge of the pupils for whom they will be responsible.

f   proven qualities of leadership and responsibility, which are evident from other aspects of his/her work

g   the necessary mental and physical fitness to undertake the proposed OAA venture without undue stress

h   appropriate competence in first aid and clear procedures to follow.

18.1.7   School staff should consider appropriate written advice from the Department for Education and Skills, local education authority (LEA), school and any other authoritative source, and seek guidance from senior management and relevant experts.

18.1.8   Systems should be in place to carry out the necessary checks to ensure that all adults, including instructors and volunteers, who will have close access to pupils during OAA ventures, are suitable to work with children. They should also ensure that all such adults are fully aware of, and able to fulfil, their duties.

18.1.9   Where an instructor is involved in the delivery of an activity, he/she is responsible for the technical aspects but the accompanying member of school staff has overall duty of care for the pupils involved.

18.1.10   When external agents or tour operators are used, systems should be in place to ensure that they are reputable, that they meet relevant statutory requirements (including financial bonding arrangements) and that they are able to fully satisfy the school's duty of care requirements.

18.1.11   Pupils should be adequately prepared for all activities and made aware of their personal responsibilities for safety.

---

1   The group leader could be a member of school staff or a centre instructor.

2   Law based on judicial decision and custom.

3   Law prescribed by parliament.

18.1.12 Pupils should share in the assessment and management of the risks associated with OAA ventures. This is an essential part of the learning process. Due to different abilities, the risk management process should be applied to individual pupils, to pupil groups and to the class as a whole.

Context

18.1.13 Employers, head teachers and governing bodies (as appropriate) should be satisfied that arrangements for OAA ventures meet insurance requirements before approving them.

18.1.14 Schools should consider the benefits of a code of conduct governing pupil behaviour, rules and discipline, which is agreed with parents and pupils prior to OAA ventures.

   ▶▶ A sample code of conduct is provided in Appendix 8.

18.1.15 Equipment and clothing should be in good condition and suitable for the intended activity and the age and size of the pupils involved. All equipment should be tested and checked well before the activity is due to take place.

18.1.16 OAA ventures can take place in a variety of different contexts. Those responsible for the activities involved should carry out a thorough risk assessment of the site and the immediate locality. Everyone involved should be made aware of any hazards present and the subsequent constraints to be observed.

18.1.17 Systems should be in place to ensure that the location and phone number of the nearest medical service or hospital is known, and that a second back-up phone number is available.

Activities away from main base

18.1.18 In case of an emergency, two responsible adults should be present, one of whom should be a competent member of school staff. More responsible adults may be required to supervise larger groups or groups with special educational needs (SEN).

18.1.19 Comprehensive information (eg route, activity locations, expected times of arrival) should be left with a responsible person at the base, together with agreed procedures to be followed by that person in the event of the schedule not being met within an appropriate time span.

18.1.20 There should be a planned means of communication between the group and the base and/or fire, medical or police services. Group leaders are advised to carry a mobile phone, but should not rely on it as the sole means of communication. The strength of the signal should be determined before setting out.

18.1.21 Equipment for use in the event of an emergency should be carried (eg torch, whistle, survival bag, high energy food (such as chocolate), spare warm clothing, first aid kit).

18.1.22 A contingency plan should be prepared for use in the event of an emergency.

Outdoor residential centres

18.1.23 Many schools use outdoor residential centres to provide pupils with experience of the outdoors. These may be run by local authorities or commercial/private agencies. There have been concerns in the past about the management, instruction and safety at some centres. School staff should therefore satisfy themselves that centres are appropriate and safe before booking them for OAA ventures.

18.1.24 Centres offering activities which are subject to licensing under the Adventure Activities Licensing Regulations 2004, must demonstrate that they meet acceptable standards of safe practice in those activities.

▶▶ See *Chapter one: Physical education and the law* for further information about the Adventure Activities Licensing Regulations 2004.

18.1.25 School staff are recommended to visit the proposed centre prior to a first booking to:

a view facilities and equipment

b meet with centre staff

c ensure that risk management procedures at the centre have been satisfactorily carried out and recorded

d ensure that the centre's fire and emergency procedures are satisfactory

e talk through and agree the entire activity programme and instruction arrangements with the centre manager.

18.1.26 School staff should resolve any unsatisfactory safety issues with the centre manager before committing to a booking. Advice should be sought from an LEA adviser or Health and Safety Officer if necessary.

18.1.27 It is advisable to ensure that the number of school staff present during OAA ventures is sufficient to enable one member of staff to accompany each group under instruction. This will help school staff to exercise their duty of care.

18.1.28 Emergency evacuation should be practised as soon as possible after arrival.

18.1.29 In the event of school staff becoming concerned that pupils may be at unnecessary or unreasonable risk during an activity, the instructor(s) involved should be approached during a safe interval and appropriate measures taken to ensure the continued safety and well-being of all the pupils.

18.1.30 School staff should hold regular meetings during the OAA venture to evaluate progress and discuss and resolve any issues that may have arisen, particularly those relating to safety.

Organisation

18.1.31   Sufficient time must be allowed for the thorough planning and risk assessment of OAA ventures to ensure that nothing is left to chance.

18.1.32   OAA ventures must conform to relevant European Union directives.

18.1.33   It is good practice to compile a written checklist and timescale covering all aspects of an OAA venture as early as possible during the planning stage. The checklist should include:

     a   preliminary visit to the intended location

     b   overall numbers

     c   adult/pupil ratios

     d   written advice (including letters and consent forms to parents)

     e   meetings

     f   travel arrangements

     g   meals

     h   accommodation

     i   activities

     j   equipment and clothing (both personal and issued)

     k   instruction

     l   responsibilities and supervision (including qualifications and experience checks)

     m   Criminal Records Bureau checks (if appropriate)

     n   finance

     o   Insurance

     p   first aid

     q   individual needs (dietary, educational and medical)

     r   contingency arrangements (for use when adverse circumstances, such as inclement weather, prevent the planned programme from taking place)

     s   emergency procedures.

18.1.34   School staff should pass a copy of all information relating to OAA ventures to a named representative of the senior management team at their school, who will act as the point of contact and communication in the event of an emergency.

18.1.35   Parents and pupils should be informed of the arrangements and requirements for OAA ventures (eg pupil groups, activities, duties, responsibilities, insurance arrangements). These details should be communicated in writing and, additionally, via meetings arranged for this purpose.

     ▶▶   A sample parent information letter is provided in Appendix 3.

18.1.36 Parental consent should be obtained for pupils to participate in the planned activities.

▶▶ A sample parental consent form is provided in Appendix 2.

18.1.37 A schedule for the supervision of pupils should be devised before an OAA venture takes place. Arrangements should also be made for the care of pupils in the event of an accident, illness or inability to participate in the planned programme.

18.1.38 School staff/instructor to pupil ratios and school staff/instructor qualifications should be in line with relevant LEA and national governing body (NGB) guidelines. A higher ratio of school staff/instructors to pupils may be required depending on factors such as previous experience, the environment, the activities to be undertaken and the availability of emergency assistance. This is particularly important when pupils with SEN, behavioural difficulties or additional educational needs are involved.

18.1.39 A minimum of two responsible adults is usually required to accompany OAA ventures, one of whom should be a member of school staff. However, more responsible adults may be required depending on the size and composition of the party, the environment and the nature of the activities to be undertaken.

18.1.40 If both male and female pupils will be involved in an OAA venture, it is advisable to have at least one responsible adult of each gender, one of whom should be a member of school staff.

18.1.41 In some circumstances (eg when working in school grounds and easily managed locations, or with small groups of more mature pupils), only one member of school staff may need to be present to provide adequate supervision.

18.1.42 Particular care should be taken to ensure that any late changes to the composition of the party are safe and realistic.

18.1.43 All activities undertaken should match the age, experience and ability of the pupils involved. Pupils should only be exposed to challenges for which they have the mental ability and physical skills and fitness required to respond. Allowances must be made for the least able pupils and activities modified as necessary to ensure their safe participation.

18.1.44 Discipline should be maintained at all times. School staff must always be prepared to intervene if pupils take potentially unsafe action.

18.1.45 Pupils should never participate in activities which are:

a not planned

b unsupervised

c not approved by the school staff leader.

18.1.46 Before taking part in more independent activities, pupils should first demonstrate sufficient skill, experience and maturity under supervision and be trained in relevant survival techniques. Adequate safeguards should be put in place and parental consent obtained prior to proceeding with these activities.

18.1.47 It is accepted practice for pupils participating in activities such as the Duke of Edinburgh's Award Scheme to undertake carefully planned expeditions with remote supervision, providing they have been properly trained to do so.

18.2 Land-based activities

18.2.1   The range of land-based OAA is extensive. During OAA ventures, combinations of different activities often take place, either one after the other or at the same time. The associated risks are considerable and it is therefore essential that great care is taken when organising and leading OAA ventures, particularly when land- and water-based activities are combined.

Camping and expeditions

> Please read the general guidance provided in *Part one* of this handbook[1] and paragraphs 18.1.1 to 18.1.47[2] before reading this section. This will help to ensure that you have a comprehensive awareness of safe practice issues affecting OAA and physical education in general.

18.2.2   There are various forms of camping, ranging from *standing camps* with some permanent on-site facilities, to *lightweight camping* during backpacking expeditions, for which lightweight equipment is used so that tents can be erected and taken down quickly. Whatever the form of camping, it is essential that all potential hazards relating to sites and activities are identified and resolved during the planning stage.

People

18.2.3   The following points should be considered in relation to the people involved in camping activities and expeditions:

a   Group leaders should be experienced in relevant styles of camping and should make a prior visit to (or have recent prior knowledge of) the site and location to be used.

b   For camping in mountainous country, group leaders should be appropriately trained and experienced. They should either hold a Mountaineering Council/Mountain Leader Training Board mountain leadership award or an alternative qualification recognised by their LEA.

c   If the party will be camping near water[3] and are likely to take part in water-based activities[4], group leaders must be familiar with the safety issues relating to the activities to be undertaken.

Context

18.2.4   The following points should be considered in relation to the context in which camping activities and expeditions take place:

a   A first camp should be held under controlled conditions and be located near to permanent shelter.

b   Sites close to quarries should be avoided.

c   Sufficient space should be allowed between tents to allow free movement between them and to prevent the spread of fire (should this occur).

1   See pages 1–124.

2   See pages 217–22.

3   The DfES/CCPR leaflet *Group Safety at Water Margins* provides useful guidance (see page 256 for full reference details).

4   See pages 240–56 for further information about water-based activities.

d The use of petrol stoves has led to serious problems in the past and is therefore not recommended.

e Gas cylinders and fuel for stoves should be stored outside tents. Fuel containers should be clearly marked (eg methylated spirits, paraffin).

Organisation

18.2.5 The following points should be considered in relation to the organisation of camping activities and expeditions:

a A ratio of one responsible adult to approximately ten pupils is recommended, depending on the composition of the party. A minimum of two responsible adults (one of whom should be a member of school staff) should normally be present in case of illness or accident, with at least one responsible adult of each gender for mixed parties. If experienced older pupils are supervised by just one member of school staff, suitable arrangements must be made for dealing with emergencies.

b Group leaders should ensure that pupils receive adequate prior training in the safe use of cooking stoves, the pitching and striking of tents and the packaging and carrying of loads.

c To prevent or minimise the risk of illness from infected food, pupils should be taught how to prepare, store and refrigerate food. Comparatively risk-free foods (eg non-cream cakes, salads, fresh fruit, fruit pies) are preferable. Eggs, chicken and similar foods must be cooked thoroughly to minimise the risk of salmonella poisoning. Pupils should be encouraged to eat food as soon as possible after it has been prepared.

d Cooking should not be permitted inside small tents.

e Naked flames should not be permitted inside tents.

f Balls games and running may be hazardous in the vicinity of the tents.

g Sewage and rubbish should be disposed of in a hygienic and safe manner in a designated area.

Caving and potholing

> Please read the general guidance provided in *Part one* of this handbook[1] and paragraphs 18.1.1 to 18.1.47[2] before reading this section. This will help to ensure that you have a comprehensive awareness of safe practice issues affecting OAA and physical education in general.

18.2.6 Underground systems, other than show caves and tourist mines, present many of the hazards associated with mountains and water, together with additional dangers associated with darkness and confined spaces. Rescue can sometimes be difficult, even from places that can easily be reached by an experienced party. Group leaders must always bear this in mind when planning caving or potholing expeditions. Great care should be taken to ensure that the risks presented are reasonable and commensurate with the abilities of the pupils involved.

---

1 See pages 1–124.

2 See pages 217–22.

People

18.2.7   Advice on suitable training and qualifications can be obtained from LEAs and/or the National Caving Association.

Context

18.2.8   The following points should be considered in relation to the context in which caving and potholing activities take place:

a   A concentration of radon gas in some caving systems has produced high levels of radiation which can be damaging to health after repeated exposure. Relevant information can be obtained from the Health and Safety Executive (Inspectorate of Mines and Quarries).

b   Industrial mines often present totally different dangers and problems from those encountered in natural cave systems, and must be treated with great care. Disused coal mines should never be used for caving. Advice should be sought from the Health and Safety Executive (Inspectorate of Mines and Quarries).

c   The minimum equipment required for each member of the caving/potholing party is as follows:

- Warm clothing

- A protective overgarment

- A protective helmet with chin strap and lamp bracket

- Strong boots with well-gripping soles

- An efficient headlamp, preferably electric.

d   If there is any possibility of prolonged exposure to water, a wetsuit, exposure suit, life jacket or other suitable gear must be worn.

e   Each member of the caving/potholing party should carry:

- lighting spares

- a whistle

- emergency food.

f   Ropes, ladders and other such equipment should be taken as required.

g   Group leaders should carry a first aid kit.

Organisation

18.2.9   The following points should be considered before going underground with a caving/potholing party:

a   A caving/potholing party should consist of a minimum of four people.

b   The recommended adult/pupil ratio for easy cave systems is a minimum of two competent adults (one of whom should be the school staff leader) to approximately ten pupils. Either adult must be capable of returning the party to the surface in the event of an emergency and know the relevant cave rescue procedures. The number of pupils should be reduced if the nature of the cave system demands it.

c   The group leader should have previously visited the cave/pothole system and be thoroughly familiar with it. Pupils should not be taken into any cave or pothole system with which the group leader is unfamiliar.

d Permission to descend should be sought from the cave/pothole owner where this is required.

e The party should be briefed on all relevant safety and cave/pothole conservation precautions, including details of the route to be followed and the features that will be encountered.

f All equipment and clothing should be checked. Care should be taken to ensure that helmets fit correctly and that all lights are working.

g Comprehensive details of the caving/potholing expedition should be left with a responsible adult back at base. These should include the names of all party members, the level of experience of all party members, the passages to be followed, the equipment being taken and the expected time of return.

h An identifying object (or person) should be left at the entrance of any cave/pothole system that is entered.

18.2.10 The following points should be considered while underground with a caving/potholing party:

a The adults involved should maintain constant contact with the front and rear of the party.

b The morale and condition of the party should be monitored. The group leader should be prepared to turn back at any stage.

c Particular attention should be paid to pupils on their first caving/potholing trip. They should be monitored for signs of physical weakness, reckless behaviour, claustrophobia, poor reaction to wet or cold, or any signs likely to hinder their safe involvement and progress.

d The party should be alerted to any hazard caused by loose chocks, falling rocks (especially below pitches), static or flowing sumps or loose flooring.

e Great care should be taken to avoid even minor injuries which could require a major rescue.

f A lifeline, handline or some other method should be used to protect pupils at places where a slip could lead to injury.

18.2.11 As soon as possible after returning above ground, the group leader must report back to the responsible adult with whom details of the expedition were left.

18.2.12 The following points should be considered when pupils have progressed to the stage of being ready to tackle vertical pitches:

a Ladder pitches or roped climbing should first be taught and practised above ground in caving attire.

b The time required for each ladder pitch should be estimated in advance and the trip and group size planned accordingly. Long waits underground should be avoided, particularly if the pupils are wet.

c All ladder pitches must be lifelined using accepted safe techniques.

d Lifelines should be held by experienced cavers or by competent pupils under constant supervision.

e No-one should be allowed on wire ladders wearing boots with hooked lacing.

f An experienced caver should descend first and ascend last, and a second experienced caver should descend last and ascend first.

Cycle touring and mountain biking

18.2.13   There are many forms of cycling, ranging from basic functional or recreational activities through to participation as varied as mountain biking, high-powered competitive sprinting and distance events. This section focuses on cycle touring and mountain biking.

18.2.14   The potential for serious accidents is high in all forms of cycling and great care should be taken when planning and organising cycling activities to minimise risk. British Cycling and the British Schools Cycling Association can provide advice on all aspects of cycling.

Cycle touring

> Please read the general guidance provided in *Part one* of this handbook[1] and paragraphs 18.1.1 to 18.1.47[2] before reading this section. This will help to ensure that you have a comprehensive awareness of safe practice issues affecting OAA and physical education in general.

People

18.2.15   Advice on training and qualifications for those leading or instructing cycling activities can be obtained from LEAs and British Cycling.

Context

18.2.16   The following points should be considered in relation to the context in which cycling activities take place:

   a   Bikes should be roadworthy, with all parts in good mechanical condition and operating correctly.

   b   Tyres should be inflated to the correct pressure.

   c   Wheels should be firmly locked in place and not buckled, with hubs running smoothly and no sideways play.

   d   Brakes should be correctly adjusted and capable of stopping the cycle and cyclist.

   e   The frame should be neither bent nor damaged. The head bearing and bottom bracket bearing should be smooth running, without play.

   f   The handlebars, brake levers and saddle should be correctly and firmly positioned.

   g   The gears should be correctly adjusted, so that the chain engages securely with the appropriate socket when using rear and front changers, and does not come off.

   h   If poor visibility is anticipated, lights should be fitted and the group leader's bike should be clearly identifiable to other cyclists.

1   See pages 1–124.
2   See pages 217–22.

l All accessories (eg pumps, tools, mudguards, lights, drinking bottles) should be securely attached.

j Luggage should be stowed in purpose-fitted saddle bags or panniers. Items should never be carried in the hands or draped over the handlebars.

k The size of the frame and the position of the cyclist on the bike are very important for both efficient and safe riding. The ideal height for the saddle is such that when the cyclist sits on the saddle with one heel placed on the pedal at its lowest point, his/her leg is only slightly flexed at the knee. When stopping, the cyclist should lean the bike over a little to enable one foot to reach the ground, or slide forwards off the saddle so that both feet can be placed on the ground. The handlebars should be set so that with the cyclist's hands within reach of the brake levers, the body is set at an angle of 45°. Young cyclists or beginners may initially prefer a more upright stance.

l Although specialist cycling clothing is available, almost any leisurewear is acceptable, providing it is not likely to become entangled in the chain or wheels. It is important for cyclists to remain warm and dry. A considerable chill factor is created by cycling and it is therefore necessary to wrap up warmly to combat this, particularly in inclement weather. Bright-coloured clothing will make cyclists more visible to other road users.

m Helmets should be worn and gloves are recommended. Helmets should conform to current British Standards European Norm (BS EN) requirements and the manufacturer's recommendations on its use and care should be followed.

n A pump, spare inner tube and basic tool kit are essential accessories and should be carried at all times.

o A first aid kit should be carried by a cyclist competent to use it.

p All cyclists should carry some form of identification (ie name and address).

Organisation

18.2.17   The following points should be considered before embarking on a cycling tour:

a Basic cycling skills are best learned in controlled conditions on a playground or other safe area before being applied on the road.

b The competence of young or inexperienced cyclists should be assessed before taking to the road. They should be familiar with road signs, traffic lights, keeping to the left, hand signals and positions on the road when negotiating roundabouts or turning left/right.

c Cyclists must be taught to avoid making any sudden actions (eg braking, changing course, slipping from the saddle) without warning.

d Care must be taken to ensure that planned rides are within the capabilities of the cyclists (their physical skills, fitness and mental application) and take account of variables such as traffic conditions, terrain, weather, speed and the duration of the ride.

18.2.18   The following points should be considered when riding on roads:

a The ratio of adults to pupils should not normally exceed one to seven.

b The group should consist of no more than 12 cyclists, including two adults. A larger party should be split into two groups, each with their own leader.

c Different groups should ride well separated (at least ten minutes apart when setting off).

d If separate groups close to within visible distance of each other, the trailing group should stop at a safe place and wait ten minutes before continuing.

e The group formation on the road should consist of two ranks when conditions are suitable, with the adults on the outside of the group – one at the front and one at the rear. This will enable them to control the speed of the group, signal effectively, call to each other and give cyclists instructions or advice.

f Each cyclist is responsible for looking ahead and should be taught to warn the cyclists behind him/her of any hazards (eg parked cars, potholes, sharp bends). Warnings should be delivered both verbally and via hand signals.

g Cyclists at the rear should warn of overtaking vehicles and those in the outside rank should give hand signals when necessary.

h When riding in two ranks, a distance of one bike length should be maintained between pairs and about half a metre between ranks. These distances may be safely reduced for experienced cyclists.

i In heavy traffic or on narrow twisting roads, single file riding is advisable. This may be achieved by the inner rank cyclists slowing slightly and the outer rank cyclists entering the space provided on the instruction of the adult at the rear. The return to two ranks may be achieved by the reverse of this manoeuvre, again on the instruction of the adult at the rear.

j In hot weather, it is essential for cyclists to carry a drink if the ride is expected to exceed 30 minutes. Food (carbohydrates) will also be necessary when rides are expected to exceed one hour.

Mountain biking (off-road touring)

> Please read the general guidance provided in *Part one* of this handbook[1] and paragraphs 18.1.1 to 18.1.47[2] and 18.2.15 to 18.2.18[3] before reading this section. This will help to ensure that you have a comprehensive awareness of safe practice issues affecting OAA and physical education in general.

Context

18.2.19 The following points should be considered in relation to the context in which mountain biking activities take place:

a Group leaders should have ridden the course recently and assessed its suitability for the party.

b Clothing should be as for cycle touring[4], although gloves should be compulsory.

c Footwear should suit the terrain and allowances should be made for changes in the weather.

d Group leaders should be equipped with a map, compass and whistle, in addition to the items for cycle touring[5].

---

1 See pages 1–124.
2 See pages 217–22.
3 See pages 227–29.
4 See paragraph 18.2.16 (points l and m) on page 228.
5 See paragraph 18.2.16 (points n to p) on page 228.

Organisation

18.2.20   The following points should be considered in relation to the organisation of mountain biking activities:

   a   Pupils should be taught off-road riding skills and assessed in appropriate locations before embarking on a mountain biking course.

   b   Staffing ratios should be as for cycle touring[1]. However, a second responsible adult should always be included in the party.

   c   If conditions become too challenging, pupils should walk with their bikes.

Horse riding and pony trekking

> Please read the general guidance provided in *Part one* of this handbook[2] and paragraphs 18.1.1 to 18.1.47[3] before reading this section. This will help to ensure that you have a comprehensive awareness of safe practice issues affecting OAA and physical education in general.

18.2.21   Horse riding and pony trekking are popular activities with many young people. Because of the inherent risks involved, trained horses and ponies should always be used within qualified riding school conditions.

People

18.2.22   Advice on training and qualifications for those leading or instructing horse riding and pony trekking can be obtained from LEAs, the British Horse Society (BHS) and the Association of British Riding Schools (or relevant home country national associations).

Context

18.2.23   The following points should be considered in relation to the context in which horse riding and pony trekking activities take place:

   a   It is recommended that any riding schools used be recognised by the BHS and/or the Association of Riding Schools (or relevant home country national association), as this will give an indication of quality instruction and suitable horses.

   b   Only licensed pony trekking centres should be used.

   c   As far as possible, riders should try to avoid traffic and busy roads. If riding does take place on roads, riders should be familiar with, and observe, relevant sections of the Highway Code.

   d   Local advice should be obtained before using routes for pony trekking which may be subject to hazards such as fog or slippery surface conditions.

   e   Horses should be fully equipped with a leather saddle, bridle and reins, which have been fitted correctly and checked carefully before use.

---

1   See paragraph 18.2.18 (points a and b) on page 228.

2   See pages 1–124.

3   See pages 217–22.

f Riders should wear suitable clothing at all times. The basic essentials include:

- a hard hat which meets current BS EN requirements

- footwear with low hard heels (training shoes or wellingtons are not suitable, as these may slip from the stirrups).

g Emergency items (eg first aid kit, mobile phone, water) should be carried during pony trekking ventures.

Organisation

18.2.24 The following points should be considered in relation to the organisation of pony trekking activities:

a Some preliminary riding instruction is advisable.

b Small groups are preferable.

c Each group should be accompanied by two responsible adults, one of whom should be appropriately qualified to lead the activity.

Orienteering

> Please read the general guidance provided in *Part one* of this handbook[1] and paragraphs 18.1.1 to 18.1.47[2] before reading this section. This will help to ensure that you have a comprehensive awareness of safe practice issues affecting OAA and physical education in general.

18.2.25 Orienteering involves completing a course while looking for prepared features at locations identifiable from information provided to participants, generally using a map and compass.

People

18.2.26 The following points should be considered in relation to the people involved in orienteering activities:

a Evidence of experience and competence is adequate for delivering a basic introduction to orienteering in school grounds or observable woodland paths.

b Advice on training and qualifications for those leading or instructing orienteering can be obtained from LEAs and the relevant NGB[3].

c Sufficient competent adults should be available to:

- monitor checkpoints

- search for any pupils who fail to check in by close-out time.

---

1   See pages 1–124.

2   See pages 217–22.

3   British Orienteering Federation, Northern Ireland Orienteering Association, Scottish Orienteering Association and Welsh Orienteering Association as appropriate.

18.2.27 The following points should be considered in relation to the context in which orienteering activities take place:

a Prior permission should be obtained to use the intended course, either from the landowner or managing agent. The existence of orienteering maps does not necessarily indicate any right of access.

b Local advice on the geography of the area should be sought as appropriate.

c Pupils should not be required to cross busy roads or negotiate major geographical hazards.

d Control points should be located well away from deep water, unsafe buildings or concealed drops in ground level.

e Appropriate clothing should be worn to suit the conditions. Complete coverage of the arms and legs is recommended for most woodland events.

f Footwear should be suitable for the course terrain and prevailing weather conditions.

g All pupils should carry a whistle during competitions.

h The address and phone number of the nearest doctor should be displayed at the base, together with the location of the nearest phone.

i First aid equipment should be readily accessible.

Organisation

18.2.28 The following points should be considered in relation to the organisation of orienteering activities:

a All hazards should be marked on orienteering maps and brought to the attention of pupils in the starting area.

b Inexperienced pupils should compete in pairs or small groups, and keep together throughout.

c Only experienced pupils should take part in night-time orienteering.

d Escape instructions may be issued to pupils to enable them to retreat safely to a pre-arranged point.

Problem-solving and improvised activities

Please read the general guidance provided in *Part one* of this handbook[1] and paragraphs 18.1.1 to 18.1.47[2] before reading this section. This will help to ensure that you have a comprehensive awareness of safe practice issues affecting OAA and physical education in general.

18.2.29 Problem-solving and associated improvised activities can be very valuable in the promotion of applied skills and team-building, using *low technology* equipment. Many activities are relatively low-risk but all should be carefully planned to ensure that pupils are not put at unnecessary risk.

1 See pages 1–124.

2 See pages 217–22.

People

18.2.30 No specific qualifications are associated with problem-solving activities. However, useful advice may be obtained from a number of sources.

Context

18.2.31 All equipment used must be adequate, in good condition, suitable and safe for the purposes for which it will be used. This is particularly important if the equipment will be used to support weight.

Organisation

18.2.32 The following points should be considered in relation to the organisation of problem-solving and improvised activities:

a Group leaders are advised to familiarise themselves thoroughly with the intended activities before using them with pupils.

b Problems should be clearly and unambiguously presented.

c Totally open-ended problems with no evident or predictable solutions should not be used.

d The safety of self and others within pupil groups should override all other considerations.

e Time limits imposed should never cause activities to be rushed or lacking in control.

f Problems involving physical challenge should be well within the capabilities of all pupils and should be closely and responsibly supervised.

Rock climbing and abseiling

Please read the general guidance provided in *Part one* of this handbook[1] and paragraphs 18.1.1 to 18.1.47[2] before reading this section. This will help to ensure that you have a comprehensive awareness of safe practice issues affecting OAA and physical education in general.

18.2.33 Rock climbing and abseiling are specialised technical activities which require the utmost attention to safe practice. Those leading activities must be fully aware of the dangers and take all reasonable steps to ensure the safety of the pupils in their charge.

People

18.2.34 Climbing and abseiling should only take place under the supervision of adults with appropriate qualifications and experience. Advice on training and qualifications for those leading or instructing rock climbing and abseiling can be obtained from LEAs and the home nation Mountaineering Councils and Mountain Leader Training Boards.

1 See pages 1–124.
2 See pages 217–22.

Context

18.2.35   The following points should be considered in relation to the context in which rock climbing and abseiling activities take place:

a   Ropes, karabiners and all other specialist equipment should meet current BS EN requirements and be in good condition. They must be checked by the group leader prior to the start of climbing/abseiling sessions.

b   Ropes should not be allowed to run directly through a rope or taped loop. A screw gate karabiner should be used as the connecting mechanism for attaching a rope to such a loop.

c   Ropes should be inspected at regular intervals for signs of wear and tear, and should be replaced when this occurs.

d   Climbers should wear safety helmets and sit harnesses which meet current BS EN requirements.

e   Gloves, which enable hands to maintain a good grip and full control of the rope, should generally be worn when belaying.

f   Footwear should provide a good grip on the rock and should be light enough to cause little damage.

Artificial climbing walls

18.2.36   The development of both indoor and outdoor artificial climbing and bouldering walls has had a significant influence on climbing. Although generally designed with safety in mind, great care is still required to ensure acceptable good practice. Group leaders should pay particular attention to the following:

a   Climbing walls should be approved by the relevant LEA or Mountaineering Council/Mountain Leader Training Board. They should be regularly inspected and maintained.

b   Ropes and equipment should be of the same standard as that required for rock climbing.

c   Any protective mattresses used should be made from high-density foam and contain a flame inhibitor. They should be covered and held firmly together by a wear sheet to prevent feet entering any gaps. They should complement (not replace) safety measures which make falls improbable.

Organisation

18.2.37   The following points should be considered in relation to the organisation of rock climbing and abseiling activities:

a   Adult/pupil ratios will depend on the level and purpose of the climbing/abseiling session, the location and the experience of the pupils involved. The following ratios are recommended:

- For introductory sessions, there should be one member of school staff and one instructor to approximately eight pupils.

- For longer climbs, one qualified adult should be responsible for no more than three pupils and each climber should be belayed individually. Climbers must remain roped throughout the climb.

- When major crags are attempted, there must be at least two qualified adults in the party, one of whom should be the school staff leader.

b   The grade of the climb should be within the capability of the least able climber in the group.

c   Climbing or bouldering should not take place unless the group leader is present and gives his/her consent.

d No-one should lead a climb without the permission of the qualified adult.

e All knots should be checked by the qualified adult before and during the climb.

f The standard climbing calls system should be used.

g Abseiling must always be supervised by the qualified adult. A safety rope should always be used and attached separately from the abseil rope.

h Sites should be as free as possible from unavoidable objective dangers such as loose rock.

i Remote sites may require the group leader to have additional *expeditioning* skills.

j Environmental sensitivities (eg bird bans) should be investigated and observed.

Skating

> Please read the general guidance provided in *Part one* of this handbook[1] and paragraphs 18.1.1 to 18.1.47[2] before reading this section. This will help to ensure that you have a comprehensive awareness of safe practice issues affecting OAA and physical education in general.

18.2.38   The guidance in this section applies to both ice, roller and in-line skating. These activities are becoming more and more popular.

Context

18.2.39   The following points should be considered in relation to the context in which skating activities take place:

a The skating surface should be regularly maintained and checked before use. Skating should only take place on an even surface.

b Pupils should wear suitable clothing which provides adequate protection.

c Elbow and knee protection is advisable.

d Beginners should wear gloves to protect their hands.

e Ice/roller boots should provide firm ankle support.

Organisation

18.2.40   The following points should be considered in relation to the organisation of skating activities:

a Skating should be supervised by school staff and a competent instructor should always be present.

b All pupils should understand and observe the rules and procedures relating to skating.

c Where possible, it is advisable for advanced skaters and beginners to skate in separate groups.

d All skaters should move in the same (anticlockwise) direction.

---

1   See pages 1–124.

2   See pages 217–22.

Skiing and snowboarding

> Please read the general guidance provided in *Part one* of this handbook[1] and paragraphs 18.1.1 to 18.1.47[2] before reading this section. This will help to ensure that you have a comprehensive awareness of safe practice issues affecting OAA and physical education in general.

18.2.41   Skiing and snowboarding can take place on natural snow or artificial slopes.

General guidance

People

18.2.42   Tuition should be provided by qualified and experienced instructors. Advice on ski/snowboarding course organisation and relevant leader and instructor qualifications can be obtained from LEAs, the British Association of Snowsport Instructors and the national ski councils[3].

Context

18.2.43   The following points should be considered in relation to the context in which skiing and snowboarding activities take place:

a   Ski helmets (when available) can provide additional head protection in the event of a collision.

b   Ski boots should provide firm support to the ankles and lower legs.

c   Skis should generally be no longer than the height of the skier (shorter for beginners).

d   Mechanisms on bindings should be correctly adjusted to individual skiers, to enable quick release in the event of a fall. These should be carefully checked and adjusted before the start of a skiing session by a trained technician or other adult with the necessary knowledge.

e   Brakes on skis should operate automatically in the event of a ski being released.

f   The length of ski sticks should be roughly equivalent to the waist height of the skier.

g   Clothing must provide adequate protection against snow, wind and cold. Essential items include:

- a ski suit or anorak

- ski trousers/salopettes (jeans are not suitable)

- gloves or mittens

- goggles

- ski hat.

---

1   See pages 1–124.

2   See pages 217–22.

3   English Ski Council, Snowsport Cymru Wales and Snowsport Scotland as appropriate.

h On dry ski slopes, clothing should be worn to protect the arms and legs from friction burns in case of a fall.

i Sun cream should be applied to prevent sunburn and lip balm to prevent chapped lips. Care should be taken to ensure that both items are suitable for individual pupils, as allergic reactions can sometimes occur. Medical advice should be sought if necessary.

Organisation

18.2.44   The following points should be considered in relation to the organisation of skiing and snowboarding activities:

a All skiing/snowboarding trips should be preceded by a programme of regular pre-ski exercises and fitness training sessions, which will help to prepare pupils for the rigours of the activities to be undertaken. The use of artificial slopes can provide valuable experience.

b A ratio of one qualified adult to approximately 12 pupils is generally acceptable, but may need to be varied in some circumstances to ensure safe supervision.

c Daily tuition of four hours (two hours in the morning, break for lunch, two hours in the afternoon) is common. If only two hours of daily instruction is provided and pupils are allowed on the slopes at other times, they must be supervised by school staff who have adequate experience and knowledge of the area, and who are competent to lead.

Skiing/snowboarding on snow abroad

Context

18.2.45   The following points should be considered in relation to the context in which skiing and snowboarding activities take place:

a When planning a ski/snowboarding trip abroad, school staff should consider the following:

- The safety of the resort and quality snow slopes with adequate lift systems for beginners through to improvers
- The safety of the hotel (or other accommodation) and adequate fire, emergency and security procedures
- The proximity of the hotel (or other accommodation) to the ski slopes
- The availability of adequate drying and storage facilities for clothing, boots and skis or boards
- The satisfactory condition of all equipment to be hired and the provision of a technician to check and adjust equipment at distribution and during the ski course
- The provision of adequate insurance cover
- A skiing guarantee in the event of poor quality snow at the selected resort.

b All members of the party should be familiar with accident and emergency procedures for fire and personal accident. A fire drill should be practised on arrival at the resort or as soon as possible afterwards.

Organisation

18.2.46   The following points should be considered in relation to the organisation of skiing and snowboarding activities:

a   There should be enough qualified adults for the size of the party (generally one qualified adult to approximately 12 pupils).

b   Recognised ski codes of practice should be known and observed by all involved.

c   Pupils should not be allowed to ski alone or outside marked ski areas and trails.

d   Supervised ski practice and all other snow activities should be carefully monitored.

e   Clear instructions should be given to pupils about the runs, tows, chairlifts, check-in times, rendezvous points and all safety procedures.

f   All skiing must be graded according to the abilities of the pupils.

g   Tired skiers should stop skiing.

h   Pupils should be adequately supervised outside of skiing sessions (eg while in the hotel/resort, including during any evening entertainment or activity).

Skiing/snowboarding on snow in Britain

18.2.47   In addition to the guidance provided on skiing/snowboarding on snow abroad[1], the following points should be considered:

a   A party should be supervised by at least two qualified adults.

b   A day's skiing on local fells should be planned in the same way as a hike in the hills or mountains[2].

c   All members of the party should wear suitable clothing to protect them from cold, wet and windy conditions.

d   All members of the party should carry food, hot drinks and spare clothing.

e   Group leaders should carry emergency equipment (eg shelter, spare clothing, food and drink, first aid kit, mobile phone).

f   All members of the party should stay together at all times.

Nordic (cross-country) skiing

18.2.48   This activity is very energetic and care should be taken to ensure that it takes place safely. Group leaders should be appropriately trained and qualified. They should also be familiar with the intended route and should ensure that it is suitable in the prevailing weather and snow conditions.

---

1   See paragraphs 18.2.45 and 18.2.46 on pages 237–38 for further information.

2   See paragraphs 18.2.49 to 18.2.54 on pages 239–40 for further information.

safe practice in physical education and school sport

Walking and mountaineering

> Please read the general guidance provided in *Part one* of this handbook[1] and paragraphs 18.1.1 to 18.1.47[2] before reading this section. This will help to ensure that you have a comprehensive awareness of safe practice issues affecting OAA and physical education in general.

18.2.49   Walking can take place in a variety of locations, from local walks on pavements and footpaths, through to high-level mountain and fell-walking in remote areas. The guidance provided in this section mainly relates to high-level walking, since the hazards are likely to be greater.

People

18.2.50   The following points should be considered in relation to the people involved in walking and climbing activities:

a Those leading walking or mountaineering groups on fells or mountains should be trained in first aid, including the treatment of hypothermia.

b Advice on training and qualifications for those leading walking and climbing expeditions can be obtained from LEAs and home nation Mountain Leader Training Boards.

Context

18.2.51   The following points should be considered in relation to the context in which walking and climbing activities take place:

a Waterproof and windproof clothing, and a spare jumper, are required at higher levels, even in summer. Boots with soles that grip well are essential. Crampons and an ice axe are required in snow and ice conditions.

b Each group member should carry as a minimum:

- a map
- a compass
- a whistle
- a torch (with spare batteries)
- pencil and paper
- food and drink.

c Every group should carry a:

- first aid kit
- group shelter
- mobile phone (or other effective means of communication)
- climbing rope (to aid scrambling if needed).

d In addition, in winter conditions, every group should carry sleeping bags (one per group member).

---

1   See pages 1–124.
2   See pages 217–22.

Organisation

18.2.52 The following points should be considered before embarking on a walking or mountaineering expedition:

a Recommended adult/pupil ratios are as follows:

- For fieldwork in less remote areas with easy access to main roads and given reasonable weather, one adult to approximately ten pupils is realistic (but with a minimum of two responsible adults, one of whom is a member of school staff).

- In more demanding terrain, the recommended ratio is one adult to approximately ten pupils (with a minimum of two responsible adults, one of whom is a member of school staff).

- Groups on unaccompanied (remotely supervised) expeditions (eg Duke of Edinburgh Award Scheme) should consist of four to seven pupils.

b The adult leader should check local weather forecasts and conditions, and mountain rescue call-out procedures.

c A route card should be left back at base indicating the date, where the group is to walk, the expected time of return and contingency escape routes. If plans are changed, the base should be informed.

d All group members should be familiar with emergency procedures.

18.2.53 The following points should be considered while walking on the hills:

a The pace should be reasonable for the slowest member of the group.

b The group should stay together, with nominated front and back markers.

c Rest and shelter should be taken in the event of exhaustion or worsening weather.

18.2.54 On returning to base, the group leader should:

a report in and collect the route card

b evaluate the expedition for future reference.

18.3 Water-based activities

General guidance

> Please read the general guidance provided in *Part one* of this handbook[1] and paragraphs 18.1.1 to 18.1.47[2] before reading this section. This will help to ensure that you have a comprehensive awareness of safe practice issues affecting OAA and physical education in general.

18.3.1 The range of water-based activities (both on and in water), and the number of people participating in them, continues to grow. This is largely due to advances in technology, which have enabled existing activities to be modified and improved, and new activities to be developed.

1 See pages 1–124.
2 See pages 217–22.

18.3.2 Great care should be taken when undertaking water-based activities. It is essential that all potential hazards are identified and managed accordingly. Following the guidance provided in this section will promote safe practice.

People

18.3.3 Group leaders should be appropriately qualified and experienced. Advice on training and qualifications in water-based activities can be obtained from the relevant NGB.

18.3.4 Group leaders should be water confident, yet always wear a life jacket/personal buoyancy aid while afloat.

18.3.5 Group leaders should have knowledge and experience of the locations and conditions in which they lead water-based activities. Advice should be sought from appropriate organisations (eg British Waterways Board, Coastguard).

18.3.6 Group leaders of water-based activities on inland waterways and canals should have suitable knowledge and experience. In particular, they should:

  a understand that the manoeuvring of boats may be limited by the narrowness of the waterway

  b be aware of, and know how to resolve, the difficulties associated with negotiating tunnels, swing bridges, sluices, weirs and low bridges (the latter can be particularly hazardous in the event of unforeseen wash from other boats)

  c possess the special boat-handling skills required to negotiate locks.

18.3.7 Pupils are generally at greater risk of hypothermia than adults because they have less body fat.

Context

18.3.8 Water-based activities should take place in suitable conditions. Weather forecasts and conditions, and water temperature and quality, should be considered when planning sessions.

18.3.9 Particular care should be taken on inland waterways and canals. Group leaders should:

  a check for potentially hazardous debris which may lie on or under the water

  b recognise the health risks associated with water contaminated by the urine and infected tissues of animals (including Weils disease (leptospirosis) which is carried by rodents)

  c take action to minimise the risk of infection – for example:

  • ensure that scratches or abrasions are covered with waterproof plasters before pupils enter the water

  • advise pupils to avoid swallowing or inhaling water

  • ensure that pupils take a shower at the end of the activity

  d ensure that pupils can get out of the water safely at any point.

18.3.10 The unpredictable nature of the sea should never be underestimated. Local shipping and weather information should always be sought from coastguards and other relevant agencies when operating in tidal environments.

18.3.11   The operational area should be clearly defined.

18.3.12   Appropriate equipment should be used, including life jackets/buoyancy aids, helmets and wet suits. These should conform to current BS EN requirements and be subject to regular and rigorous safety checks.

18.3.13   Appropriate clothing and footwear should be worn.

18.3.14   Everyone involved should understand the appropriate emergency and rescue procedures, and how they will be implemented.

Organisation

18.3.15   Pupils need to develop confidence on and in water, in order to experience water-based activities safely and enjoyably. Group leaders should ensure that pupils have the level of water confidence and competence required for the intended activity (including the moving and handling of boats).

18.3.16   Pupils should receive adequate water safety training (eg safe swimming, in-water survival techniques, self-rescue, rescue of others) before taking part in all water-based activities. This should take place in water of a realistic temperature for the intended activities.

18.3.17   The emphasis should at all times be on appropriate challenge within an agreed, planned framework for the activities to be undertaken.

Angling

Please read the general guidance provided in *Part one* of this handbook[1] and paragraphs 18.1.1 to 18.1.47[2] and 18.3.1 to 18.3.17[3] before reading this section. This will help to ensure that you have a comprehensive awareness of safe practice issues affecting OAA and physical education in general.

18.3.18   Angling is popular with many young people. It provides opportunities to develop environmental awareness, address conservation issues and promote regard and respect for other water users.

People

18.3.19   The following points should be considered in relation to the people involved in angling activities:

   a Group leaders of angling activities should:

   • be active and proficient anglers

   • have practical experience of the waters in which angling will take place

   • be qualified in accordance with National Federation of Anglers recommendations.

1   See pages 1–124.
2   See pages 217–22.
3   See pages 240–42.

b When fishing from a boat, group leaders should be:

- knowledgeable about the local waters, tides and weather

- proficient in boat-handling, rowing and engine operation, or otherwise engage the services of a professional boatman.

c Advice on training and qualifications for those leading or instructing angling can be obtained from LEAs and the National Federation of Anglers.

d Group leaders are strongly recommended to ensure that at least one member of the angling party is trained in lifesaving and first aid.

Context

18.3.20   The following points should be considered when bank or shore angling takes place:

a Pupils should be made aware of any potential hazards, such as crumbling banks, variations in the height and speed of tides, slippery weed-covered rocks, unexpectedly large waves, tidal bores and quicksand.

b Studded felt-soled waders should be worn where appropriate.

c Extra care should be taken when fishing from wave-washed rocks and those surrounded by deep water – a rescue line or line-throwing buoy should be available.

18.3.21   The following points should be considered when fishing from a boat:

a The boat should be adequate for the purpose and appropriately licensed.

b There should be sufficient space for the number of pupils taking part.

c If hired, the boat should conform to requirements laid down by the appropriate marine safety agency or other authority.

18.3.22   In addition, the following points should be considered when fishing from a boat at sea:

a The boat should be equipped with spare and emergency equipment, including two-way radio communication if fishing will take place some distance from the shore.

b Pupils should wear bright-coloured windproof and waterproof clothing, and carry spare warm jumpers.

c Food and drink should be available (including emergency supplies).

d Steps should be taken to prevent seasickness if this is anticipated.

Organisation

18.3.23   The following points should be considered when bank or shore angling takes place:

a The recommended supervision ratio is a minimum of two responsible adults (one of whom should be a member of school staff) to ten pupils.

b Group leaders should emphasise the dangers of wading in fast and unfamiliar waters.

c Pupils should receive adequate instruction in recovery techniques and the use of wading sticks.

18.3.24   When fishing from a boat, group leaders should ensure that pupils are always accompanied – they should never fish alone.

Canoeing and kayaking

> Please read the general guidance provided in *Part one* of this handbook[1] and paragraphs 18.1.1 to 18.1.47[2] and 18.3.1 to 18.3.17[3] before reading this section. This will help to ensure that you have a comprehensive awareness of safe practice issues affecting OAA and physical education in general.

18.3.25 Canoeing and kayaking are potentially hazardous. Risks must be reasonably assessed and managed, without detracting from the challenge and spirit of adventure which form the very essence of these activities.

People

18.3.26 The following points should be considered in relation to the people involved in canoeing activities:

a The British Canoe Union has a qualification system of graded awards for instructors relating to both placid and moving (ie flowing, tidal and white) waters and to the use of different types of craft (ie open- and closed-cockpit kayaks and canoes). Group leaders should be suitably qualified and experienced for the intended level of instruction to be provided, the type of craft to be used and the type of water on which canoeing/kayaking will take place. The activities they lead should be well within their personal canoeing/kayaking competence and experience.

b All group leaders must be capable of performing expired-air resuscitation and must also know how to recognise and treat hypothermia.

c On open, exposed water, an assistant leader with the ability to perform deep-water rescues is recommended.

d All members of the canoeing party should have sufficient experience and should be physically fit enough to participate in the prevailing weather and water conditions.

Context

18.3.27 The following points should be considered in relation to the context in which canoeing activities take place:

a Group leaders should assess local conditions, including currents, tides and any potentially dangerous features (eg weirs), by studying guides, maps, charts and tide tables. Great care should be taken when strong tides combine with offshore winds, as canoes and kayaks will be swept out to sea quite quickly. Landing opportunities will change according to the prevailing conditions.

---

1 See pages 1–124.

2 See pages 217–22.

3 See pages 240–42.

safe practice in physical education and school sport

b Local weather forecasts should be obtained – these are available in coastal areas from Marine Call[1]

c Canoes and kayaks, when brightly coloured, are clearly visible. Some form of identification is helpful.

d The materials used to repair canoes and kayaks may be hazardous and great care must be taken when storing and using them for repair work. The chemicals and dust may present a fire risk and, if inhaled, may cause skin irritation or internal damage. Guidance should be sought from the Health and Safety Executive.

e Canoes and kayaks should be fitted with buoyancy. If buoyancy bags are used, these should be firmly secured and distributed at the bow and stern, with 13.5 kilograms of buoyancy at either end, so that in the event of a capsize they remain in place, do not suffer damage or deflation from water pressure and cause the craft to float horizontally.

f Painters, if fitted fore and aft, must be secured to keep them well clear of the cockpit. Toggles are generally preferable.

g Footrests should be substantial and be designed to prevent canoeists from sliding forwards on impact. They should be easily adjustable and should not rotate.

h Spray decks should be used on graded water and the sea. They should be easily removable in the event of a capsize. Pupils must be trained in the removal of spray decks and progressively become accustomed to using them.

i Items to be carried should be packed in waterproof bags or containers, stored so that the trim of the craft is maintained, and secured firmly. Equipment in a kayak must not be packed in the cockpit or stored beside the paddler's legs.

j Any new equipment purchased should conform to current BS EN requirements.

k Waters in and around the United Kingdom are almost always cold. Clothing and footwear should therefore provide adequate warmth and protection from the elements, particularly during extended periods afloat. The following items are essential:

- Lightweight clothing (heavy clothing should never be worn)
- Waterproof anoraks
- Wetsuits (in conditions where hypothermia may occur)
- Hard helmets
- Lightweight footwear (wellingtons should never be worn).

l The condition and suitability of canoes, kayaks, equipment and clothing (eg windproof anoraks, wetsuits, footwear) should be checked.

m During every canoeing or kayaking expedition, group leaders must carry and keep readily available:

- a first aid kit
- a tow line
- distress flares (for sea and open water)
- spare paddles and a spray cover (for kayaks)
- a survival bag

---

1   Refer to the local phone directory for contact details.

- the means for providing hot drinks

- a whistle.

  NB During extended expeditions, each pupil should also carry the items listed above

n Group leaders should carry a mobile phone if there is a reasonable chance of getting a reception.

Organisation

18.3.28 The following points should be considered before embarking on canoeing activities:

a Progressive activities should be provided for beginners. These should start on placid water (eg a swimming pool) and gradually develop pupils' readiness and capabilities to safely take part in increasingly challenging activities.

b The recommended supervision ratio is one qualified adult to approximately eight pupils on placid waters and one qualified adult to approximately six pupils on moving or tidal waters. In both cases, a minimum of two responsible adults is recommended. The condition of the water may necessitate smaller groups of pupils.

c The capsize drill should form an early part of basic training and be practised thoroughly. In the event of a capsize occurring, the following action should be taken:

- The kayak should be left upside down for use as a buoyancy aid.

- The canoeist should remain with the craft unless to do so would be dangerous (eg if drifting towards rocks, a sluice or weir).

- If close to land, the canoeist should move to one end of the craft and tow it to shore by swimming using backstroke.

- In open water, deep-water rescue methods should be employed. The group should have learned and mastered the skills required in practice conditions.

d A signalling system should be agreed with all members of the canoeing party.

e Details of any route to be followed on unsheltered waters (eg a coastal trip), or of any passage across a large area of exposed inland water, should be given to the local coastguard or police. The same authorities must be informed on the party's safe return.

18.3.29 The following points should be considered while on the water:

a The slowest paddlers should go at the front of each group and the slowest groups should go first. (This may need to be modified when on moving water.)

b Care should be taken to ensure that individuals do not become isolated from the group.

c The leader of each group should be positioned according to the wind and current, and to the configuration of the group.

d A leading canoeist and last canoeist should be appointed from among responsible members in each group, whose task it is to ensure that the group stays together.

e An inspection should be carried out at the top of short rapids, from the bank if necessary. If safe to do so, canoeists should then descend the rapids individually and wait at the side in slack water until the whole party is safely through.

f The descent of the group through any rapid should be adequately monitored and controlled.

g Portaging (carrying canoes on land) should be undertaken where the assessed risks of paddling through a rapid are unreasonable.

h Stops should occur in sheltered places and extra clothing should be put on if necessary.

i Mishaps should be dealt with as quickly as possible to prevent the rest of the party from getting cold.

Coasteering

> Please read the general guidance provided in *Part one* of this handbook[1] and paragraphs 18.1.1 to 18.1.47[2], 18.2.33 to 18.2.37[3] and 18.3.1 to 18.3.17[4] before reading this section. This will help to ensure that you have a comprehensive awareness of safe practice issues affecting coasteering activities, OAA and physical education in general.

18.3.30   Coasteering is an emerging activity which is still being developed. It takes place on rock faces located above the sea and involves traversing the rock close to (and sometimes in) the sea. The wide range of skills and techniques employed are similar to those for rock climbing, although the horizontal direction of travel and close presence of the sea provides a varied dimension and challenge. The activity is physically demanding and potentially very hazardous.

People

18.3.31   Coasteering activities must be led by competent and experienced rock climbers, who are thoroughly familiar with the location and route.

Organisation

18.3.32   The following points should be considered in relation to the organisation of coasteering activities:

a Supervision ratios will vary according to the circumstances. In some cases, experienced adults may need to work with pupils on a one-to-one basis.

b Pupils should be made aware of all access and escape routes.

1   See pages 1–124.
2   See pages 217–22.
3   See pages 233–35.
4   See pages 240–42.

Rafting

> Please read the general guidance provided in *Part one* of this handbook[1] and paragraphs 18.1.1 to 18.1.47[2] and 18.3.1 to 18.3.17[3] before reading this section. This will help to ensure that you have a comprehensive awareness of safe practice issues affecting OAA and physical education in general.

18.3.33   Rafting is an increasingly popular activity. It may be used to provide either task-centred learning exercises (task-centred rafting) or experience of paddling inflatables on white water rivers (white water rafting). In both cases, it is essential that all potential hazards are identified and managed accordingly.

Task-centred rafting

People

18.3.34   Group leaders should be experienced in construction techniques, since constructed rafts will distort when placed on the water and care will be needed to avoid entrapment.

Context

18.3.35   The following points should be considered in relation to the context in which task-centred rafting activities take place:

a   The construction criteria used should include safety advice.

b   The materials used should be suitable for the purpose.

Organisation

18.3.36   The following points should be considered in relation to the organisation of task-centred rafting activities:

a   Safety boats are advisable on open stretches of water.

b   Appropriate procedures should be followed in the event of a capsize or emergency.

White water rafting

> Please read paragraphs 18.3.25 to 18.3.29[4] in addition to this section. This will help to ensure that you have a comprehensive awareness of safe practice issues affecting white water rafting.

1   See pages 1–124.
2   See pages 217–22.
3   See pages 240–42.
4   See pages 244–47.

People

18.3.37 Group leaders should be highly qualified and very knowledgeable about the waters to be used and the nature, location and management of all known hazards. Group leaders are recommended to obtain the British Canoe Union Raft Guide Award.

Organisation

18.3.38 Appropriate procedures should be followed in the event of a capsize or emergency.

Rowing

> Please read the general guidance provided in *Part one* of this handbook[1] and paragraphs 18.1.1 to 18.1.47[2] and 18.3.1 to 18.3.17[3] before reading this section. This will help to ensure that you have a comprehensive awareness of safe practice issues affecting OAA and physical education in general.

18.3.39 Rowing is a strenuous activity and care should be taken to ensure that pupils are thoroughly physically prepared for it.

People

18.3.40 Advice on training and qualifications for those leading or instructing rowing can be obtained from LEAs and the relevant NGB[4].

Context

18.3.41 The following points should be considered in relation to the context in which rowing activities take place:

a Group leaders are responsible for ensuring that the conditions for rowing are appropriate.

b A named person should be put in charge of the boat.

c Suitable equipment should be used.

d Life jackets/personal buoyancy aids should be worn, particularly when young rowers are involved.

Organisation

18.3.42 The following points should be considered in relation to the organisation of rowing activities:

a Before being allowed on the water, pupils should be fully briefed on:

• local navigation rules

• the effects of currents, weirs, sluices and winds

• the rights and customs of other water users.

---

1 See pages 1–124.
2 See pages 217–22.
3 See pages 240–42.
4 Amateur Rowing Association, Irish Amateur Rowing Union, Scottish Amateur Rowing Association and Welsh Amateur Rowing Association as appropriate.

b Practical experience should be provided, at an appropriate stage, of emergency procedures in the event of a capsize or other accidents while rowing.

Sailing

Please read the general guidance provided in *Part one* of this handbook[1] and paragraphs 18.1.1 to 18.1.47[2] and 18.3.1 to 18.3.17[3] before reading this section. This will help to ensure that you have a comprehensive awareness of safe practice issues affecting OAA and physical education in general.

18.3.43   Sailing is a long-established, traditional activity which has become a core feature of many OAA programmes. It can be undertaken individually (eg solo handling of small craft) or in groups (eg group handling of large sailing vessels). The physical skills required are complemented by those of thoughtful planning, communication and leadership in an activity which promotes awareness of, and respect for, the natural environment.

People

18.3.44   The following points should be considered in relation to the people involved in sailing activities:

a Advice on training and qualifications for those leading or instructing sailing can be obtained from the Royal Yachting Association (RYA) and the National Schools Sailing Association. The RYA Dinghy Instructor Award is the benchmark qualification for leading sailing activities.

b Power boat drivers should hold at least the RYA Power Boat Level 2 qualification. For sea activity, they should also hold a coastal endorsement.

c All sailing instructors should be experienced in first aid, including:

- administering expired-air resuscitation

- dealing with severe bleeding

- recognising hypothermia at an early stage and taking preventative measures

- treating shock, concussion and fractures.

NB RYA instructor awards are only valid when supported by a current first aid certificate.

Context

18.3.45   The following points should be considered in relation to the context in which sailing activities take place:

a All dinghies should be checked to ensure that they are seaworthy and have adequate secure buoyancy and emergency equipment.

b Appropriate, warm clothing should be worn and protected by waterproofs when necessary. At certain times of the year and in cooler weather, wetsuits may be required for some forms of sailing.

---

1   See pages 1–124.

2   See pages 217–22.

3   See pages 240–42.

safe practice in physical education and school sport

Organisation

18.3.46   The following points should be considered before embarking on sailing activities:

a   The number of pupils per dinghy during instruction should be in line with recommendations in the RYA *Principal's Pack*[1].

b   The probability of capsizing is always high when dinghy sailing. Capsize procedures should be practised as a part of training, along with techniques for righting the dinghy, sailing on and bailing water. In the event of a capsize which cannot be righted, all pupils should remain with their boats and be accounted for as soon as possible.

c   If larger dinghies, which may not be practical to capsize, are used (eg *day* boats), a thorough risk assessment based on a limited practical scenario should be carried out.

d   Arrangements should be made for an appropriately equipped and manned safety boat to accompany the fleet[2].

e   If sailing in open coastal or tidal waters, comprehensive details of the fleet and itinerary should be left with the coastguard.

f   All pupils should be informed of the agreed sailing area and the group recall signal.

18.3.47   The following points should be considered when on the water:

a   The sailing area should be well defined and known and observed by all involved.

b   A simple code of easily visible and/or audible signals should be understood and used by all involved.

c   Instructors should determine the need to reef sails or otherwise take account of prevailing conditions.

d   Great care should be taken in the event of light winds directly off-shore and a strong outgoing tide, as boats may be taken some distance out to sea and returning to land under sail may prove difficult and laborious.

Sub-aqua activities

> Please read the general guidance provided in *Part one* of this handbook[3] and paragraphs 18.1.1 to 18.1.47[4] and 18.3.1 to 18.3.17[5] before reading this section. This will help to ensure that you have a comprehensive awareness of safe practice issues affecting OAA and physical education in general.

18.3.48   Underwater exploration often begins with snorkelling, but the use of breathing apparatus with appropriate techniques provides greater scope for enthusiastic divers. As with all water-based activities, basic safety requirements must be followed.

---

1   Contact the RYA for a copy of the latest version.

2   Advice on suitable safety boats can be obtained from the RYA.

3   See pages 1–124.

4   See pages 217–22.

5   See pages 240–42.

People

18.3.49   The following points should be considered in relation to the people involved in sub-aqua activities:

   a Advice on training and qualifications for those leading or instructing sub-aqua activities can be obtained from LEAs, the British Sub-Aqua Club (BSAC) and the Professional Association of Diving Instructors.

   b Skippers of boats used by divers should be suitably qualified and experienced. BSAC Diver Coxswain Level III is recommended as a minimum qualification.

   c Snorkellers should be confident swimmers who are able to swim at least 50 metres.

   d Scuba divers should be over 15 years of age and should have taken the BSAC proficiency test.

   e All divers should know and observe the BSAC code of conduct[1].

   f All divers should know rescue and expired-air resuscitation techniques.

   g A rigorous risk assessment should be carried out before pupils with epilepsy, diabetes and certain other medical conditions, which can result in coma, take part in sub-aqua activities.

Context

18.3.50   The following points should be considered in relation to the context in which sub-aqua activities take place:

   a When diving takes place in UK waters, some form of protective clothing (eg drysuit or wetsuit) should be worn.

   b All equipment, including masks, snorkels and aqualungs, should conform to current BS EN requirements.

   c All divers should wear suitable life jackets (carbon dioxide or air inflated).

   d Each aqualung group should use a surface marker buoy.

Organisation

18.3.51   The following points should be considered before embarking on sub-aqua activities (whether in a pool or open water):

   a Recommended supervision ratios are as follows:

	Pool training	**Open water**
Snorkelling	One instructor for up to ten pupils	One instructor for up to four pupils
Aqualung training	One instructor for up to four pupils	One instructor for no more than two pupils

   b Adequate provisions should be made for emergencies (including training in appropriate safety drills).

---

1   A copy of the code of conduct is provided in BSAC's *Diving Instructor's Manual* (see page 256 for full reference details).

18.3.52   The following points should be considered during open water dives:

   a A support boat should always be present, with at least one stand-by diver.

   b The group leader must be satisfied that pupils are sufficiently physically fit and have received appropriate instructions to complete the dive safely.

   c No-one suffering from fatigue, a cold or other infection should be permitted to dive.

   d Divers should normally work in pairs for both snorkelling and aqualung diving.

   e Diving without a partner should only be allowed when a lifeline is used and an experienced diver is present.

Surfing

> Please read the general guidance provided in *Part one* of this handbook[1] and paragraphs 18.1.1 to 18.1.47[2] and 18.3.1 to 18.3.17[3] before reading this section. This will help to ensure that you have a comprehensive awareness of safe practice issues affecting OAA and physical education in general.

18.3.53   Surfing requires the same vigilance as all other water-based activities, whether instructing, supervising or participating.

People

18.3.54   The following points should be considered in relation to the people involved in surfing activities:

   a Group leaders should be appropriately trained and qualified. The British Surfing Association's National Coaching Accreditation Scheme provides a course for surfing instructors. The Surf Life Saving Association and Royal Life Saving Society UK provide specialist training and qualifications in surf life saving and first aid.

   b Pupils should be very able swimmers and capable of swimming strongly for a considerable period of time in rough water conditions.

   c Surfers should be paired with shore-based people who are responsible for observing them.

   d In addition, an active lifeguard should be present at all times.

Context

18.3.55   The following points should be considered in relation to the context in which surfing activities take place:

   a The teaching locations selected should be appropriate for pupils' levels of ability and experience.

   b Pupils should be made aware of local conditions, particularly local surf zones.

   c Boards should have adequate flotation for pupils' varying physiques and levels of fitness.

   d Wetsuits (preferably those which cover the arms and legs) should be worn.

1   See pages 1–124.
2   See pages 217–22.
3   See pages 240–42.

Organisation

18.3.56   The following points should be considered in relation to the organisation of surfing activities:

a The recommended supervision ratio is one instructor to approximately six pupils.

b Surfers should be briefed on, and keep to, the planned incoming and outgoing lane system.

c Surfers should stop surfing as soon as they start to feel tired.

Swimming in open water

Please read the general guidance provided in *Part one* of this handbook[1], *Chapter nineteen: Swimming, diving and lifesaving activities*[2] and paragraphs 18.1.1 to 18.1.47[3] and 18.3.1 to 18.3.17[4] before reading this section. This will help to ensure that you have a comprehensive awareness of safe practice issues affecting swimming activities, OAA and physical education in general.

18.3.57   Swimming in the sea, lakes or rivers is a potentially hazardous and life-threatening activity. It requires very careful risk assessment and must always be adequately supervised.

People

18.3.58   Swimming activities in open water should be supervised by people capable of carrying out rescue resuscitation procedures.

Context

18.3.59   The following points should be considered in relation to the context in which swimming activities in open water take place:

a The condition of the lake or sea bed should not be deemed hazardous for swimming (eg weeds, rocks, underwater obstacles).

b The water should be free from pollution and locally recognised as suitable for swimming.

c Strong and dangerous tidal undertows are often present in attractive shore locations.

d The depth of water can change very rapidly.

e Local knowledge and information provided on markers and signs should always be sought and respected.

f Swimming areas should be clearly defined and pupils briefed and frequently reminded about them.

1   See pages 1–124.
2   See pages 263–75.
3   See pages 217–22.
4   See pages 240–42.

254   2004 edition   **safe practice** in physical education and school sport

Organisation

18.3.60   The following points should be considered in relation to the organisation of swimming activities in open water:

a   Parental consent for swimming in open water should be obtained.

b   School staff should be able to account for all group members at all times (whether swimming or not).

c   Pupils should never swim alone.

d   Weaker swimmers must always keep to areas where they can stand if they need to.

e   Swimmers should be constantly aware of other water users (eg powered boats).

f   Swimming time should be strictly limited in cold water.

g   Diving should not be permitted except from designated diving platforms.

Water-skiing

> Please read the general guidance provided in *Part one* of this handbook[1] and paragraphs 18.1.1 to 18.1.47[2] and 18.3.1 to 18.3.17[3] before reading this section. This will help to ensure that you have a comprehensive awareness of safe practice issues affecting OAA and physical education in general.

18.3.61   Water-skiing and jumping are very specialised, strenuous activities, which usually take place on stretches of water reserved for that purpose. They are potentially hazardous and should only take place in highly controlled conditions under suitably qualified leadership. If older pupils of secondary age should, by choice, have the opportunity to take part in water skiing, they should be both excellent swimmers and physically very fit. School staff are advised to seek advice and guidance from the British Water Ski Federation.

Windsurfing

> Please read the general guidance provided in *Part one* of this handbook[1] and paragraphs 18.1.1 to 18.1.47[2] and 18.3.1 to 18.3.17[3] before reading this section. This will help to ensure that you have a comprehensive awareness of safe practice issues affecting OAA and physical education in general.

People

18.3.62   The RYA Windsurfer Instructor Award is the benchmark qualification for leading windsurfing activities.

---

1   See pages 1–124.
2   See pages 217–22.
3   See pages 240–42.

Context

18.3.63   The following points should be considered in relation to the context in which windsurfing activities take place:

a Land simulators are useful for teaching windsurfing techniques. However, they should be used carefully to ensure safe practice. They should be low, stable and meet RYA standards.

b The use of tethering boards should be considered when working with beginners during the very early stages of learning on water.

c The wearing of wetsuits is recommended in all weather conditions, in order to reduce the likelihood of physical injury. Soft-soled shoes are also recommended for protection purposes.

Organisation

18.3.64   The following points should be considered in relation to the organisation of windsurfing activities:

a The recommended supervision ratio when working with beginners during the very early stages of learning is one qualified adult to approximately six pupils. The number of pupils per qualified adult may be increased when working with more experienced windsurfers. Refer to the RYA *Principal's Pack*[1] for further details.

b Strong wind and tide conditions can take windsurfers a long way in a short time, even when capsized. Rescue craft crew should be vigilant to ensure the safety of windsurfers.

Further reading

- British Sub-Aqua Club (2003) **Diving instructor's manual.** Revision 2. Ellesmere Port, British Sub-Aqua Club

- CCPR, DfES (2003) **Group safety at water margins.** London, CCPR and DfES. Ref no: 0270/2003

- Ellerby, D (2004) **Dive leading**. Ellesmere Port, British Sub-Aqua Club. ISBN 0 9538991 94 1

- RYA (2004) **Guidance notes for inspection of RYA recognised teaching establishments**. Southampton, RYA

1   Contact the RYA for a copy of the latest version.

Risk management

People

- **Pupils should share in the assessment and management of the risks involved**.

- Pupils should be sufficiently physically fit, knowledgeable, skilled and confident to take part in the intended activity.

- Pupils should have the necessary skills and knowledge required to save themselves in the event of an emergency.

- OAA instructors should have an appropriate NGB award and be sufficiently experienced to lead or assist the intended activity.

Context

- The intended location should be compatible with pupils' skills and competences.

- All equipment should be checked and approved prior to use.

- Pupils should be suitably clothed and equipped to keep them relatively warm and dry for the duration of the activity.

Organisation

- Group leaders should obtain a reliable weather forecast, evaluate the consequences of it and, if necessary, adapt the programme of activities.

- Comprehensive information (eg route, activity locations, expected times of arrival) should be left with a responsible adult back at base.

- Group leaders and pupils should be suitably equipped to deal with emergency situations.

▶▶ See *Chapter two: Risk management* for more detailed, general guidance on risk management issues.

Questions and answers

People

Qu 1   **For a number of years, I have organised and led a four-mile walk across low fells for upper Key Stage 2 pupils. The activity takes place during the summer term and is very popular. I have considerable personal experience as a rambler with a group and know this particular terrain very well, but am aware that I hold no formal qualification for leading such walks. Should I continue with this activity?**

Ans   It is essential to consult your employer in the first instance and to check local regulations. Some may insist that a qualification is held.

The issue here is one of competence. This can be based on qualification resulting from formal training and assessment, from personal experience and involvement in an activity, or from working alongside a colleague who is an expert in the field. Often, it will be a combination of these factors which results in competence.

In your case, experience of the activity counts for a lot. Your personal involvement in your rambling group will no doubt have provided you with many varied circumstances on which to exercise judgement. This experience will have direct practical relevance to the activity you undertake with pupils.

Ensure that you carry out an adequate risk assessment of the activity both before and during the walk. Providing you do this, there is no reason why you should not continue to lead the walks. If necessary, a specific evaluation could be made by a technical expert.

Qu 2   **Should I allow pupils who are non- or weak swimmers to participate in water-based activities?**

Ans   It is clearly desirable that pupils who take part in water-based activities should be confident and capable both on and in water, and should be able to cope and stay safe in circumstances, which may foreseeably arise (intentionally or otherwise).

The National Curriculum requirements for swimming are intended to provide pupils with the opportunity to learn to swim and be water safe, thus providing a good foundation for a wider range of activities on and in water. However, some pupils may find swimming difficult and remain non- or weak swimmers. School staff will not wish to deprive such pupils of beneficial water-based experiences, providing the associated safety issues can be successfully assessed and managed.

Life jackets or personal buoyancy aids should be worn regardless of swimming ability, to ensure flotation in water. Wetsuits help to insulate the body and retain body heat, and are recommended for use in cold water. In many cases, lifeguards and manned safety boats are also recommended.

The skills required for water-based activities are best introduced and learned under well controlled conditions, using the warmer water of a swimming pool and shallow water as appropriate. In-water confidence and capability can be developed, and subsequently transferred to other water-based activities.

For all water-based activities, it is essential that safety management arrangements take account of the pupils involved and their varying abilities, the intended activity and the context in which the activity will take place.

Qu 3 **As an experienced teacher and ski course leader, I am planning a ski course abroad for pupils at my school. Interest has been expressed by two pupils who are known to be disruptive and disobedient. How should I proceed?**

Ans This is a difficult situation which must be handled with care and sensitivity. It is recognised that some pupils who cause difficulties in school may behave quite differently in a residential setting where they are motivated by their interest in the activity, and that the experience can have a beneficial effect on their subsequent performance in school.

You have a clear responsibility to your head teacher, the governors and the parents of all the pupils who will be involved, to ensure that the ski course is conducted in a safe and acceptable manner. You must therefore assess the risks associated with any foreseen problems at an early stage. All pupils and their parents should be made aware of the requirements for participation, including acceptance of a code of behaviour with which pupils will be expected to conform during the ski course.

You should draw up a strategy for dealing with the two disruptive pupils and discuss this with your head teacher. The pupils and their parents need to be made fully aware of your concerns and the conditions under which they can take part in the course. This could involve a written agreement on acceptable behaviour in school with continuous monitoring and recording by school staff to ensure that the pupils conform to it. Failure to reasonably comply by either pupil may result in that pupil being excluded from the course.

Skiing is an activity which requires a significant degree of self-control and discipline. You would be unwise to include any pupil on your course who was considered likely to put either him/herself or others at risk through poor behaviour.

Context

Qu 4 **Where can I obtain a reliable weather forecast?**

Ans Weather is a very important factor for outdoor activities. A torrential downpour, sudden snowstorm or appearance of fog can impact significantly, and even tragically, on an outdoor venture. Prior knowledge of anticipated weather conditions is essential in determining the measures required to manage outdoor activities safely. In some cases, this may mean postponing the intended activities altogether and implementing contingency arrangements.

Coastguards are one useful source of reliable weather forecasts, particularly for very localised areas. Weather conditions in coastal regions can vary considerably and this is not always conveyed by national weather predictions. Shipping forecasts are broadcast regularly on the radio and TV, and are an accurate and useful source of information for activities at sea.

Local knowledge of weather patterns can also be useful, but should not be solely relied upon and should be used in conjunction with forecasts from authoritative sources (eg Met Office website).

Organisation

Qu 5 **I intend to take a group of 40 Year 6 pupils (boys and girls) with three other members of school staff and two parent volunteers on a three-day summer residential youth hostelling and walking venture in the Peak District in Derbyshire. I have previous experience as a group leader and have already visited the area and planned the routes in conjunction with the youth hostel warden. Is the venture viable? What general advice do you have on school staff/pupil ratios for such visits and the roles of accompanying parents?**

Ans With the widespread publicity which inevitably accompanies outdoor activity ventures when something goes tragically wrong, it is not surprising that this question has arisen.

You have prepared well for your venture by visiting the location in advance and, by discussing the walking itinerary with the hostel warden, you have benefited from local expertise and knowledge.

Four members of school staff should be adequate to cope in the event of an emergency. Having an even split of male and female staff would help you share your duties equitably, particularly if you are required to deal with an emergency during the night at the hostel. At least one member of school staff should be capable of administering first aid.

You should make sure that the two parents fully understand (and accept) their own role, and that of the party as a whole, before the venture takes place. Their contribution as responsible adults could be very useful. If necessary, disclosure procedures should be followed to ensure that they are suitable to work closely with young people. In addition, you and the other members of school staff will be responsible for managing them during the venture.

Recommended supervision ratios will vary according to the nature of the activities you plan to provide and the pupils involved. For example, for a walk in the countryside on well known, safe terrain where no traffic will be encountered, a ratio of one member of school staff to 15 pupils could be adequate. However, there may be occasions when the risk factor increases and the ratio will need to be adjusted accordingly. A higher ratio of school staff to pupils will be required if pupils with SEN are taking part in the venture. In some cases, one-to-one support (using a responsible adult) may be required. A further consideration may be to split the pupils into two groups, each of which would operate independently of the other and should be appropriately led.

Regardless of the number of pupils, the minimum staffing requirement is two. This could be a member of school staff plus a carefully chosen responsible adult, who have a clear understanding and acceptance of their respective roles, especially in the event of a foreseeable emergency. For a party of boys and girls, the minimum staffing requirement is one male and one female.

In the first instance, you should submit your complete planning schedule (including a risk assessment) to your head teacher and school governors for approval. You should also obtain written parental consent for all the pupils taking part in the venture.

Qu 6   **Who should I inform when embarking on a sea or long-range water expedition?**

Ans   It is very important to leave comprehensive details about any outdoor venture, which involves a trek or expedition, back at base, especially one which takes place on water. Details should include the size and composition of the party, means of travel (eg canoes), place and time of departure, intended route and place and expected time of return.

The details should be left with a responsible adult who will be able to take appropriate emergency action if necessary. It would also be advisable to inform the local coastguard in case a lifeboat or helicopter search is required.

Care must be taken to ensure that the same people are informed as soon as possible after the safe return of the party. This will avoid unnecessary and expensive emergency action being taken.

Qu 7   **What specific advice would you give to a party leader on planning a residential visit to a commercial centre, which has not been used by the school before, and where the activities are led and conducted by instructors employed by that centre?**

Ans   The first step is to find out whether any schools in your area have used the commercial centre before and, if so, to ask a selection of them for copies of the evaluations of their visits. If these prove satisfactory or better, the school staff leader and deputy leader at your school are highly recommended to visit the centre before any firm booking is made. This will enable them to assess the suitability of the premises, fire risks and evacuation procedures.

During this preliminary visit, a suitable programme of proposed activities could be drawn up, with due regard to the age, experience, ability and any SEN of the pupils who will take part in the visit. This should include contingency arrangements in case the main programme is adversely affected by factors such as inclement weather. The centre's instructors should be involved in this process or, at the very least, arrange for a representative to be present to discuss your school's requirements. You should ensure that the centre is licensed by the Adventure Activities Licensing Authority to offer OAA (eg sailing, canoeing, caving, climbing).

The question of whether or not the centre's instructors should take sole charge of groups of pupils may arise. You are strongly advised to ensure that a member of school staff (or responsible adult within the party who knows the pupils) accompanies each group. This will help to ensure that duty of care is fulfilled.

You should ensure that all aspects of the visit are planned in accordance with your school's policy on residential visits and advice provided by your Educational Visits Coordinator.

safe practice in physical education and school sport

Chapter nineteen

Swimming, diving and lifesaving activities

19.1 Swimming activities

> Please read the general guidance provided in *Part one* of this handbook[1] before reading this chapter. This will help to ensure that you have a comprehensive awareness of safe practice issues affecting swimming activities and physical education in general.

19.1.1 Swimming can be enjoyed by people of all ages and has many health benefits. Learning to swim provides the essential foundation for many other water-based activities and is appropriately included in the National Curriculum. It is essential that as many young people as possible are taught basic swimming skills.

19.1.2 Due to the evident risk of drowning, great care must be taken by all involved in the teaching and learning of swimming and water safety.

19.1.3 This section focuses on swimming in swimming pools. Additional considerations should be taken into account when swimming in open water.

▶▶ See *Chapter eighteen: Outdoor and adventurous activities* for guidance on swimming in open water.

People

19.1.4 The Health and Safety at Work Act 1974 places responsibilities on swimming pool owners, managers and users to establish sound procedures which reasonably ensure that swimming activities are carried out safely.

▶▶ See *Chapter one: Physical education and the law* for further information about The Health and Safety at Work Act 1974.

1   See pages 1–124.

19.1.5   Schools often use swimming pools on premises other than their own. By law, pool managers must ensure that their facilities are safe and present no risks to the health and well-being of visiting groups. The same applies when schools use swimming pools belonging to other schools. These are regarded in law as a place of work under the responsibility of the host school.

19.1.6   Specialist swimming teachers may be employed by schools or local education authorities (LEAs) to assist with swimming sessions and provide essential lifesaving cover. Their role is to complement the skills and experience of school staff in the safe delivery of a swimming programme. However, the overall responsibility for pupils remains with school staff at all times. Similarly, school staff are responsible for monitoring the progress of pupils, regardless of who leads the swimming sessions.

19.1.7   It is essential that school staff and swimming teachers enjoy a good working relationship and that they communicate effectively with each other.

19.1.8   School staff responsible for the delivery of programmed aquatic activities in swimming pools[1] should be aware of Health and Safety Executive (HSE) recommendations on appropriate lifesaving and lifeguard qualifications for swimming teachers, coaches and lifeguards.

19.1.9   It is recommended that those directly responsible for the supervision of swimming pools hold a current, nationally recognised pool lifeguard qualification, such as the Royal Life Saving Society UK (RLSS UK) National Pool Lifeguard Qualification. This is jointly recognised by the Amateur Swimming Association (ASA), the RLSS UK, the Institute of Swimming Teachers and Coaches and the Swimming Teachers' Association (STA).

19.1.10   It is recommended that swimming teachers and school staff responsible for classes hold appropriate ASA, STA and RLSS UK teaching and lifesaving awards. However, it should be remembered that these may not indicate up-to-date competence in lifesaving, unless they are renewed on a regular basis. Employers should ensure that swimming teachers and school staff are offered frequent opportunities to obtain and update relevant qualifications.

19.1.11   When swimming activities take place in school swimming pools, pupils must always be supervised by qualified adults. It is recommended that school staff responsible for the safety of a programmed session (eg swimming lesson) hold a current swimming pool lifesaving award, such as the National Rescue Award for Swimming Teachers and Coaches.

19.1.12   School staff/swimming teachers should regularly practise their previously learned lifesaving skills.

19.1.13   In addition to recognised lifesaving qualifications, specialist knowledge is required to supervise activities such as canoeing and scuba diving in swimming pools.

▶▶   See *Chapter eighteen: Outdoor and adventurous activities* for further information about these and other water-based activities.

---

1   A programmed aquatic activity has a formal structure and is supervised, controlled and continuously monitored from the poolside. Examples include school swimming lessons, coaching sessions and other relevant tuition.

19.1.14   It is essential that pupils are well behaved during all swimming activities. School staff/swimming teachers should explain the required procedures and reasons for them.

19.1.15   Pupils should be encouraged to look out for, and report, unacceptable behaviour, particularly when safety may be compromised.

19.1.16   Pupils should share in the assessment and management of the risks associated with swimming activities. This is an essential part of the learning process. Due to different abilities, the risk management process should be applied to individual pupils, to pupil groups and to the class as a whole.

Context

Facility

19.1.17   Leisure pools (particularly those with special water features and irregular shapes) may have potential supervisory blind spots. These should be checked regularly.

19.1.18   The water temperature should be approximately 29°C to ensure that pupils are comfortable and do not become cold during swimming sessions. The ambient air temperature should be slightly above that of the water to avoid condensation.

19.1.19   Pool depths and any potential risks should be clearly indicated on signs on the walls. School staff/swimming teachers should explain their significance to pupils, especially beginners. All signs must conform to the appropriate British Standards European Norm (BS EN) requirements and be clear to pupils who may have difficulty reading them.

19.1.20   If non-swimmers are present, a pool divider (usually a rope) should be positioned to mark shallow and deep water areas.

19.1.21   The water should be sufficiently clear to ensure that the bottom of the pool is visible at all depths.

19.1.22   Glare across the water surface from natural or artificial light may restrict visibility to the bottom of the pool. In these circumstances, it may be necessary for those supervising to move around the pool (or take other appropriate action) in order to maintain maximum visual awareness.

19.1.23   Swimming pool managers should ensure that outlet pipes at the bottom of the pool are covered by securely fastened grilles. The holes in the grilles should not be large enough for fingers to become trapped.

19.1.24   Entrance doors to school pools should be kept locked when the pool is not in use.

Standard operating procedures

19.1.25   Standard operating procedures should be written for all swimming pools in conjunction with the swimming teachers, coaches, school staff and all others who accompany groups of pupils to swimming pools. Standard operating procedures are simply day-to-day organisational systems based on risk assessment and typically include the following information:

     a   Responsibility for safety

     b   Staffing levels and qualifications

     c   Pool design and depth

     d   Potential areas of risk

     e   Pool safety and equipment

     f   Water quality

     g   Clothing and equipment

     h   First aid provision

     i   Supervision and pupil conduct

     j   Maximum numbers

     k   Arrangements for swimming sessions

     l   Arrangements for pupils with particular needs (eg very young pupils, pupils with special educational needs (SEN) or medical conditions).

19.1.26   All those responsible for the safety of pupils using a swimming pool (whether during curriculum time or out-of-school-hours learning (OSHL) activities) should be aware of, and follow, the standard operating procedures of the pool being used. These may vary according to the particular circumstances of the pool and the pupils involved.

19.1.27   Standard operating procedures should be reviewed on a regular basis in order to maintain up-to-date, consistently applied standards of practice.

Emergency procedures

19.1.28   A risk assessment should be carried out to identify foreseeable emergencies. An emergency action plan should subsequently be written, outlining who is responsible for managing emergencies and the action to be taken in the event of circumstances such as those listed below:

     a   Serious injury to a swimmer

     b   Dealing with casualties in the water

     c   Sudden overcrowding in a public pool

     d   Sudden lack of water clarity

     e   Outbreak of public disorder

     f   Emergency evacuation in the event of a:

        •   fire alarm

        •   bomb threat

        •   power failure

        •   structural failure

        •   toxic gas emission.

19.1.29　　Adequate lifesaving equipment, buoyancy aids and first aid equipment (including a blanket) should be readily accessible.

19.1.30　　Special stretchers for recovering patients (especially those who may have suffered head and/or neck injuries) are available and are strongly recommended. School staff and those on poolside duty should know how to assemble and use them.

19.1.31　　A phone providing direct contact with the emergency services should be available and made known to everyone.

19.1.32　　All those responsible for the safety of pupils using a swimming pool (whether during curriculum time or OSHL activities) should be aware of, and follow, the emergency action plan of the pool being used.

19.1.33　　Standard emergency procedures should be practised at regular intervals (eg each term). Evacuation of the pool should be initiated by a specified signal (both audible and visual), with which all adults and pupils are familiar.

Equipment and clothing

19.1.34　　School staff/swimming teachers should check that all lifesaving equipment is adequate, in good condition and readily accessible.

19.1.35　　Goggles or masks should only be worn in exceptional circumstances when chemicals in the water may adversely affect pupils' eyes. Any goggles or masks used should be made of unbreakable plastic or rubber. Pupils should be taught to remove them by slipping them off their head, rather than by stretching the retaining band.

19.1.36　　Pupils should wear appropriate swimwear. If, for cultural and/or religious reasons, pupils are allowed into the water in clothing other than usual swimwear, they should be restricted to shallow water until they have shown that they are able to swim competently. School staff are advised to liaise with relevant community leaders about special clothing requirements.

19.1.37　　All personal effects should be removed or made safe prior to taking part in any swimming activity.

19.1.38　　The chewing of food, sweets or gum immediately before or during swimming activities should never be allowed. Chewing can result in choking, which can have serious, even fatal, consequences.

Organisation

National governing body directives

19.1.39　　National governing bodies (NGBs) sometimes issue directives concerning the safe management of swimming activities. When a competition takes place under the remit of an NGB (eg affiliated competitions), any relevant directives should be considered as rules, which need to be followed. However, NGBs have no authoritative remit in the context of the National Curriculum, OSHL activities or friendly competitions. In these circumstances, NGB directives have the same status as that of this handbook – well intentioned guidance which managing staff should consider in relation to their particular situation.

Adult/pupil ratios

19.1.40   Safe adult/pupil ratios should be determined by swimming pool owners/operators/occupiers under the terms of the Health and Safety at Work Act 1974 and The Management of Health and Safety in the Workplace Regulations 1999.

> ▶▶ See *Chapter one: Physical education and the law* for further information about The Health and Safety at Work Act 1974 and The Management of Health and Safety in the Workplace Regulations 1999.

19.1.41   As swimming pool designs and environments vary greatly, it is not possible to give a definitive set of adult/pupil ratios. For example, shallow learner pools are much easier to supervise than large public pools, where the presence of public swimmers can present problems. However, in all cases, adequate supervision must always be provided by adults capable of carrying out rescue and cardio-pulmonary resuscitation procedures. Changing rooms must also be adequately supervised.

19.1.42   In order to determine appropriate adult/pupil ratios for specific situations, thorough risk assessments must be carried out based on the people (ie adults and pupils), context and organisation involved. The adult/pupil ratio should be such that it safely meets the varying risks imposed by these three factors. Any local (eg LEA) requirements must be met.

19.1.43   Consideration should be given as to whether pupils will have sole or shared use of the pool. The HSE has clearly identified that swimmers are substantially less at risk when taking part in programmed activities compared to swimming during public sessions in public pools. If pupils will share the pool with public swimmers, school staff/swimming teachers should ensure that the associated implications for supervision and overall responsibility are satisfactorily addressed.

General considerations

19.1.44   Pupils must be registered or counted both before and after all swimming sessions. It is also a good idea to carry out regular head counts throughout sessions, particularly when young pupils are involved.

19.1.45   Pupils should be informed about standard procedures, deep and shallow water, and relevant notices both before and at the start of their first visit to the pool. They should also be reminded at the start of all subsequent visits.

19.1.46   Pupils should be encouraged to carry out the usual hygiene procedures before entering the water.

19.1.47   Pupils should not be permitted to run on the pool surrounds.

19.1.48   School staff/swimming teachers should be able to see all the pupils throughout the swimming session.

19.1.49   Apart from in emergencies, school staff/swimming teachers should not enter the water if this would leave no supervising adult on the poolside.

19.1.50   Pupils should be taught to report any mishaps to school staff/swimming teachers. It is a good idea to operate a *buddy* system whereby pupils are paired up and required to check on the well-being of their partners at regular intervals.

Special considerations

Very young pupils

19.1.51   Infants and young primary pupils are best taught in shallow water beginner pools and with appropriate floatation aids.

19.1.52   Care should be taken when teaching very young non-swimmers who are unable to touch the bottom of the pool. The pupils should wear appropriate floatation aids to ensure confidence. Additional adult support in the water may be considered according to the age, ability and confidence of the pupils involved.

Pupils with special educational needs

19.1.53   When pupils with SEN take part in swimming activities, the class size may have to be reduced to take account of the age, ability, confidence, specific needs and experience of the pupils involved. This decision should be based on risk assessment.

▶▶   See *Chapter ten: Pupils with special educational needs or medical needs* for further information about teaching pupils with SEN.

Pupils with medical conditions

19.1.54   Written parental consent must be obtained before pupils with serious medical conditions are allowed to participate in school swimming programmes.

19.1.55   Pupils with epilepsy require careful observation, as shimmering water or flickering light may trigger a seizure. It is good practice to establish a *buddy* system of observation or, in severe cases, to have a responsible adult in the water.

▶▶   See *Chapter ten: Pupils with special educational needs or medical needs* for further information about teaching pupils with medical needs.

19.2   Diving activities

> Please read the general guidance provided in *Part one* of this handbook[1] and paragraphs 19.1.1 to 19.1.55[2] before reading this section. This will help to ensure that you have a comprehensive awareness of safe practice issues affecting swimming and diving activities, and physical education in general.

1   See pages 1–124.
2   See pages 263–69.

19.2.1 Diving, by its very nature, can be dangerous and a number of serious diving accidents have been recorded in recent years. Safe practice is essential to avoid such accidents reoccurring.

19.2.2 This section focuses on diving in swimming pools. Diving should not be permitted when swimming in open water except from designated diving platforms.

▶▶ For further information about scuba diving and other sub-aqua activities, see paragraphs 18.3.48 to 18.3.52[1].

People

19.2.3 Diving sessions should be supervised by school staff or specialist swimming teachers who are thoroughly familiar with current diving techniques and practices.

Context

19.2.4 When diving forms part of swimming sessions, the water depth should ideally be at least full standing height plus arms and fingers fully extended. However, very few existing swimming pools can meet this requirement for adults or tall children. If this is the case, the deepest water available should be used (at least 1.8 metres deep) and great care taken to ensure that dives are performed safely.

19.2.5 Areas appropriate for diving should be clearly signposted.

19.2.6 Appropriate warning signs should be clearly displayed and regularly drawn to pupils' attention.

19.2.7 Pupils should be thoroughly familiar with the diving environment. Diving should never take place in unknown waters.

19.2.8 The pool freeboard (ie the distance from the poolside to the surface of the water) should be less than 0.38 metres high.

19.2.9 A sufficient area of forward clearance (ie the horizontal distance over which the minimum depth of water is maintained) is required.

19.2.10 Diving areas should be clearly designated and controlled.

19.2.11 To avoid the risk of collision during simultaneous dives, there should be:

a sufficient pool space

b sufficient forward clearance (ie the horizontal distance over which the minimum depth of water is maintained)

c no underwater obstructions.

Organisation

19.2.12   The number of pupils should be sufficiently low to allow school staff/specialist swimming teachers to observe all divers.

19.2.13   No other swimmers should be allowed in or through the diving area while diving is in progress.

19.2.14   Great care should be taken to ensure that dives are performed safely.

19.2.15   Prolonged underwater swimming after a dive should be discouraged.

Jumping into water

19.2.16   Care should be taken when jumping feet-first into shallow water, as the feet may strike the bottom of the pool with force, causing damage to the arches of the feet. Generally, entry into water, which is less than 1.5 metres deep, is best effected from a sitting position on the side of the pool.

Plunge diving

19.2.17   All pupils should be taught to perform a plunge dive from the side of the pool and understand when to use it. It is important to ensure that any pupils taking part in a competitive swimming race, which starts with a plunge dive, are competent enough to do so safely, especially when starting blocks will be used.

19.2.18   Pupils should not be allowed to dive from starting blocks or the side of the pool unless there is a minimum depth of 1.5 metres, until they have demonstrated the ability to perform an efficient, competitive start.

19.2.19   The minimum water depth required for vertical entries or a tuck dive or back dive is three metres. Pupils should be taught the technique of extending the hands at the wrists immediately after entry, in order to level and raise the body to the surface.

Board diving

19.2.20   Only one diver should be allowed on any part of the board at any one time.

19.2.21   Before performing a dive, both the diver and the adult supervisor should check that the water is clear of swimmers and obstructions.

19.2.22   Board divers should demonstrate their competence at lower levels before progressing to higher levels.

19.3   Lifesaving activities

Please read the general guidance provided in *Part one* of this handbook[1] and paragraphs 19.1.1 to 19.1.55[2] before reading this section. This will help to ensure that you have a comprehensive awareness of safe practice issues affecting swimming and lifesaving activities, and physical education in general.

19.3.1   Only reaching and throwing rescues should be taught to pupils under the age of eight.

19.3.2   Contact rescues should not be taught to pupils under the age of 14.

19.3.3   RLSS UK can provide advice and associated guidance on appropriate lifesaving awards for the different Key Stages in primary and secondary education.

Further reading

- HSE (2003) **Managing health and safety in swimming pools**. 3rd edition. Sudbury, HSE Books. ISBN 0 7176 2686 5

- Institute of Sport and Recreation Management (2001) **Safe supervision for teaching and coaching of swimming**. 2nd edition. Loughborough, Institute of Sport and Recreation Management. ISBN 1 900 738 16 3

Risk management

People

- **Pupils should share in the assessment and management of the risks involved.**
- School staff/swimming teachers should be suitably qualified and experienced.
- School staff/swimming teachers should have a sound knowledge of pupils':
  - ability
  - behaviour patterns
  - medical conditions
  - confidence levels.
- Effective communication between school staff/swimming teachers and pool staff is essential.

Context

- School staff/swimming teachers and pupils should be familiar with the layout of the facilities being used.
- The water clarity and temperature should be checked before the start of swimming sessions.
- Pool depths and any potential risks should be clearly signposted and pupils' attention drawn to them.
- Rescue equipment and teaching aids should be readily accessible.

Organisation

- Group sizes should be appropriate.
- Additional supervision should be provided where necessary.
- Activity levels should be appropriate for the pupils involved.
- The same high level of supervision required in structured swimming sessions should also apply to informal play activity sessions.
- Regular head counts should be carried out (ie onto and off the poolside, and during swimming sessions).
- School staff/swimming teachers should regularly scan the whole pool.
- Teaching positions should enable observation of maximum numbers and maximum space.
- School staff/swimming teachers should be able to see the bottom of the pool at all times.
- Pupils should be monitored for signs of fatigue, stress, fear and cold.
- Emergency signals, procedures and equipment should be known and applied by everyone involved.
- School staff/swimming teachers should walk around the pool at the end of swimming session.

  ▶▶ See *Chapter two: Risk management* for more detailed, general guidance on risk management issues.

Questions and answers

Organisation

Qu 1　**As the only member of school staff responsible for a class of eight-year-old pupils at a public swimming pool, I am concerned that I cannot supervise the boys' changing rooms adequately. What should I do?**

Ans　Ideally, a male and female member of staff should accompany each class in order to fully supervise the changing rooms. However, due to staffing pressures, this may not be possible and an adult volunteer of the appropriate gender may be used. He/she may need disclosure clearance to ensure that he/she is suitable to supervise pupils getting changed.

If neither of these suggestions is feasible, it may be possible to arrange for pool staff to supervise the other changing rooms. Formal arrangements should be made with the pool manager.

If this suggestion is not feasible and you are the only suitable adult present, it is essential to at least establish procedures for dealing with any emergencies that may arise in the other changing rooms. You will also need to be able to trust them to behave appropriately. For example, you could arrange for one of the pupils to alert you outside the changing rooms, so that you could subsequently enter the other changing rooms to deal with the situation.

If none of these suggestions are acceptable, it may be necessary to combine classes and take single gender groups, providing appropriate staffing is available.

Qu 2　**I have been told that there are set ratios of school staff/swimming teachers to pupils for teaching swimming. Must I follow these? What happens if the number of pupils in my group is one greater than the set ratio?**

Ans　If your employer (eg governors, LEA) sets specific ratios, you must follow them.

Some NGBs recommend maximum ratios. Although this is well-intentioned guidance, it does not take into account the varying circumstances school staff/swimming teachers may encounter.

You should carry out a risk assessment based on the people (ie school staff/swimming teachers and pupils), context and organisation involved in your swimming sessions. From this, you should be able to determine an appropriate maximum ratio for your specific circumstances.

For example, a confident swimming teacher with a well-behaved group of non-swimmers, using a well-equipped, shallow pool, may feel able to manage more than 12 pupils safely by him/herself. However, the same person, with the same group and the same resources, is likely to want to significantly reduce the number of pupils if the swimming session will take place in a large, steeply shelving pool, which will be shared with the public.

If possible, it is advisable for an additional adult to be present on the poolside, even if they just act as a *second pair of eyes*.

safe practice in physical education and school sport

Qu 3   **How soon after a meal (eg sandwiches or school dinners at lunch time) should pupils be allowed to take part in swimming activities?**

Ans   It is wise to allow a reasonable amount of time after the end of a meal before pupils are allowed to enter the water. This will enable them to digest their food sufficiently and minimise the risk of vomiting during the swimming session, which could be life threatening if their airway became blocked.

If a swimming session takes place immediately after the midday lunch break, it is advisable for pupils to eat lightly and as early as possible to allow sufficient time for them to digest their food before the start of the swimming session.

Chapter twenty

Educational visits

> Please read the general guidance provided in *Part one* of this handbook[1] and paragraphs 18.1.1 to 18.1.47[2] before reading this chapter. This will help to ensure that you have a comprehensive awareness of safe practice issues affecting educational visits and physical education in general.

20.1 Introduction

20.1.1 Educational visits are a valuable part of school life. They take many forms and have the potential to deliver a range of educational objectives relating to learning, skill acquisition and cultural and personal development. BAALPE endorses the detailed guidance provided in the Department for Education and Skills (DfES) document *Health and Safety of Pupils on Educational Visits* and related supplements[3].

20.1.2 Schools are strongly recommended to nominate a competent member of school staff trained as an Educational Visits Coordinator to oversee and monitor the arrangements for all educational visits in their school, including outdoor and adventurous activities (OAA).

20.1.3 All forms of educational visits require sound planning and organisation, regardless of whether or not they involve potentially hazardous activities. It should be remembered that an element of risk is always associated with any off-site activity.

▶▶ A range of useful forms relating to educational visits are provided in Appendices 2, 3, 7 and 8.

20.1.4 Figure 3 on page 278 summarises the main considerations that should be applied to any proposed educational visit. School staff are strongly recommended to refer to the diagram when planning educational visits, as it will greatly assist the risk assessment and management process which is central to pupil safety and well-being.

20.1.5 Many educational visits involve OAA for which activity leaders are usually required to hold an appropriate national governing body qualification. In these circumstances, school staff should consider a wide range of specific safety issues in addition to those outlined in Figure 3 on page 278.

▶▶ See *Chapter eighteen: Outdoor and adventurous activities* for further guidance.

1 See pages 1–124.
2 See pages 217–22.
3 See page 280 for full reference details.

Figure 3: Safe practice on educational visits

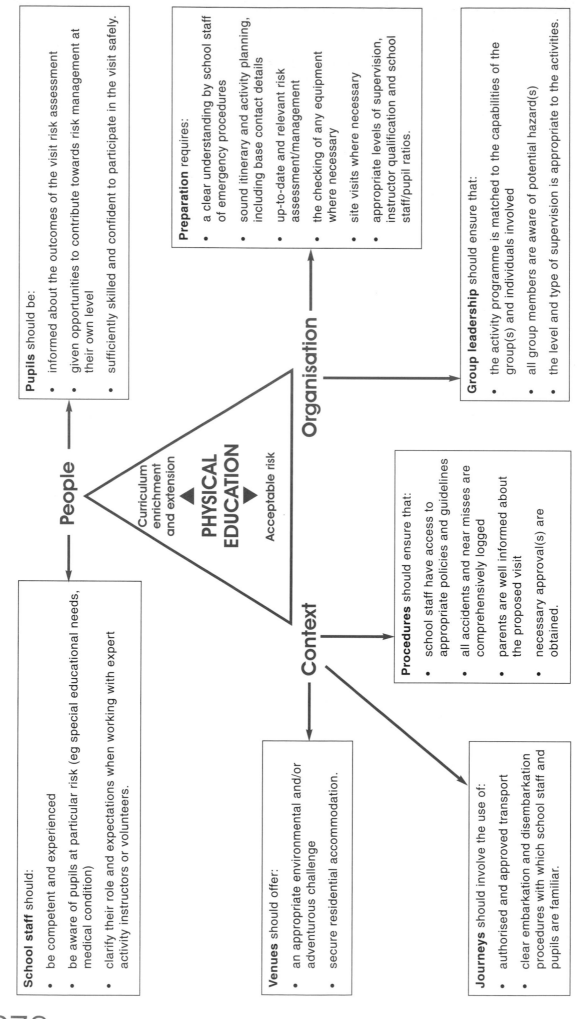

School staff should:
- be competent and experienced
- be aware of pupils at particular risk (eg special educational needs, medical condition)
- clarify their role and expectations when working with expert activity instructors or volunteers.

Pupils should be:
- informed about the outcomes of the visit risk assessment
- given opportunities to contribute towards risk management at their own level
- sufficiently skilled and confident to participate in the visit safely.

People

PHYSICAL EDUCATION

Curriculum enrichment and extension ◄ ► Acceptable risk

Organisation

Preparation requires:
- a clear understanding by school staff of emergency procedures
- sound itinerary and activity planning, including base contact details
- up-to-date and relevant risk assessment/management
- the checking of any equipment where necessary
- site visits where necessary
- appropriate levels of supervision, instructor qualification and school staff/pupil ratios.

Group leadership should ensure that:
- the activity programme is matched to the capabilities of the group(s) and individuals involved
- all group members are aware of potential hazard(s)
- the level and type of supervision is appropriate to the activities.

Context

Venues should offer:
- an appropriate environmental and/or adventurous challenge
- secure residential accommodation.

Journeys should involve the use of:
- authorised and approved transport
- clear embarkation and disembarkation procedures with which school staff and pupils are familiar.

Procedures should ensure that:
- school staff have access to appropriate policies and guidelines
- all accidents and near misses are comprehensively logged
- parents are well informed about the proposed visit
- necessary approval(s) are obtained.

20.2   Residential settings

20.2.1   School staff have a duty of care for the pupils in their charge, which applies 24 hours a day, extending beyond the main activity schedule to include unprogrammed time and night-time.

Arrangements should be made to provide continuous supervision during the day and evening, and for the action to be taken in the event of an emergency during the night.

Bedrooms should provide adequate space and storage for pupils, without overcrowding.

Lighting should be provided in dark areas to enable pupils to pass through them safely.

Pupils should be made familiar with the interior of the building and the immediate surrounds to which they will have access during their stay as soon as possible after arrival.

Care should be taken to ensure that the proprietor/manager of the residential building has taken all possible fire precautions and that adequate evacuation procedures are in place.

All members of the party should be familiar with accident and emergency procedures for fire and personal accident. A fire drill should be practised on arrival at the residential building or as soon as possible afterwards.

It is essential to ensure that adequate security arrangements are made in relation to the accommodation provided in the residential building. If the school party will have sole use of the building, it should be possible to lock the outer doors. If this is not feasible, school staff should:

a   consider the location of the reception area in relation to the main exits

b   consider the location of the school staff's bedrooms in relation to the pupils' bedrooms and the main exits

c   ensure that pupils' bedroom doors are not locked at night in case of the need for emergency evacuation

d   inform pupils of the location of the school staff's bedrooms

e   encourage pupils to inform them of any strangers seen in the residential building.

Overseas ventures

Educational visits include planned ventures abroad, the organisation of which requires particular care and attention.

Overseas ventures must meet UK emergency procedure requirements.

20.3.3   Reciprocal health insurance arrangements can be arranged for overseas ventures to European Union countries, providing the essential paperwork is carried out well beforehand. The appropriate Government department[1] will provide the necessary information and forms.

---

1   Currently the Department of Health.

20.3.4   Collective passports are suitable for group travel. Advice from the United Kingdom Passport Service should be sought well in advance of the overseas venture, as some pupils may not qualify for inclusion under Home Office regulations and special arrangements may be necessary in individual cases.

20.3.5   Visas may be required to visit some countries or for some individual pupils. Advice from the appropriate consulate office should be sought well in advance of the overseas venture.

20.3.6   Vaccinations may be required to visit some countries. Advice from local health authorities should be sought well in advance of the overseas venture.

20.3.7   When external agents or tour operators are used, school staff should ensure that they are reputable, that they meet relevant statutory requirements (including financial bonding arrangements) and that they are able to fully satisfy the school's duty of care requirements.

Further reading

- BAALPE, DfES, NCSS (2004) **Guidance on the organisation of inter-school fixtures and area sports events**[1]

- DfEE (1998) **Health and safety of pupils on educational visits**. London, DfEE. Ref no: HSPV2

- DfES (2001) **Health and safety: responsibilities and powers.** London, DfES Publications. Ref no: DfES/0803/2001

- DfES (2002) **A handbook for group leaders.** London, DfES Publications. Ref no: DfES/0566/2002

- DfES (2002) **Standards for adventure.** London, DfES Publications. Ref no: DfES/0565/2002

- DfES (2002) **Standards for LEAs in overseeing educational visits.** London, DfES Publications. Ref no: DfES/0564/2002

[1]   Visit the BAALPE website (www.baalpe.org) for further details.

safe practice in physical education and school sport

Questions and answers

People

Qu 1   **I am a newly qualified teacher (NQT) – is it appropriate for me to lead a residential visit?**

Ans   It would not normally be appropriate for an NQT to lead an educational visit. Before being given this responsibility, it would be better for you to assist with a number of visits under the guidance of an experienced member of school staff, who can mentor you through the process involved.

Qu 2   **Is both male and female supervision required for mixed gender residential visits?**

Ans   Yes – it is essential that both male and female adults are present to supervise mixed residential visits.

▶▶   See also Qu I, Qu 2 and Qu 3 in *Chapter eighteen: Outdoor and adventurous activities* (pages 258–59).

Context

Qu 3   **I have been asked by my head teacher to organise a visit of historical interest to a site unknown to the school. What preparations do I need to make?**

Ans   In order to carry out a meaningful risk assessment for the visit, it is essential to find out as much information as possible about the intended venue. The best way to do this is to pay an initial visit to the site to obtain first-hand information and identify any potential hazards. The knowledge gained can be used to inform the planning of your visit.

If such a visit is impractical, you should consult closely with those who have a good knowledge of the venue and are able to provide the necessary information (eg your local education authority, a neighbouring school which has already visited the site).

▶▶   See also Qu 4 in *Chapter eighteen: Outdoor and adventurous activities* (page 259).

Organisation

Qu 4   **We are planning a day visit to a local country park to do some environmental work with classes of Key Stage 1 and Key Stage 2 pupils. What qualifications should the staff hold and what level of supervision should be provided?**

Ans   Assuming that the visit will not involve any hazardous activities, at least one member of the supervisory staff should be a qualified teacher. School staff/pupil ratios should comply with local requirements. The younger the pupils, the more generous the staffing provision will have to be.

A typical ratio for Key Stage 1 pupils on such a visit would be one responsible adult to six pupils. For older Key Stage 2 pupils, a ratio of one responsible adult to ten pupils may be appropriate. However, when deciding on appropriate schoolstaff/pupil ratios, you should always take into account the behaviour and maturity of the pupils involved, and whether any of them have special educational needs.

Qu 5   **What adult/pupil ratios would be required for an educational visit attended by the parents of some of the pupils involved?**

Ans   The assistance of parents during educational visits is often required to comply with the required adult/pupil ratios. If a supervising parent's own child is involved in the visit, it will normally be sufficient to recruit one extra adult (ie non-parent) to the supervisory staff. For example, a Key Stage 2 visit to a local environmental centre involving 40 pupils would normally require at least four adult supervisors (1:10), one of whom should be a competent member of school staff. If one (or more) of the four adults is a parent of a pupil involved in the visit, an additional adult (ie non-parent) would be required, bringing the total number of supervisory adults to five. However, local regulations relating to parental assistance during educational visits should always be consulted, as specific adult/pupil ratios may be recommended.

Qu 6   **During a primary school visit to a local heritage site, pupils express a wish to spend some time exploring on their own. As the member of school staff leading the party, how much freedom should I allow the pupils?**

Ans   Although you will want the visit to be enjoyable and not too restrictive, it would be very unwise to allow the pupils to explore on their own, as they will be in unfamiliar surroundings. There may be hazards which they are unaware of or they may be tempted to take risks which would not be permitted under your risk assessments. You would be placing yourself in an untenable position should an accident occur during unsupervised activity.

▶▶   See also Qu 2 in *Chapter ten: Insurance* (page 114) and Qu 5, Qu 6 and Qu 7 in *Chapter eighteen: Outdoor and adventurous activities* (pages 260–61).

Chapter twenty-one

Play in the school environment

> Please read the general guidance provided in *Part one* of this handbook[1] before reading this chapter. This will help to ensure that you have a comprehensive awareness of safe practice issues affecting play activities and physical education in general.

21.1 Introduction

21.1.1 School play areas, particularly in primary schools, provide opportunities for pupils to engage in active, safe, purposeful play, and also to experience quiet and environmental areas.

21.1.2 Play area safety and supervision is essential, both during informal and instructed play.

21.2 Play area design

21.2.1 School staff (and pupils where possible) should be fully involved in the planning of inventive and innovative play areas.

21.2.2 When new schools are built and/or play areas are constructed, it is important for school staff to be fully involved in minimising hazards (eg flower beds, access to nursery class rooms).

21.2.3 Play areas should be designed so that all pupils are visible at all times to those designated to supervise.

21.2.4 Full use should be made of the space available.

21.2.5 Differently coloured surfaces and impact absorbing surfaces make play areas easy to identify, and young pupils find the varied colours exciting.

21.2.6 Signs in play areas should be drawn to pupils' attention. This will help to raise their awareness of safety issues and promote the development of a safe play environment.

21.2.7 Play areas for pupils with special educational needs should be planned carefully. These should include quiet areas, board games on tables, nature areas, chess boards marked on paving stones and other similar areas.

---

1   See pages 1–124.

21.3 Play area markings

21.3.1   Play area markings should be in line with manufacturers' and local education authority (LEA) guidelines. They should be appropriate to pupils' needs, the ethos of the school, and the availability of trained, experienced and qualified school staff.

21.3.2   Where possible, pupils should be involved in the design of play area markings.

21.3.3   Observing play is fascinating and rewarding, and can also inform the design of play area markings to enable creative and safe play.

21.4 Play area surfaces

21.4.1   Play area surfaces should be even, maintained in good condition and free from loose grit. Hazards (eg uncapped tennis post sockets, vandalised or damaged fencing wire, crevices in the surface) should be removed or remedied.

21.4.2   Steep slopes and sudden changes in level should be avoided.

21.4.3   School staff should carry out daily, weekly and monthly inspections of play area surfaces. These should form part of a risk assessment record, which should be acted upon by senior management.

21.4.4   If a surface becomes temporarily unsuitable for use, the affected area should be coned off or, at worst, the whole area should be placed out of bounds until repair work has been carried out.

21.5 Environmental hazards on play areas

21.5.1   An audit of hazards should enable school staff to identify those that could be of significant risk to pupils using play areas. These hazards can then be addressed. This process of good practice is known as *risk management*[1] and should be present in all aspects of physical education and play.

21.5.2   The types of hazards that may be encountered include the following:

a **Play area surface:**

- Uneven or cracked
- Loose grit
- Slippery in wet weather
- Vegetation growing on or through

b **Play area drainage:**

- Standing water after rain
- Drain grids below general level
- Drain grids with over-sized spaces
- Drain grids broken or missing

---

1   See *Chapter two: Risk management* for further information.

c **Play area built on sloping ground:**

- Steep steps

- Lack of secure handrail

- Condition of steps

- Presence of rubbish or vegetation on steps

- Possibility of pupils over-running off play area

- Possibility of stones etc rolling onto play area

d **Buildings around play area:**

- Exposed external corners adjacent to play areas

- Projections below head height (adult)

- Outward opening windows

- Outward opening doors

- Non-toughened glass

e **Surrounding plants/shrubs etc:**

- Possibility of pupils over-running into plants/shrubs etc

- Type of plants/shrubs etc (eg shrubs with large thorns)

- Possibility of poisonous berries

f **Access to play area:**

- Possibility of unsupervised pupil access (environmental or task-orientated)

- Possibility of vehicular access

- Vehicular deposits on play area if used as car park outside school hours

- Use as public right-of-way

g **Fixed climbing equipment:**

- Lack of inspection and repair schedule

- Inappropriate surrounding surface

- Proximity to other hazards (eg windows, projections).

21.6   Supervision of play areas

21.6.1   Supervision should be provided by trained and experienced personnel.

21.6.2   It is essential that all those who promote, supervise and control play in a school environment take advantage of professional development opportunities.

21.6.3   Risk assessments should be carried out to determine the number of people required to supervise play areas in order to maximise supervision.

School staff

21.6.4 It should not be assumed that school staff are automatically competent to supervise play areas.

21.6.5 It will therefore be necessary to provide professional development opportunities to make all school staff aware of their responsibilities. This should include discussion of major supervision issues (eg observation points, sight lines, separation of activities) and a review of standard procedures for accidents that take place in play areas.

▶▶ See *Chapter eleven: Accidents, incidents and first aid management* for further information about standard accident procedures.

Lunchtime supervisors

21.6.6 The role of lunchtime supervisors may include facilitating play activities in addition to their supervisory roles.

21.6.7 Training will be necessary to enable play facilitators to perform their role effectively and safely.

21.6.8 Many LEAs and colleges of further education offer specific courses for lunchtime supervisors. It is good practice for schools to arrange and pay for their lunchtime supervisors to attend such courses.

21.6.9 Lunchtime supervisors should be invited to attend staff meetings whenever play facilitation is included on the agenda.

Play monitors

21.6.10 Play monitors in primary schools can provide useful support to school staff and lunchtime supervisors in developing play activities.

21.6.11 It is necessary for play monitors to receive some form of training in order to ensure their own safety and that of the pupils they work with.

21.6.12 Play monitors should only work under the direct guidance of a member of school staff or lunchtime supervisor.

21.7 Managing play activities

21.7.1 Through the management and promotion of play across the curriculum, school staff can change attitudes, set safe parameters and modify pupil behaviour towards others.

21.7.2 In order to provide opportunities for purposeful play, it is essential that play activities are planned for curriculum time, as well as for before school, break times, lunchtimes, and after school. Related policies, procedures and rules must be established, implemented and made known to everyone involved, including parents.

21.7.3   Active play times are rewarding when they are planned, led and supervised by school staff. As well as providing pupils with opportunities for safe play and skill development, they also offer continuing professional development (CPD) and team-building opportunities.

21.7.4   Where possible, a structure should be provided for active play times. However, the use of balls and bats in crowded areas is hazardous. Careful planning is therefore essential in order to minimise risk and provide a play environment in which everyone is comfortable.

21.7.5   Creative play can be part of curricular physical education and can take many forms. In all cases, it should be well planned and structured. However, pupils should be provided with adequate equipment and opportunities to enable them to invent games. This will encourage them to use their imagination and develop play-related skills.

21.7.6   Overcrowding can be avoided if play areas are designated and play times/break times are staggered. These are both good examples of risk management.

21.7.7   Some schools have an extended day with post-school play activities. It is important that all school staff involved are suitably trained and experienced, and that they continue to fulfil their duty of care.

21.7.8   The quality of pupil behaviour is a key factor in the safe management of play. Pupils should understand that appropriate behaviour and attitudes create a safe play environment.

21.7.9   Pupils should be made aware of what constitutes unacceptable behaviour and that this will be challenged and that sanctions may be applied. All school staff should adopt a consistent approach to discipline.

21.8   Climbing equipment

21.8.1   School staff should consider whether play area climbing equipment is necessary, meets pupil needs, can be adequately supervised, is the best use of space and extends pupils during climbing activities. They should obtain advice from their local Health and Safety Officer (HSO).

21.8.2   All surfaces and their installation should meet appropriate British Standards European Norm (BS EN) requirements[1]. They should be level, non-slip and even.

21.8.3   Research has shown that recommended impact absorbing surfaces reduce injuries. It is essential to bear this in mind when selecting play area surfaces.

21.8.4   An appropriate surface should be provided beneath and around all new equipment. This should extend at least 1.75m beyond the outermost points of the base of the frame. Impact absorbing surfaces are not required beneath frames that are less than 600mm high. However, it is good practice to do so, as this helps to cover all eventualities and displays an attention to detail in risk assessments.

21.8.5   Frames surrounding wood bark impact absorbing surfaces can be a hazard. Care should therefore be taken when constructing them, with particular attention being paid to their proximity to potential landing sites for falls from heights.

1   Contact the National Playing Fields Association (NPFA) for further details (www.npfa.co.uk).

21.8.6   All climbing equipment should be appropriate for the age and developmental needs of the pupils who will use it. It should ideally meet appropriate BS EN requirements[1].

21.8.7   Bars (sometimes described as *monkey bars*) should be discouraged, as statistics show that they increase the risk of foreseeable accidents.

21.8.8   Signs displaying instructions on how to use climbing equipment can aid supervision.

21.8.9   After installation, all climbing equipment should be inspected and approved prior to use by the local HSO. Written confirmation that the equipment is safe to use should be obtained.

21.8.10   All supervisory staff must be familiar with the play area climbing equipment and the abilities of the pupils involved. They should be competent, confident, trained and fully aware of their responsibilities. They should not accept any additional responsibilities beyond their level of confidence or competence. Untrained staff may assist, but should not be placed in sole charge.

21.8.11   No adult should be placed in sole charge of a lunchtime play area and climbing equipment at the same time.

21.8.12   The maximum number of pupils, who can safely use the whole climbing area and individual items of equipment at any one time, should be determined by senior management. All school staff and pupils involved should be made aware of these limits.

21.8.13   Pupils must wear appropriate footwear that provides good traction between the feet and the frame. Smooth soles may be dangerous.

21.8.14   Young pupils, who may be timid (eg nursery age pupils), should not use climbing equipment at the same time as older pupils. Suggested rota systems to enable this could be included in school play policies[2].

21.8.15   Climbing frames should not be used in inclement weather.

21.9   Soft play and inflatables

21.9.1   When schools hire an inflatable for a fund-raising event, it is essential that a written agreement is made with the manufacturer/hirer to clarify the responsibilities of each party, safety recommendations, supervision and insurance. The agreement should be signed, countersigned and dated.

21.9.2   Safety rules should be established and displayed on appropriate signs when the inflatable is used. The attention of all users and/or parents should be drawn to them. Such rules should be dated to show that they were clearly in operation on the day of any reported accident.

21.9.3   Supervision must be consistent and be provided by trained and experienced adults.

1   Contact the NPFA for further details (www.npfa.co.uk).

2   See Section 21.10 on pages 289–90 for further information about school play policies.

safe practice in physical education and school sport

21.9.4   Particular attention should be paid to the following issues:

a The permission of the head teacher and governors should be obtained before hiring an inflatable.

b Any technical advice provided by the manufacturer/hirer should be followed and their expectations met.

c All equipment should be in good repair and should have been subject to a regular inspection and repair programme.

d Generators should be positioned and regularly checked so as not to cause injury.

e High-sided, integral, padded walls should be provided on three sides of the inflatable to prevent children falling over the edge and onto the ground. The fourth (open) side is for access, egress and observation.

f A sloping safety apron or thick mattresses should be provided at ground level along the open side, and a sufficient number of mature *spotters* should be situated at arm's length intervals to assist children climbing on and off, and to prevent children falling over the exposed edge when bouncing.

g The number of children bouncing at any one time should be kept sufficiently low to reduce the possibility of them colliding with each other.

h Guidance on the wearing of socks and shoes should be followed.

i Rotational movements in the air, and running from wall to wall, should not be permitted.

j Beginners should only bounce on their feet (eg they should not perform seat bounces).

k Only children of similar sizes should be allowed on the inflatable at any one time.

l The time allowed per bouncing session should not be unduly long, so that children do not tire and lose concentration or control.

m Children who are known to experience difficulties with their physical control may require one-to-one assistance, holding hands while bouncing. At such times, the number of children bouncing may need to be reduced accordingly.

n Arrangements may need to be made for the bouncing surface to be cleaned and sterilised from time to time. When this occurs, the bouncing surface should be thoroughly dry before activity recommences.

o Onlookers should not be permitted to distract those who are bouncing by shouting or calling out.

p Hired ball pools should be checked to make sure they are clean.

21.10   School play policy and guidelines

21.10.1   Head teachers and school governors are responsible for establishing a school play policy for the use and supervision of play areas in a recreational context.

21.10.2   Head teachers and school staff should determine the guidelines necessary to implement the policy to enable them to fulfil their duty of care and thereby ensure safe practice.

21.10.3   These guidelines should include means of communicating the policy and guidelines to all school staff, new appointments, lunchtime supervisors, volunteers and paid coaches.

21.10.4   School play policies and guidelines should be reviewed at regular intervals, particularly following any accident or incident.

Apparatus and equipment

21.10.5　Guidelines, which are determined by the school play policy, should govern the safe use of apparatus and equipment, and should be rigorously applied by those supervising play activities.

21.10.6　These guidelines should include statements such as those listed below:

a Wheeled equipment (eg trikes) should only be used in specified areas.

b Hitting and striking games should be sited so that participants hit away from quiet areas.

c Invasion games should be restricted to a specific court, so as not to place other children at risk.

d Pupils using climbing equipment must conform to related school rules (eg clothing, personal effects, overcrowding).

21.10.7　It is common practice that climbing equipment used during curriculum lessons is not used during play activities. This is to prevent schools having dual standards in relation to safe practice on climbing equipment. During lesson time, pupils work under direct supervision, they wear appropriate clothing and footwear, they will have removed any personal effects, they work towards a specific task and overcrowding is not possible. These factors are not present during unsupervised play activities.

Further reading

- BAALPE, DfES (2003) **The use of volunteers and paid coaches (contractors) in physical education and school sport**[1]

- BAALPE, PEA UK, Sport England, sports coach UK (2003) **School induction pack for teachers and adults other than teachers**. Leeds, Coachwise Solutions. ISBN 1 902523 44 X

- HSE (1999) **Entertainment sheet no 11: the new European standards for outdoor playground equipment.** Sudbury, HSE Books

- ILAM, NPFA and RoSPA (1999) **Indoor play areas – guidance for safe practice**. Reading, Institute of Leisure and Amenity Management. Ref no 25342 (**Note:** This resource has been superseded by, and should be read in conjunction with, BS8409:2002 *Soft Indoor Play Areas – Code of Practice*)

- NPFA (1997) **Impact absorbing surfaces for children's playgrounds**. London, NPFA. ISBN 0 9460 8535 X

- Performance Textiles Association[2] (2003) **Safe use and operation of inflatables, including bouncy castles**[3]

1　Visit the BAALPE website (www.baalpe.org) or DfES website (www.dfes.gov.uk) for further details.

2　In partnership with the HSE.

3　Visit www.pipa.org.uk for further details.

Risk management

People

- **Pupils should share in the assessment and management of the risks involved.**

- Pupils should be aware of the behaviour and discipline expected of them in play situations.

- School staff should be aware of their duty of care to pupils before, during and after school hours.

- School staff should understand which activities they are qualified to supervise.

- New members of school staff should receive an induction on the school play policy.

Context

- Play areas should have separate, designated zones for different age groups, active games and wheeled play equipment.

- School play policies should:

  - conform to the requirements of The Children Act 1989[1], other relevant regulations and employer guidelines

  - state who is responsible for the supervision of play areas at various times of the school day (ie before school, play times, lunch times, after school)

  - state who is responsible for the closure of play areas during inclement weather.

- Vehicles should only be allowed access to play areas when escorted by an adult. This applies before, during and after school hours.

- Accidents and incidents in play areas should be discussed by all relevant staff as part of their ongoing CPD.

- Equipment and apparatus should be formally checked on a monthly basis. All such checks should be recorded in writing.

- Pupils should wear appropriate clothing and footwear for play activities.

Organisation

- Specific risk assessments are required for adventure playgrounds, fixed climbing equipment and inflatable apparatus.

▶▶ See *Chapter two: Risk management* for more detailed, general guidance on risk management issues.

---

1 See *Chapter one: Physical education and the law* for guidance on The Children Act 1989.

Questions and answers

People

Qu 1 **As head teacher, school staff often complain to me that the playground is not kept clear of debris. Whose job is it to do this?**

Ans As the head teacher, and therefore manager, of your school, it is ultimately your responsibility. However, you will delegate the day-to-day responsibility to relevant staff – usually to your site manager. Your risk assessment should determine the actions required to ensure that the playground is kept clean and safe. Responsibility for these actions should be written into the job description of the appropriate person. However, it will still be necessary for school staff to ensure that the playground is safe prior to using it.

Qu 2 **Should lunchtime supervisors be allowed to take responsibility for responding to accidents that occur in the playground at lunchtime?**

Ans As a head teacher, you should follow your employer's safe practice policy. Check that their insurance policy covers all school staff and volunteers who administer first aid. You should also ensure that your lunchtime supervisors are fully aware of the school's accident procedures.

Qu 3 **I appreciate that a school has a duty of care for its pupils. When does that duty start and finish?**

Ans This has always been a grey area. In 2000, a High Court judge ruled that a school's responsibility, during normal school attendance, starts and ends at the school gate. However, schools should be aware that duty of care extends outside the school gates when a pupil is taken off site under the supervision of school staff.

Context

Qu 4 **It is obvious that a change of school policy is necessary if active play is to become a normal part of our school day. Which school documentation needs to be updated to ensure safe practice?**

Ans The following documentation should be reviewed and updated in line with the guidance provided in this handbook:

a School handbook/prospectus

b School safety policy

c Physical education safety policy

d Parents' handbook

e Person and job specifications for:

- Physical education coordinators
- Lunchtime supervisors.

Writing and re-writing policy documents is only the start – it is putting policies into practice that ensures safety. Check that appropriate guidelines exist and that all members of school staff are aware of them.

Qu 5 **Vehicles often cross our playground during the school day. These vary from private cars to delivery vehicles. It has been argued that we always have responsible adults on duty in the playground to ensure the safety of the pupils. Could you comment?**

Ans It is unreasonable to allow free access to vehicles to cross your playground. There will be times when school staff are not on duty. It would be advisable to devise a system that prohibits vehicular traffic, except under escort. Drivers would be required to seek permission to cross the playground and could only do so under escort.

Qu 6 **A local firm has donated a sum of money to the nursery unit for the purchase of wheeled play equipment. Do you have any suggestions?**

Ans Your school should examine the project in detail before moving forward. A complete risk assessment should be carried out for the proposed activity, covering the actual equipment to be purchased, the environment to be used and the method of use.

You may find the following guidelines useful:

Equipment

a Aim for quality, not quantity. Remember that the equipment will be used a lot more than it would in the home.

b Purchase four- and three-wheeled equipment, rather than two-wheeled.

c Arrange for the equipment to be added to your annual inspection and repair programme for physical education equipment.

Environment

a Segregate the *wheeled play* from the *general play* area.

b If space permits, develop a road system, so that road safety can be incorporated into play activities.

c Introduce a one-way system from the outset.

Task

a Ensure that school staff are aware of their responsibility to examine equipment prior to each use.

b Train children not to enter the *wheeled play* area from the *general play* area.

c Do not allow double riding.

d Your risk assessment may determine that wheeled equipment should only be used by children wearing head protection. This should be taken into account when purchasing the equipment.

Note: Please be aware that these are just suggestions and do not constitute a definitive list.

Organisation

Qu 7   **When parents are waiting to pick up their children at the end of the school day, they often allow their younger offspring to play on the outdoor climbing apparatus. I believe this to be an excellent community exercise. Do you agree?**

Ans   Although this demonstrates a good, caring attitude, there are associated problems. It is unlikely that your employer's insurance policy for school activities would cover such practice. It is essential to check this. If a child was injured, it could be argued that the child had not been taught how to use the apparatus safely and that he/she was not supervised by a knowledgeable person. It may also be argued that the child was incorrectly dressed. Taking issues like these into account, you may come to the conclusion that it would be best to prohibit the use of the apparatus outside official school sessions.

▶▶   See also Qu 4 in *Chapter eight: Environment and equipment* (pages 101–02).

Appendices

People

Appropriate
challenge

▲

PHYSICAL
EDUCATION

▼

Acceptable risk

Context

Organisation

Appendix 1

Risk assessment form

School: _____ Work area: _____

ASPECTS TO CONSIDER	RISK RATING	WHO IS AFFECTED?	IS FURTHER ACTION REQUIRED? (CONTROL MEASURE – ACTION REQUIRED TO REDUCE RISK TO ACCEPTABLE LEVEL)		
Only list actual hazards	Low (L) Medium (M) High (H)	Pupils (P) School staff (S) Visitors (V)	What?	Who?	Completed?
PEOPLE • School staff: • Volunteers/paid coaches: • Pupils: • Others:					
CONTEXT • Facility: • Procedures: • Equipment: • Transport: • Others:					

ASPECTS TO CONSIDER	RISK RATING	WHO IS AFFECTED?	IS FURTHER ACTION REQUIRED? (CONTROL MEASURE – ACTION REQUIRED TO REDUCE RISK TO ACCEPTABLE LEVEL)		
Only list actual hazards	Low (L) Medium (M) High (H)	Pupils (P) School staff (S) Visitors (V)	What?	Who?	Completed?
O R G A N I S A T I O N • Preparation: • Class organisation: • Teaching style: • Emergency action: • Progression: • Others:					

Signed: Head teacher _____   Date of assessment: _____

       Subject leader _____   Review 1: _____ (date) _____ (initials)

                                                             Review 2: _____ (date) _____ (initials)

                                                             Review 3: _____ (date) _____ (initials)

Appendix 2

Parental consent and medical information form for educational visits, overnight stays and outdoor and adventurous activities

This form should be completed in full by parent(s) and returned to the school.

School _____

1   Details of visit

Visit to _____

From _____ (date/time) to _____ (date/time)

I agree to my son/daughter/ward

Full name _____ Form/class _____

taking part in the above stated visit and having read the information sheet, agree to his/her participation in any or all of the activities described. I acknowledge the need for good conduct and responsible behaviour on his/her part.

2   Emergency details

a I agree to my child being given any medical, surgical or dental treatment, including general anaesthetic and blood transfusion, as considered necessary by the medical authorities present.

b I may be contacted by telephoning the following number(s):

Home (full number) _____

Work (full number) _____

My home address is _____

_____

c Please provide details of an alternative contact:

Tel number _____

Name _____

Address _____

_____

(continued)

d Child health service details:

Medical card number _____

Family doctor:

Name   _____

Address   _____

_____

Tel number   _____

3   Medical information

Does your child suffer from any of the following conditions?
(delete as applicable)

Asthma	Yes / No	Bronchitis	Yes / No
Chest problems	Yes / No	Diabetes	Yes / No
Epilepsy	Yes / No	Fainting attacks	Yes / No
Heart trouble	Yes / No	Migraine	Yes / No
Raised blood pressure	Yes / No	Tuberculosis	Yes / No

If **Yes**, please provide full details:

_____

_____

_____

_____

_____

Does your child suffer from any other   Yes / No *(delete as applicable)*
condition requiring medical treatment,
including medication?

If **Yes**, please provide full details:

_____

_____

_____

_____

_____

(continued)

Is your child allergic or sensitive to any   Yes / No *(delete as applicable)*
medication, insect bites or food?

If **Yes**, please provide full details:

_____

_____

_____

_____

Has your child been immunised against the following diseases?

Poliomyelitis   Yes / No *(delete as applicable)*

Tetanus (lock jaw)   Yes / No *(delete as applicable)*

If **Yes** to tetanus, please give date if known _____

Is your child taking any form of   Yes / No *(delete as applicable)*
medication on a regular basis?

If **Yes**, please give full details indicating the type of medication and dosage:

_____

_____

_____

Please ensure that your child has adequate supplies of medication.

To the best of your knowledge, has your child   Yes / No *(delete as applicable)*
been in contact with any contagious or infectious
diseases, or suffered any recent condition that
may become infectious or contagious?

If **Yes**, please give full details:

_____

_____

_____

_____

(continued)

4   Insurance cover

I understand that the visit is insured in respect of legal liabilities (third party liability) but that my child has no personal accident cover unless I have been specifically advised of this in writing by the organiser of the visit.

I also understand that any extension of insurance cover is my responsibility unless advised differently by the school.

5   Declaration

- I have read the information provided about the proposed educational visit and the insurance arrangements.

- I consent to my child _____
  taking part in the visit and, having read the information sheet, declare my child to be in good health and physically able to participate in all the activities mentioned.

- I have noted where and when the pupils are to be returned, and I understand that I am responsible for ensuring that my child gets home safely from that place.

- I am aware of the levels of insurance cover.

- I have completed the required medical form and return it with this consent form.

- I will notify the school prior to the visit of any change of circumstances which will affect my child's participation in the visit.

Signature of parent   _____

Print name   _____

Address   _____

_____

Appendix 3

Information on proposed educational visit or journey

Dear Parent

The Governors and I have given approval to the following educational visit/journey, in which it is hoped that you wish your child to participate. This letter contains information intended to help you make this decision.

Details of visit/journey _____

Date(s) _____ to _____

Activities to be included in the visit/journey _____

_____

_____

_____

Party leader _____ Deputy leader _____

Other school staff _____

Other adults _____

Age range of group _____ Probable number: Boys _____ Girls _____

Accommodation arrangements _____

_____

_____

Travel arrangements _____

_____

_____

Insurance arrangements _____

_____

(Note: The party leader can provide details of instances when private insurance will be taken out by the school on behalf of the pupils.)

Any special requirements (clothing etc) _____

_____

(continued)

For the visit/journey to be a valid and safe educational experience, sensible active involvement is required from all participating pupils. To ensure that the maximum value is gained from the visit/journey, the school has particular requirements regarding behaviour and application. These are contained in a code of conduct, a copy of which will be sent to you to make both you and your child aware of the expectations.

If you require further details, please do not hesitate to contact _____, the party leader.

or

A parents' evening will be organised by _____, the party leader, at which further details of the visit/journey will be made available and the opportunity provided for you to ask questions.

If, after considering all the details, you wish your child to be included on the visit, please inform me accordingly by completing and returning the slip at the end of this letter. I will then arrange for the necessary forms to be sent to you for you to complete.

Yours sincerely

_____ (Educational Visits Coordinator/Head Teacher)

- -

_____ School school visit/journey

I would like my child _____ in form _____

to be included in the school visit/journey

to _____

on _____

Please send the following forms for me to complete and sign:

1   Agreement and medical details

2   Code of conduct

Signed   _____

Relationship to child   _____

Date   _____

Appendix 4

Sample consent form for the use of digital imagery in school

Digital imagery may be used in a number of school activities. The following sample letter does not specifically refer to physical education and should be seen as a means of obtaining parental consent for the use of digital imagery in all school-related activities.

Dear Parent

Digital imagery is an exciting new medium, which can motivate and inspire pupils. Although the associated risks are minimal, schools have a duty of care towards pupils.

(school name) recognises the need to ensure the welfare and safety of all young people. In accordance with our child protection policy, we will not permit photographs, videos or other images of pupils to be taken without the consent of the parents and pupils involved.

(school name) has policies relating to the use of photographs and videos. Copies can be obtained from *(named person)*.

(school name) will take all necessary steps to ensure that any images produced are used solely for the purposes for which they are intended. Photographs may be used in our printed publications for display around the school, as teaching resources within the curriculum and on the internal school website. Video clips may also be used as teaching aids within the curriculum and for staff training and educational purposes at both local and national level. At no time will the images be sold or made available for wider publication without further parental approval.

Please complete, sign and return this form to *(named person)* at *(school name)*

Name of child   _____

Name of parent   _____

Address   _____

                     _____

                     _____

I consent to *(school name)* photographing and videoing my child as described above.

Signature   _____

Date   _____

Queries regarding this form should be addressed to *(school name and address)*

Appendix 5

Standard accident procedures

It is essential that all school staff and pupils are aware of the standard accident procedures (SAP) adopted by their school. This will help to ensure that they all respond to an emergency in the same way, thus minimising the time spent between the accident occurring and the injured pupil(s) receiving first aid.

This appendix contains a sample SAP. Please note that it does not attempt to constitute an authoritative legal interpretation of the provisions of any enactment, regulations or common law. That interpretation is exclusively a matter for the courts.

The suggested format for an SAP is illustrated in the three flow charts on pages 307–09:

1 **Red procedure:** for serious accidents that require immediate hospitalisation.

2 **Yellow procedure:** for an accident that can be referred to a doctor, clinic or hospital by transport by parent or school.

3 **Green procedure:** for accidents that can be dealt with in-house.

The red procedure should always be used when:

a   there is any doubt about the level or nature of the injury

b   concussion occurs as a result of an accident.

Red accident procedures

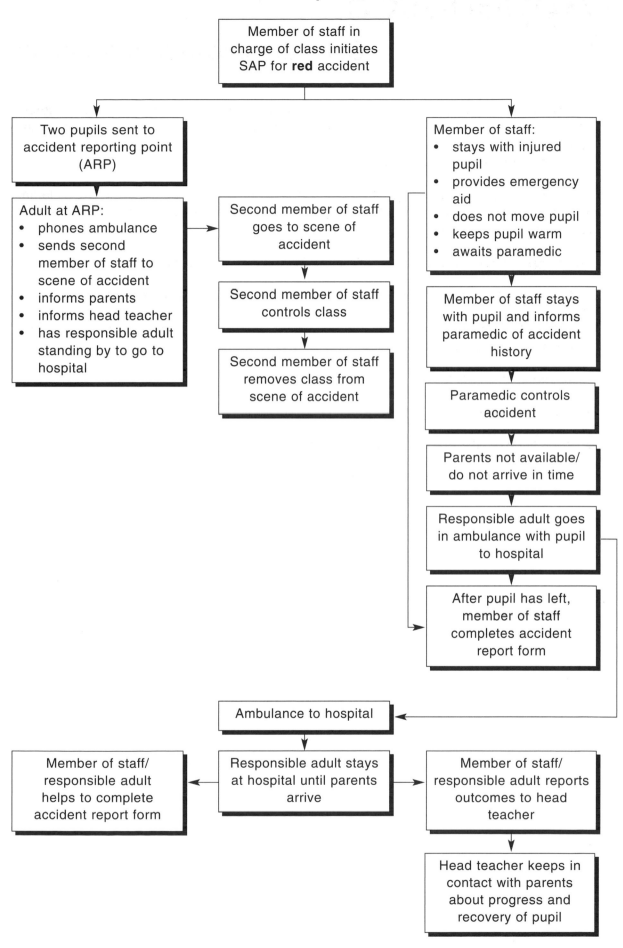

Member of staff in charge of class initiates SAP for red accident

Two pupils sent to accident reporting point (ARP)

Adult at ARP:
- phones ambulance
- sends second member of staff to scene of accident
- informs parents
- informs head teacher
- has responsible adult standing by to go to hospital

Second member of staff goes to scene of accident

Second member of staff controls class

Second member of staff removes class from scene of accident

Member of staff:
- stays with injured pupil
- provides emergency aid
- does not move pupil
- keeps pupil warm
- awaits paramedic

Member of staff stays with pupil and informs paramedic of accident history

Paramedic controls accident

Parents not available/ do not arrive in time

Responsible adult goes in ambulance with pupil to hospital

After pupil has left, member of staff completes accident report form

Ambulance to hospital

Member of staff/ responsible adult helps to complete accident report form

Responsible adult stays at hospital until parents arrive

Member of staff/ responsible adult reports outcomes to head teacher

Head teacher keeps in contact with parents about progress and recovery of pupil

Yellow accident procedures

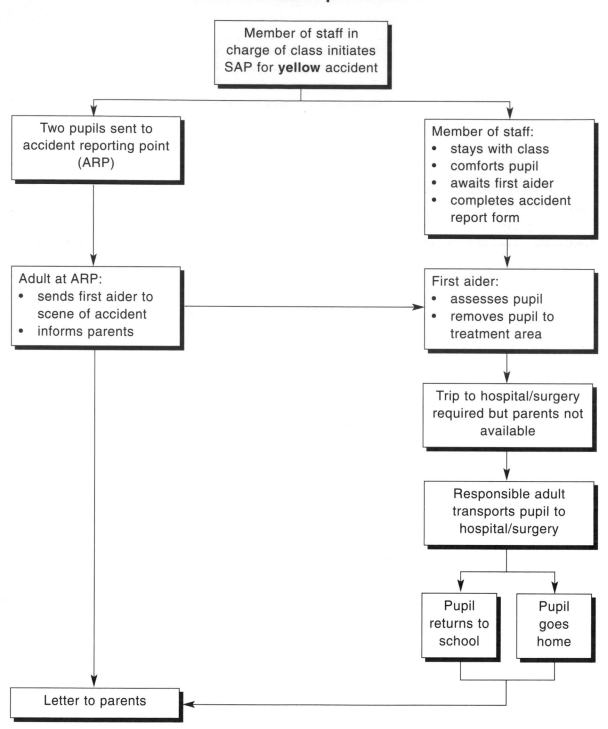

Member of staff in charge of class initiates SAP for **yellow** accident

Two pupils sent to accident reporting point (ARP)

Member of staff:
- stays with class
- comforts pupil
- awaits first aider
- completes accident report form

Adult at ARP:
- sends first aider to scene of accident
- informs parents

First aider:
- assesses pupil
- removes pupil to treatment area

Trip to hospital/surgery required but parents not available

Responsible adult transports pupil to hospital/surgery

Pupil returns to school

Pupil goes home

Letter to parents

Green accident procedures

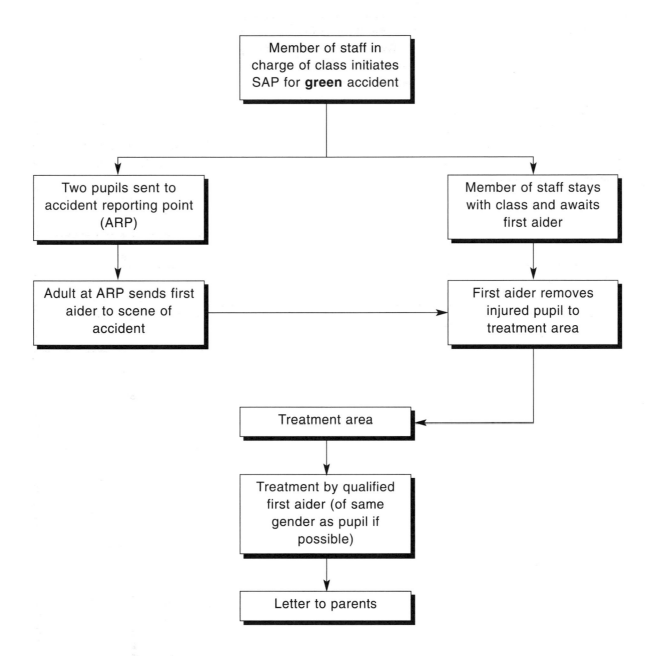

Member of staff in charge of class initiates SAP for **green** accident

Two pupils sent to accident reporting point (ARP)

Member of staff stays with class and awaits first aider

Adult at ARP sends first aider to scene of accident

First aider removes injured pupil to treatment area

Treatment area

Treatment by qualified first aider (of same gender as pupil if possible)

Letter to parents

Appendix 6

School accident report form

(This form could supplement the employer's accident report form)

Accident details

Pupil's name [　　　　　　　　　] Age [yrs][mths] Sex [　　　　] Height [m][cm]

Pupil's home address [　　　　　　　　　　] Tel no [　　　　　]

Class [　　　　] No in class [　　] No of boys [　　] No of girls [　　]

Teacher in charge of lesson [　　　　　] Other adults present [　　　　　]

Type of lesson [　　　　] Unit no [　　] Lesson no [　　]

Nature of injury [　　　　　　　　　]

Approx time of accident [　　　　]

Location [　　　　　　　　　　　　　]

a   In the space above, draw a plan of the location of the accident showing the position of:
  i   any apparatus, equipment etc
  ii   the pupil involved in the accident
  iii   any adults present
  iv   two witnesses.

b   Give approximate measurements (in metric) to show the relative relationship of the people to apparatus and each other.

Other persons involved

1   Names of any school staff sent to assist at the scene of the accident

[　　　　] [　　　　] [　　　　]

2   Name of person who carried out emergency aid [　　　　　]

3   Names of witnesses [　　　　] [　　　　]

   Statements obtained from witnesses *(circle appropriate response)*   Yes   No

4   Name of person who contacted:

   a   ambulance service [　　　　]   b   pupil's parents [　　　　]

   (continued)

safe practice in physical education and school sport

Post-accident procedures

1 Assessment of the nature of the injury determined that the pupil should be treated by
(tick appropriate box):

a school only ☐   **b** hospital A&E department ☐   **c** pupil's doctor ☐

2 Treatment at school

   a Name of person who carried out treatment [   ]

   b Brief details of that treatment

   [   ]

3 Treatment at A&E department

   a Approximate time between accident
   and arrival of ambulance [   ]

   b Name of paramedic (if possible) [   ]

   c Who accompanied pupil to hospital? | Parent | School staff |
   (circle appropriate response)

   d If school staff, state name [   ]

      i Did hospital ask member of staff | Yes | No |
   to sanction any action or form of
   treatment prior to arrival of parents?
   (circle appropriate response)

      ii If **Yes**, specify action or treatment [   ]

   e Approximate time parents arrived
   at hospital [   ]

   f Was pupil admitted to hospital following | Yes | No |
   treatment in A&E?
   (circle appropriate response)

(continued)

Follow-up procedures

1 Completion of employer's accident report form

a Form completed by

b Date forwarded to employer

NB The school is legally obliged to complete and submit the form to the employer as soon as possible after the accident so that the employer can comply with RIDDOR regulations.

2 Risk assessment

a Risk assessment of the lesson reviewed by

b Date carried out

c Was a change to procedures recommended? *(circle appropriate response)*

Yes	No

d When were these changes implemented?

3 Contact with parents

a Who contacted parents to ascertain pupil's progress?

b How soon after the accident was contact made?

c Brief details of information received

4 Pupil's return to school

a Date of return to school

b Date of restart of physical education

c Any restrictions on pupil's involvement in physical education laid down by medical profession

Form completed by

Signed   Date

Note: Schools may choose to attach additional information to this form (eg employer's accident report form, witness statements, risk assessment form covering activity, photocopy of register covering the four weeks prior to the accident).

Appendix 7
Code of conduct for pupils on educational visits

It is good practice for schools to agree a code of conduct with parents and pupils before pupils participate in educational visits. Acceptance of a code will provide party leaders with the necessary authority to carry out their responsibilities. The agreed code of conduct should be formalised and sent to parents, with the consent and medical forms, for them and their child to sign. Suggested items for inclusion in the code of conduct are listed below.

All pupils should:

a   observe normal school rules

b   cooperate fully with leaders at all times

c   fulfil any tasks or duties set prior to and during the visit

d   participate fully in all activities and sessions during the visit

e   be punctual at all times

f   not leave group sessions or accommodation without permission

g   always return to the meeting point or accommodation at agreed times

h   be in groups of not less than three pupils if granted indirectly supervised time

i   avoid behaviour which may inconvenience others

j   be considerate to others at all times

k   respect all requests made by school staff and accompanying adults

l   behave at all times in a manner which reflects positively on themselves, the party and the school

m   abide by the laws, rules and regulations of the countries and places visited

n   comply with customs and duty-free regulations

o   not purchase or consume alcohol, tobacco products or purchase dangerous articles such as explosives and knives

p   consult with school staff if in doubt about any issues

q   accept that a full written report of any misconduct will be forwarded to the Educational Visits Coordinator/head teacher and their parents.

Appendix 8

Notification of proposed educational visit or journey

This form should be completed by the party leader and submitted to the Educational Visits Coordinator/head teacher for information and the approval of the head teacher and governors.

School _____ Party leader _____

Educational visit/journey reference number _____

Accompanying school staff (first named to be deputy leader) _____

_____

Other accompanying adults _____

Outline details of visit/journey (eg costs, itinerary) _____

_____

Date(s) _____ to _____

Pupil age range _____ Probable number of boys _____ girls _____

Travel arrangements _____

All proposed activities _____

Does the party leader have previous experience of leading groups which
involve these activities?   Yes / No

Relevant qualifications/experience of party leader _____

Relevant qualifications/experience of school staff and other adults listed above

_____

_____

Staff/adults with first aid/emergency aid qualifications _____

If school minibus to be used, name of driver(s) _____

_____

Will special insurance cover be arranged?   Yes / No

If **Yes**, name of company and brief details of cover _____

_____

Will the visit/journey be arranged through a commercial company?   Yes / No

If **Yes**, name of company _____

Will the visit/journey be covered by ABTA?   Yes / No

Signed _____ (Party leader)

Date _____

Date passed to head teacher _____

Visit/journey approved?   Yes / No   Signed _____ (head teacher)

Date _____

Appendix 9

Useful contacts

Adventure Activities Licensing Authority
www.aala.org.uk

British Waterways
www.britishwaterways.co.uk

Central Council of Physical Recreation (CCPR)
www.ccpr.org.uk

Contact a Family (CAF)
www.cafamily.org.uk

Criminal Records Bureau (CRB)
www.crb.gov.uk

Department for Education and Skills (DfES)
www.dfes.gov.uk

Department of Education Northern Ireland
www.deni.gov.uk

Department of Health
www.dh.gov.uk

DfES Publications
www.dfespublications.gov.uk

Disclosure Scotland
www.disclosurescotland.co.uk

Health and Safety Executive (HSE)
www.hse.gov.uk

Institute of Leisure and Amenity Management (ILAM)
www.ilam.co.uk

Learning Wales
www.learning.wales.gov.uk

Met Office
www.met-office.gov.uk

National Council for School Sport
www.ncss.org

National Playing Fields Association (NPFA)
www.npfa.co.uk

Qualifications and Curriculum Authority (QCA)
www.qca.org.uk

Royal Society for the Prevention of Accidents (RoSPA)
www.rospa.com

Scottish Executive
www.scotland.gov.uk

Sport England
www.sportengland.org

sports coach UK
www.sportscoachuk.org

Sports Council of Northern Ireland
www.sportni.net

Sports Council for Wales
www.sports-council-wales.co.uk

sportscotland
www.sportscotland.org.uk

St John Ambulance
www.sja.org.uk

UK Sport
www.uksport.gov.uk

United Kingdom Passport Services (UKPS)
www.ukpa.gov.uk

Index

1   See also guidance for specific activities in *Part two*.

---

1   See also guidance for specific activities in *Part two*.

safe practice in physical education and school sport